PERSONAL FINANCE

John Edwards

PERSONAL FINANCE

The A–Z of Investment and Money-Management

GRAFTON BOOKS

A Division of the Collins Publishing Group

LONDON GLASGOW
TORONTO SYDNEY AUCKLAND

Grafton Books
A Division of the Collins Publishing Group
8 Grafton Street, London W1X 3LA

Published by Grafton Books 1989

British Library Cataloguing in Publication Data

Edwards, John
 Personal finance: the A–Z of investment
 and money management.
 1. Great Britain. Personal finance
 I. Title
 332.024′00941

ISBN 0-246-13284-1
ISBN 0-246-13595-6 (Pbk)

Phototypeset by Computape (Pickering) Ltd.
North Yorkshire

Printed in Great Britain by
William Collins Sons & Co. Ltd, Glasgow

CONTENTS

PREFACE

This is a book for the growing number of people needing to know more about money, investment and all other aspects of personal finance.

In recent years the number of shareholders in the UK has grown enormously following the government drive to encourage wider share ownership through privatization issues, company profit-sharing schemes and by direct tax relief through Personal Equity Plans.

Big changes have taken place too in other key aspects of saving and borrowing, offering a much wider range of choice. But, with this increase in choice and freedom to shop around, there is also a greater need for guidance from an independent source. My book does not seek to give advice on how to make a fortune. The purpose is rather to provide basic information, in the form of an easy-to-use reference work. The idea for writing this book originally came when I first started writing about personal finance for the *Financial Times*, having moved from another section of the paper to edit the Family and Finance pages in the Weekend *FT*. Initially I found myself in a mysterious world, full of jargon and phrases incomprehensible to the outsider, even to an experienced financial journalist. Although there are lots of books about personal finance, I couldn't find a single one that provided basic information in an understandable and comprehensive form covering all aspects of the subject.

So I decided to fill the gap. The choice of entries included in this book is comprehensive. I have tried to judge what anyone, ranging from the complete novice to those in the financial services industry, may want to look up to have the meaning, and background, explained.

I have also highlighted, with extra long entries, certain sectors where there have been big changes in recent years, such as mortgages, pensions, tax reform and the system for investor protection.

The entries are in strict alphabetical order, including initials. For example, if you want to look up the meaning of SERPS, the first step would be to look under Se... You will then see a cross reference to STATE EARNINGS RELATED PENSION SCHEME where you will find a full explanation and cross reference to other relevant entries. At the back of the book are lists of useful addresses and currencies for different countries.

It is a book to be used. I hope it will prove a valuable addition to bookshelves in the home, libraries, offices and schools as a constant source of information on matters that affect all our lives at one time or another.

JE
April 1989

ACKNOWLEDGEMENTS

Many thanks to my wife, Stephanie, for her invaluable help in producing this book. Not only in the actual preparation, but also in providing constant encouragement and support.

Out of the many sources of reference consulted, I would recommend in particular: the *Which* books on different aspects of finance, published by the Consumers Association; the *Guardian Money Book* by Margaret Dibben; *Fidelity's Investors A–Z* by Rosemary Burr; *The Family Money Book* by Douglas Moffitt; *Fair Shares* by Simon Rose; the *Longman Dictionary of Business English* by J. H. Adam; and the *Penguin Business Dictionary* by Michael Greener.

A

'A' shares Special type of share in a company, they give the same dividend payments as normal ordinary shares but do not allow the holder voting rights. 'A' shares are often used as a method for one group of shareholders to retain control of a company, while allowing an additional body of shareholders to receive dividends.

Accepting (acceptance) house Name given to certain banking companies in the City of London which qualify for membership of the Accepting Houses Committee. Their traditional business was to 'accept' bills of exchange used in commodity trading, so that the buyers and sellers were able to settle their payments immediately for the supply of goods. Nowadays they act in a similar way to merchant banks in helping to finance international trade generally.

Account period General term for a specified time during which money has been received and paid, such as monthly statements provided by banks or annual accounts issued by public companies.

Also London stock market term for the trading periods (normally two weeks) in which shares can be dealt in before any charges are made. Investors can both buy and sell shares (but not government securities) within the account period without any immediate financial outlay, provided their credit is good with the stockbroker. At the end of each account period, all the purchases and/or sales made by a stockbroker on a client's behalf are totalled in order to find the amount due for payment either by the broker or by the client. The resulting total is then paid on account, or settlement, day. Details of the account periods, and settlement days, can be obtained from the Stock Exchange or stockbrokers, or from newspapers and magazines carrying financial reports.

Accountant 'Someone who keeps and examines business accounts', according to the dictionary definition. They have a reputation for being dull and boring, possibly because of the nature of their traditional job – poring over accounts and dealing with the Inland Revenue – although their work covers a much wider and more interesting spectrum these days. Many accountants are chief executives or finance directors of companies through their training and expertise in financial matters.

Qualified accountants have to pass a series of examinations to become members either of the Institute of Chartered Accountants of England and Wales, of Scotland or of Ireland, or the Chartered Association of Certified Accountants. Once qualified, they can put after their name either ACA (Associate Chartered Accountant) or FCA (Fellow Chartered Accountant), or ACCA and FCA in the case of certified accountants. The difference between chartered and certified accountants lies in the examinations set by the different organizations. Generally, however, certified accountants tend to work in industry for companies, while chartered accountants join private partnerships or set up as sole practitioners, claiming to be better qualified than certified accountants.

Accountancy firms are never limited companies; instead, they are composed of partners or operate as individuals. Some of the partnerships can be very large indeed, with several hundred partners, annual turnover of millions of pounds and offices throughout the world.

The nature of accountancy businesses can vary widely, with some partnerships concentrating primarily on auditing the accounts of companies, while others deal with private individuals, handling tax returns, giving advice on tax, and general financial planning. They charge fees for their services, either a flat rate or by the hour or a mixture of both. See CERTIFIED and CHARTERED ACCOUNTANTS.

Accrual rate   Amount by which a pension builds up each year in a final salary or average-earnings pension scheme. The higher the accrual rate, the higher the pension received. If the accrual rate is 1/80th a year, then after 40 years the pension would equal 40 × 1/80th, or half the salary, at pensionable age. An accrual rate of 1/60th would give two-thirds of the salary: 40 × 1/60th.

Accrued benefits   Payments due under a pension scheme or life policy, representing the proceeds accumulated up to a specified period.

Accrued interest   Undistributed interest on capital that has not been paid out to the investor. With National Savings Certificates, for example, the interest earned on the original investment is accrued, and paid only when the certificate is cashed in.

Accumulation and maintenance trusts   Special type of trusts, set up under a trust deed, used to provide financial benefits for children and grandchildren under the age of 25. Used primarily in order to reduce the payment of INHERITANCE TAX.

Accumulation units   Used by investors in unit trusts who do not want to receive dividends or interest payments, which instead are re-invested in the fund, after the tax payable has been deducted. Accumulation units, therefore, have a higher value than income units in the same fund.

But, to add confusion, accumulation units in a regular premium life insurance fund are different, since all the dividend and interest payments are re-invested anyhow. In that case, for the first few years the premiums go into capital units, from which very high charges are deducted to recoup the expense involved in setting up and maintaining the fund – the commission and costs of launching the fund. Only later are the premiums put into accumulation units, when the unfortunate policy-holder finally starts to get value for the money invested, instead of paying the insurance company's expenses.

Active assets   See ASSETS.

Active bond   See BOND.

Active money   Money being put to use in buying and selling, instead of being held on deposit.

Act of God   Term used in insurance policies to exclude providing financial compensation for events caused by natural forces beyond the control of humans, such as an earthquake or lightning.

Actuarial report   A statement showing the financial state of a pension fund, or insurance policy, at a specified date. Often used by employers to decide the rate of contributions needed to fund pension schemes.

Actuary Member of the Institute of Actuaries (or Faculty of Actuaries in Scotland), who have special skills and training in assessing and evaluating risks by mathematical means. Actuarial tables record details of past experience, which are used to project future probabilities. Actuaries are employed primarily by life assurance companies and pension funds to set premium rates and contribution levels based on their calculation of likely future trends. They are key figures who have statutory obligations to ensure that the policy or fund remains financially viable. There is a special Government actuary who gives guidance to company actuaries in line with government policy.

Added years The extra benefits, sometimes gained when moving jobs or pension schemes, that provide more 'years' in exchange for the value of the rights transferred from the previous pension scheme.

Additional voluntary contributions (AVC) Way for employees to obtain extra pension benefits. Members of a company pension scheme can choose to make additional voluntary payments to top up their eventual pension either to the managers of the company scheme or with another completely separate pension provider. The latter is known as FSAVC (free-standing additional voluntary contributions).

In the 1989 Budget proposals were put forward to abolish many of the rules and regulations previously imposed by the Inland Revenue. The most important change was that the excess funds earned by (FS)AVC that cannot be used to provide benefits over the maximum limits, will in future be returned to the employee,

instead of merely reducing the occupational pension paid by the employer. However, the refunded amount will be subject to a special tax charge. See PENSIONS.

Adjuster Professional used by insurance companies to act on their behalf in valuing losses and settling claims. Comparable to an ASSESSOR, who plays a similar role but acts on behalf of the insured making the claim.

Administration bond See BOND.

ADR See AMERICAN DEPOSITORY RECEIPTS.

Ad valorem Tax or duty that is based on a percentage of the value of the product or service being taxed.

Advisers See INDEPENDENT FINANCIAL ADVISERS, STOCKBROKERS.

AFBD See ASSOCIATION OF FUTURES BROKERS AND DEALERS and USEFUL ADDRESSES.

Age allowance A special additional amount that can be earned before income tax becomes payable that is given to people over 64 years of age before the start of the tax year on 6 April, or a married couple with one member over 64. The threshold for this relief is regularly adjusted in line with inflation. There is a further extra allowance for older people, which in the 1989 Budget was extended to include anyone over 75 years old, instead of 80 years as previously. In both cases, the extra allowances are added on, and are therefore additional, to the normal personal tax-free allowance given to those under 64. However, unlike the personal allowance, the age allowance is reduced in line with the 'total income' being received over and above the top limit of the allowance. This is known as the age allowance 'trap' since extra income can result in the loss of some or all the tax relief. The formula used, which was adjusted in the 1989 Budget, is that the age allowance tax relief is reduced by £1 for every £2 of income received above the limit.

'Total income' for the purpose of age allowance includes income received from investments like interest on bank or building society accounts, as well as from life assurance policies and investment bonds. So it makes sense in some cases for older people to switch to tax-free investments, like National Savings Certificates, to avoid losing the age allowances.

Agency broker A stockbroker who deals on behalf of clients, but is not a principal market maker in the stocks or shares. See MARKET MAKER.

Agent Person, or organization, with the power to act on someone else's behalf. This can be simply selling or dealing in products or goods, like an auctioneer, broker, insurance salesman or estate agent, or representing the wider interests of a principal (company or person) generally, like a land agent. See COMMISSION and DEL CREDERE AGENTS.

Agent of necessity An agent who acts on behalf of another person only in those conditions where immediate action is required, without there being time to refer to the principal for instructions. An example is the captain of a ship being forced to jettison some cargo in order to save the rest.

AGM See ANNUAL GENERAL MEETING.

Agreed bid When a company making a takeover offer for another company receives the support of a majority of the shareholders in the company being taken over. Some companies will only make agreed takeover bids, on the grounds that it is much better to have a willing partner and retain the goodwill of the staff and business than to force through a bid. Very often, for an agreed bid, extra incentives are offered to shareholders of the company to be taken over in order to avoid a costly and possibly lengthy takeover battle.

Aleatory contract An insurance policy to cover losses resulting from a chance event.

All moneys debenture Arrangement with a bank that the size of a loan can be increased without renegotiating the basic terms or providing additional security.

Allotment With a new issue of shares in a company, the shares are allotted to those applying for them on the terms outlined in the prospectus. Where demand for the shares exceeds the number available – as happened with several of the privatization issues – an allotment is made based either on the number applied for or on a random basis by ballot.

Allotment letter The formal letter or document certifying that the recipient has been allotted a specified number of shares in a company, subject to payment. This letter is later exchanged for a share certificate; but it can be used in the meantime to demonstrate proof of ownership in dealing in the shares or borrowing money to purchase them. See RENUNCIATION.

Allowances Money given to someone for a particular purpose, like a dress allowance, pocket money, motor car or expense allowances. Alternatively, allowances can be forms of discount for damaged goods or in respect of large or special orders. Tax allowances are the amounts that can be offset against the amount of tax to be paid, such as personal allowance for earned income, blind person's allowance, etc.

All risks Rather misleading term used to describe type of insurance cover provided under a household contents or travel policy. It does *not* cover all risks but rather a wide range of risks within certain specified categories, normally against theft and accidents. It is used mainly to insure personal possessions and valuables that may be taken out of the home or moved from place to place when travelling.

Alpha shares Most actively traded shares of the leading companies dealt on the London stock market. Under the trading system introduced by the stock market in October 1986, the shares of companies traded were divided into several categories – Alpha, Beta, Gamma and Delta – based on the size, available stock and type of company. Alpha category includes the biggest and most popular shares, which are the easiest both to buy and to sell, since there is normally plenty of available stock and of market makers willing to deal at the prices quoted on the SEAQ (Stock Exchange Automated Quotes System) screens. Alpha shares, as the most actively traded, tend to have the lowest 'spread' (difference between the buying and selling prices) and to be less volatile in price movements than smaller companies. Many Alpha shares are known as Blue Chip companies. See BIG BANG and STOCK EXCHANGE.

Alternative investments Usually refers to non-conventional investments: antiques, books, coins and medals,

commodities, diamonds, furniture, paintings and other works of art, precious metals and wines. Also a wide range of collectibles like stamps, toy soldiers or teddy bears. Advocates of alternative investments argue that, as assets with a basic intrinsic value, they provide better protection, especially during times of high inflation, than 'paper' money or share certificates. The returns can certainly be much higher, but so are the risks, and alternative investments do not provide dividends or interest. Nevertheless many conventional investors, including big funds, consider it prudent to put a proportion of their money into some alternatives, notably gold, platinum and silver.

American Depository Receipts (ADR) Special certificates, for trading on the American stock markets, issued by banks confirming that they hold a specified number of a particular company's shares available for trading. ADRs are denominated in dollars and traded on the US stock markets as American securities, although they normally represent non-US companies. They thus provide a means for US investors to trade in the shares of foreign companies on their own domestic stock markets.

American Stock Exchange (AMEX) Rival stock market in New York to the New York Stock Exchange, but much smaller in the number of stocks listed and the trading turnover.

AMEX Abbreviation for AMERICAN STOCK EXCHANGE and also for American Express, the US-based international banking and charge card group.

Amortize Pay off a debt or loan gradually over a period of time, often by setting aside money in a sinking fund each year in order to cover the capital repayments. Amortization is also used in company accounts to write off (reduce the value) of assets that in themselves are not depreciating in value, for example a lease on a building or property over a fixed period. These types of assets cannot be depreciated, so they are amortized instead. See DEPRECIATION and SINKING FUND.

Analyst Someone who is employed, normally by investment companies or stockbrokers, to examine 'all the known facts' and investigate the future outlook. The analyst can deal with specific companies or cover a much wider brief, ranging from the world economies to long-term trends affecting inflation, property values and the development of particular countries or sectors of industry. Fundamental analysts tend to look at the underlying value and basic forces at work, while technical analysts rely more on past price movements and developments in order to project future trends. Neither one is necessarily right, but they can have considerable influence on share price movements and, on occasion, the ability of a company to borrow sufficient money to keep going.

Angels Popular name given to people, or organizations, who provide financial backing for a new venture, particularly a theatrical show or a film. Normally they give loans in return for a share in any profits made and special benefits, such as privilege booking rights. It is a very risky form of investment, since any return depends on the venture being a financial success and the failure rate of theatrical shows tends to be very high.

Annual exemption See CAPITAL GAINS TAX.

Annual General Meeting All public limited companies have to hold a meeting once a year to report to shareholders on the previous twelve months. The AGM, as it is familiarly known, is the time when shareholders are given the opportunity to find out how their company is faring with the presentation of the report and accounts by the directors and auditors; the declaration of the planned dividend payment, if any; and the re-appointment of the auditors and any directors whose term of office has expired and who offer themselves for re-election.

Shareholders can show disapproval of the way the company is being run by refusing to approve the report and accounts, opposing the re-election of directors or auditors, and making their views known publicly in the case of companies whose shares are quoted on the stock exchange.

Be wary of companies which hold their AGMs in places that are difficult for shareholders to attend. AGMs are one of the few occasions when the directors and managers of public companies meet their shareholders face to face. They are normally boring, formal affairs, and as a result are attended by few shareholders unless the company actively encourages them to attend. On occasions, however, they can be the scene of dramatic happenings, especially if a company is pursuing a policy disliked by a section of its shareholders, or has been performing badly or has become involved in a take-over battle.

Annual percentage rate of charge (APR) Standardized method for calculating the true cost of borrowing, or credit, by taking into account all charges incurred and the timing of the repayments. It was introduced by the government, under the Consumer Credit Act in 1984, to try and stamp out the use of misleading rates of interest by money lenders, and to provide a proper comparison of different interest rates. It is now compulsory for all lenders, including banks and building societies, to quote the APR equivalent of the interest and costs being charged. There is a complicated standard mathematical formula, published by the Office of Fair Trading, for the calculation of the APR.

Essentially, it measures the flow of money going out and coming in. Regular monthly repayments, for example, have a much higher APR than a single annual repayment, since the monthly repayments gradually reduce the debt to the benefit of the lender. At the same time, if charges (such as an arrangement fee) are included, these have to be added to the total sum borrowed, so the APR is variable according to the length of the repayment period. Special Consumer Credit tables are also issued by the Office of Fair Trading to help with the complicated methods of calculating the APR.

Annual report Produced each year, supposedly to let shareholders know the progress of a company during the previous twelve months, although they are often difficult to understand. Annual reports must by law include certain details and be examined by independent auditors. Each report should contain a statement by the directors of the company summarizing developments during the past year and giving a view (normally over-optimistic) of future prospects; a profit and loss account showing the result of the company's activities in financial terms; and a balance sheet at the end of the company's financial year, providing a 'snap-shot' of its financial health on a particular date. A statement on funding shows how the company was financed and the use made of money received from various sources.

Annuitant Someone receiving an annuity payment.

Annuity A fixed sum of money paid at regular intervals. A retirement annuity, for example, is another name for a pension. Annuities can also be bought for a capital sum from insurance companies, paid for in advance or in arrears. The buyer of an annuity (the annuitant) receives a regular payment, normally until death. There are tax advantages: annuity payments are viewed by the Inland Revenue as being split into two parts – repayment of the original capital outlay which is tax free, and interest that is taxable. The cost of annuities varies, according to prevailing interest rates, the sex (women tend to live longer so are charged more) and the age of the purchaser and the potential recipient. Because of the commitment to pay until death, younger people are charged a lot more; as a result, annuities are normally advisable only for older people and those without dependants, who would otherwise inherit the capital sum spent to acquire the annuity. Temporary annuities, for specified periods such as five or ten years, are also offered for sale, usually by insurance companies, as a way of providing income in a tax-efficient way. See HOME INCOME PLANS and PENSIONS.

Annuity bond See BOND.

APP See APPROPRIATE PERSONAL PENSION.

Appeal bond See BOND.

Appointed company representatives Advisers or salesmen who are tied to sell products or introduce clients to one particular company, even though they are not employed by that company on a full-time basis. See TIED AGENTS.

Appropriate personal pension (APP) Type of pension introduced in July 1988 which allows employees to leave (contract out of) the State Earnings Related Pensions Scheme (SERPS) and to receive a rebate of National Insurance contributions plus the special incentive of 2% National Insurance contributions being paid by the government until 1993 in order to encourage people to leave SERPS. See PENSIONS.

APR See ANNUAL PERCENTAGE RATE (of charge).

Arbitrage Dealing simultaneously in separate markets in order to take advantage of any difference in price, with a view to making a guaranteed profit by buying the undervalued asset and selling the overvalued. This mechanism to some extent keeps different world markets in line. It can be used for stocks and shares, commodities, futures contracts, currency or bills of exchange. Arbitrageurs, professional market traders employed to undertake arbitrage operations, also deal in various assets with indirectly related values – soyabean meal and soya-oil, for example, both produced from soyabeans – or shares whose prices are related, either as members of the same parent company or in the same sector.

Arbitrageurs Professional market traders who undertake arbitrage transactions. In the United States, however, the term is used more widely to cover professional traders generally.

Arrangement fees Polite term for charging extra costs, used by banks, building societies and mortgage lenders for arranging overdrafts and business transactions.

Assented bond See BOND.

Assessments Official valuation of goods insured against loss or damage. Tax assessments, based on details supplied by the tax payer, are used by the Inland Revenue to decide the amount of tax liability.

Assessor Professional employed by those making a claim under an insurance policy to value the loss or damage. See ADJUSTER.

Asset backed Normally used to describe investments in companies with tangible assets, notably property. In other words, the assets could be sold and the proceeds distributed to the shareholders if the company fails to make the grade.

Assets General term used to describe any possession, held by an individual or a business, which has a monetary value that can be realized. Assets come in many shapes and sizes. These include:

active or productive assets – those which earn interest or income;

available or liquid assets – cash in hand, or anything that can be turned quickly into cash;

capital or fixed assets – possessions of a long-lasting or permanent nature, like land, buildings, machinery and trade investments;

contingent assets – possessions or gains that will not be realized until a particular event takes place;

current, circulating or floating assets – possessions which may be used up or turned into cash fairly quickly (usually within a year) in the normal course of business, such as raw materials, stocks and debts;

deferred assets – unused part of an expenditure, which has been paid wholly or partly in advance;

equitable assets – special kind of asset which is part of a property left by someone who has died but which can be applied to the settlement of the deceased person's debts only after a court order has been obtained;

fictitious or nominal assets – assets of no real value which nevertheless have to appear on a company balance sheet for accounting purposes;

frozen assets – possessions which cannot be turned into cash immediately either because of some restriction, such as a court order, or because their sale would result in a serious loss;

hidden assets – where a possession is given, normally in a company balance sheet, a value considerably less than its real market value;

illiquid or slow assets – those which cannot be sold for cash at short notice;

intangible assets – possessions with no material form that are difficult or impossible to turn into cash, but which still have value, such as goodwill, copyrights and trademarks;

legal assets – part of the property left by someone who has died, but not including any equitable assets;

net assets – the excess of assets over liabilities or a combination of current and fixed assets which, after deduction of current liabilities, is used to calculate the capital employed in a company;

personal assets – any possessions such as personal goods and interests in leasehold property or land;

quick or realizable assets – cash or possessions that can be quickly turned into cash without serious loss;

real assets – possessions other than money, such as land, buildings and machinery;

tangible assets – possessions with physical form that can be turned into cash fairly quickly, such as share certificates and cheques;

wasting assets – fixed assets which are gradually being used up, such as a quarry or oil-well.

Asset stripping A way of making money by taking over a company and then selling its assets to realize a quick profit. The proceeds are either distributed to the shareholders or retained in the company as a cash shell. This practice is frowned upon, since selling its assets can ruin a perfectly good and profitable company.

Asset value Total worth of a company, calculated by adding together the value of the assets. All the liabilities shown in the balance sheet (such as bank overdrafts) and prior capital commitments (like loan stock) are deducted from the asset value, and are then divided by the number of shares to give the net asset value per share. See NET ASSET VALUE.

Associated operation A device used normally for taxation purposes in order to generate artificial profits or losses. One operation is linked to another in order to achieve a transfer of value.

Association of Futures Brokers and Dealers (AFBD) One of the self-regulatory organizations, set up under the umbrella of the Securities and Investment Board, to implement the provisions of the 1986 Financial Services Act and provide suitable protection for investors. It regulates the activities of firms operating in the futures and options markets and deals with complaints from investors. See SELF-REGULATORY ORGANIZATIONS and USEFUL ADDRESSES.

Association of International Bond Dealers (AIBD) Organization that regulates the activities of firms trading in overseas bond markets to ensure that they comply with the rules laid down to protect the interests of investors.

Assumed bond See BOND.

Assurance Insuring for an event that will definitely happen one day, like death or retirement, as opposed to insurance which covers events that may or may not happen, such as accidents, damage or theft. Assurance companies traditionally, therefore, deal in life and pensions policies. See INSURANCE.

Assured tenancy schemes New type of Business Expansion Scheme (BES) introduced in 1988 to encourage the creation of more rented accommodation in order to try to relieve the housing shortage. Investors are offered special tax reliefs to put money into enterprises which buy or convert properties for renting under assured tenancies introduced in 1989 that give the landlord greater powers to dispose of the properties and evict the tenants. See BUSINESS EXPANSION SCHEMES.

Attendance allowance Special benefit paid by the government to the severely disabled, either mentally or physically, who require constant help. A lower allowance is paid for those needing either day or night care, while a higher sum can be claimed if 24-hour care is required.

At best Instruction to a broker or dealer to buy or sell something at the most favourable level currently available in the market.

ATM See AUTOMATED TELLER MACHINE.

At-the-money A term used in the options market when an option is bought at approximately the same price as the value of the underlying security or commodity.

Attorney Someone, normally a lawyer, with power to act on another person's behalf, especially on legal matters. See POWER OF ATTORNEY and ENDURING POWER OF ATTORNEY.

Audit An official examination and check of the annual accounts of an organization or company by an independent qualified person (auditor). Audits are normally carried out annually, since the auditor has by law to be appointed by shareholders at each annual general meeting. But some big companies operate a continuous audit throughout the year.

Auditor A person who audits accounts. By law, for limited companies the auditor must be qualified as a member of an officially-recognized organization of professional accountants and must not be an official or employee of the company being audited.

As a representative of the shareholders, appointed each year, the auditor has wide-ranging powers to find out the true financial position of the company. The auditor's report, accompanying the balance sheet and annual accounts, must by law contain an indication – through a form of words – as to how much information has been provided and the auditor's view of the company's financial state. A qualified report is a serious matter for the company, which then has to answer any questions as to why the auditor is unwilling to give a 'clean' report.

Authorized (share) capital The amount of capital that a limited company is allowed to raise, usually expressed as a specific number of shares with a nominal face-value. This is usually substantially higher than the issued, or paid-up, capital but fixes a ceiling on the amount of extra capital a company can raise without altering its memorandum or articles of association. See SHARE CAPITAL.

Authorized unit trusts Unit trusts that comply with the rules and regulations laid down by the UK Government and the Securities and Investment Board (SIB).

Automated teller machines (ATMs) The hole-in-the-wall cash dispenser machines widely used by banks and building societies. Originally designed simply to dispense money on demand, they now provide a whole range of services, from paying bills to giving account balances.

Available assets See ASSETS.

AVC See ADDITIONAL VOLUNTARY CONTRIBUTIONS (pension).

Averaging Investing over a period of time to achieve an 'average' cost. Particularly useful for long-term investments with volatile short-term price movements. Regular savings schemes in investment or unit trusts, with the investor paying a fixed amount each month, achieve what is called 'pound cost averaging' by acquiring more shares or units when prices are low and fewer when prices are high. Alternatively, an investor wishing to build up a holding over a period of time will choose a certain price level at which to 'average in' purchases, or when selling may 'average out' at a specified price level.

Averaging also refers to the reduction of an insurance claim payment because of underinsurance. The payment is reduced in line with the percentage of the underinsurance against the true value.

B

Baby bond Special endowment policy offered by Friendly Societies for children under 18 years old, giving totally tax-free returns. The Inland Revenue, however, limits the number that can be offered for sale. See FRIENDLY SOCIETIES.

Back-to-back loans Method used by investment groups to provide protection against risk from unpredictable movements in currency values. Two transactions are involved: a loan is taken out in one foreign currency and secured with a deposit for a similar amount in another currency.

Backwardation Has two separate meanings. On the stock market, it refers to the charge made by a buyer of shares when the seller fails to deliver the stock on the due settlement day. On the commodity and financial futures markets, it refers to a situation when the cash (or spot) price for immediate delivery is higher than the price for delivery at some time in the future; it signifies a shortage of immediately available supplies. A backwardation highlights that the market is not in a normal state; prices for goods to be delivered at a future date should in theory be higher, since they include the cost of carrying (storage and insurance) until delivery is made by the seller. See CONTANGO.

Bad debts insurance See CREDIT POLICY.

Baggage insurance Policy that compensates the insured for loss of luggage and personal possessions when travelling.

Balance sheet A statement, normally issued at the end of a company's financial year, showing its assets and liabilities on a specific date. Under the 1981 Companies Act, a balance sheet has to be included in the annual report of limited companies, accompanied by an auditors' report confirming that it is a 'true and correct' record. The balance sheet is an important guide to the company's financial state. It outlines the effect of the past year's trading and, by including details of money owed and due, helps assess the future prospects.

Ballot Used when a new share issue attracts too many applications for the number of shares available. Some, or all, of the applications are put together and withdrawn at random, like a lottery or raffle. Those picked out receive all, or some, of the shares applied for, while those not selected are returned to the applicants. With a weighted ballot, the allocation of shares can be influenced as required by excluding certain groups of applications from the ballot. This technique was used in some of the government's privatization issues in order to favour the small investor.

Baltic Exchange Building in the City of London where shippers and shipbrokers meet to negotiate freight rates – the cost of transporting goods by dry-cargo ships or oil-tankers from place to place in the world. Different routes have different rates which are decided primarily by the availability of ships or tankers on the dates required. The Baltic, as it is called, offers a free market alternative to the fixed rate or conference lines set by shippers in consultation with customers. Brokers on the Baltic act as intermediaries, selling surplus space on behalf of the ship owners, and also acting for buyers wishing to charter space. A similar service for chartering aircraft for freight and passengers is operated by specialist brokers.

With modern communications, these days most of the chartering is done outside the Exchange, which remains as a symbolic meeting place and centre, providing standard rules and regulations for contracts. The Exchange also houses several futures markets, for grain and other agricultural products, as well as Biffex (Baltic International Freight Futures Exchange). See FUTURES and USEFUL ADDRESSES.

Band earnings The salary range, with lower earnings and upper earnings limit, on which the level of National Insurance contributions is based. See NATIONAL INSURANCE.

Bankable asset Something with an acknowledged value and which will therefore be accepted by a bank or other lender as security for a loan.

Bank charges Sums charged by banks, and often deducted direct from customers' accounts, for services provided. It is necessary, therefore, constantly to check bank statements to ensure the right charges have been made. Most of the big retail banks make no charge nowadays on accounts in which a credit balance is maintained or only a small overdraft is

incurred. With some high interest accounts, the banks make separate charges for cheques and other withdrawals, which can on occasion exceed the interest earned. There is also a wide variety of charges made for extra services, such as storing share certificates and legal documents, and arranging loans and mortgages.

Bank draft A form of cheque often more acceptable to a recipient because it is issued by a bank in its own name and is therefore certain to be honoured, provided it is not a forgery. It is thus considered to be the equivalent of cash and is often used to pay over large sums in situations where it might be difficult to provide cash and where a personal cheque would entail an element of risk for the recipient.

Banker's order An instruction given by customers to a bank to pay out certain specified sums at regular intervals – monthly, quarterly or annually. Better known as a STANDING ORDER. Not much liked by banks, since they involve non-computerized work, they have been replaced to a large extent by DIRECT DEBITS.

Bank for International Settlements (BIS) Originally formed in Western Europe to co-ordinate payments for damages caused by the First World War. Nowadays, with a headquarters in Basle, Switzerland, it is a clearing point for CENTRAL BANKS and works closely with the INTERNATIONAL MONETARY FUND.

Bank giro system Way of paying bills quickly and cheaply. By filling in a giro form and providing the required cheque, a bank customer can make any number of payments free to other parties, although a charge is made for payments to someone with a bank account. Not to be confused with the national Girobank system operated by the Post Office in Britain. See GIRO and NATIONAL GIROBANK.

Bank guarantee An undertaking by a bank to cover a debt or provide credit facilities. Particularly useful for supporting a financial transaction without having to put money 'up front' or provide some kind of collateral or security, although the bank itself usually insists on security and makes a charge. Bank guarantee can also apply to a third party agreeing to pay a loan on behalf of someone else, if the borrower fails to pay by the required date.

Banking ombudsman Independent official appointed to run an office that arbitrates in disputes between banks and their customers. The ombudsman will agree to act only after the normal channels for complaints have been exhausted without any agreement being reached. The ombudsman has the power to award compensation if one of the member banks is found to be at fault and to have acted wrongly or unfairly. The complainant, however, can take legal action, even if the complaint is not supported by the ombudsman. See OMBUDSMAN and USEFUL ADDRESSES.

Bank note Printed paper money, normally issued by the government's central banks, promising to pay the bearer a specified sum in the local currency of the country. See LEGAL TENDER.

Bank of England Became the UK Government's state-owned central bank when it was nationalized in 1946. It was originally a finance company. When Charles II confiscated the gold deposited by the goldsmiths of London in the Treasury, the depositors hit on a new scheme for banking their gold: they formed a company, whose subscribers were known as the Governor and Company of the Bank of England. Over the years, the Bank worked closely with the government, lending it money and helping to raise a National Debt. It became the government's banker and became the only bank allowed to issue bank notes in England and Wales. Under a special Act of Parliament, three Scottish banks are empowered to issue bank notes in Scotland. The Bank of England continues to operate like a normal bank, although its main customers are the UK government, other domestic banks, overseas central banks and international organizations. It does, however, keep a few special private customer accounts.

The Bank acts as a lender of the last resort to its customers – the commercial banks, acceptance and discount houses – and controls the amount of money in circulation in accordance with government policy.

The ability of the clearing banks to lend money is geared to their balances held at the Bank of England, which calls for special deposits when seeking to control the supply, and also sets the lending rates.

The Bank acts as registrar for government securities (gilts), stocks issued by nationalized industries and stocks of some local authorities, public boards and Commonwealth governments. It is thus involved in sending out millions of dividend payments each year.

As the agent for the UK government, the Bank acts on its behalf in the foreign exchange markets by buying and selling different currencies to try and lift or depress their values; it also monitors developments in the City of London, particularly in the banking sector, financial markets and institutions.

The Governor of the Bank of England is appointed by the Prime Minister and its activities are supervised by the Chancellor of the Exchequer via the Treasury.

Bank overdraft Amount of money that the customer owes the bank, as a result of having drawn out more money than is deposited. Also known as being 'in the red', since debit balances used to be shown in red ink on bank statements. Bank managers are prepared to negotiate overdraft facilities, which allow the customer to be overdrawn up to a specified maximum amount for a specified period. The interest rate charged by the bank depends on the size of the overdraft and the considered risk of lending (i.e. the financial standing or whether any security has been provided) to the customer.

However, banks penalize unauthorized overdrafts with very high rates of interest and will on occasion 'bounce' (refuse to pay) cheques if the customer runs up an unauthorized overdraft or exceeds the agreed overdraft limit, especially if reminder letters have been ignored. Small overdrafts are normally arranged between the customer and the local bank manager, who has some discretion over the terms.

Bank rate Originally was the lowest rate at which the Bank of England would discount approved bills of exchange and was used by other banks as the basis for the interest rates on deposits, loans and discounts. In October 1972 it was replaced by the Minimum Lending Rate, and nowadays is used as an alternative name for the base rate. See BASE RATE and MINIMUM LENDING RATE.

Bank reference Assurance given by a bank that a customer has an account with it and is believed to be creditworthy. Usually required by suppliers of goods or services as a precaution before giving any credit or business to a new client.

Bank run Heavy and urgent demands by customers to withdraw their money, normally caused by fear that the bank itself may be in financial trouble. One of the worst things that can happen to a bank, since even an unjustified run on a bank can wipe out its reserves and force it into bankruptcy.

Bankrupt When someone is unable to pay debts in full, an application for a bankruptcy order is made to the High Court either by the debtor or by any creditor owed more than £50. If a bankruptcy order is made, the Court appoints a receiver who takes possession of the debtor's entire property (with the exception under the Bankruptcy Act 1914 of the tools of his/her trade and some clothing) and compiles a list of the debts and assets. The creditors and debtor can then agree to a scheme of arrangement by which each creditor may be paid wholly or in part. If such an arrangement is not agreed, however, then the debtor is declared bankrupt and the court appoints a trustee who will share out the debtor's property among the creditors. Once this has been done, the debtor can apply to be discharged from bankruptcy but has to prove to the Court that everything reasonably possible has been done to settle the debts.

A certified bankrupt is someone who, on being discharged, is given by the Court a 'certificate of misfortune' stating that the bankruptcy was not caused by any wrongful or dishonest act. An undischarged bankrupt may not act as a director or take part in the management of a company; may not sit or vote in the House of Lords or House of Commons; may not be appointed or act as a Justice of the Peace; and may not hold the office of mayor, alderman, councillor or county councillor.

There are strict limits on the amount of credit an undischarged bankrupt may obtain, and on entering into contracts.

A company cannot be declared

bankrupt. Instead it is put into liquidation and its assets turned into cash for distribution to the creditors. See INSOLVENCY.

Banks Originally formed, as a successor to storehouses for valuables, to look after other people's money and keep it secure, banking services have widened considerably over the years into providing loans for individuals and companies, as well as investment, insurance and legal facilities. They charge for all these services in various ways – either directly, as with their money-lending side, or indirectly by making a profit on the money deposited with them. In the UK, banks have to be authorized under the Banking Acts and are subject to strict regulations. Clearing, commercial or retail, banks deal mainly with the general public, while also helping to finance businesses.

In contrast merchant banks have traditionally been mainly concerned with trade and industrial finance.

These days there is a great deal of overlapping, with both kinds of bank offering investment products and services and venture capital for business. The main clearing banks all have merchant banking subsidiaries. See CLEARING, COMMERCIAL and MERCHANT BANKS.

Bank statement A record, supplied by banks to customers, giving details of all payments and receipts over a specified period of time, often monthly or quarterly. Nowadays statements are usually supplied on loose-leaf sheets, prepared by a computer, and give few details of the individual transactions. In most cases they simply add up the payments and receipts to state whether there is a credit or debit balance in the account. Some small 'private' banks continue to provide more detailed statements identifying individual

transactions, but they tend to charge for this service.

Bank transfer A method of transferring funds between different accounts or different banks without the use of cheques or drafts. Normally used for making payments to accounts overseas. The bank is instructed to pay a stated sum to a named account abroad and does so through its branch, agent or correspondent in the foreign country. It deducts the sum, and its charges, direct from the payer's account; it is one of the best ways of transferring capital sums from one country to another. It can be the quickest too, if the instructions can be passed on by the bank by telegraph, cable or telex. See TELEGRAPHIC TRANSFER.

Bargain Terms used on the stock market to describe a sale or purchase. It does not imply that the transaction was made at a cheap or favourable price, simple that the deal was concluded.

Barometer stocks Shares of leading companies whose price movements are seen as mirroring the underlying mood of the whole market. See BLUE CHIPS.

Base date Important element in calculating an index. Movements in an index are often expressed as variations above or below its original starting point – the base date. The current figure of an index, therefore, is only relevant when compared with the figure, normally 100, on its base date.

Base metals Non-precious metals, used by industry for manufacturing purposes. Leading base metals are aluminium, copper, lead, nickel, tin and zinc. The main centre for trading base metals, and helping to fix current prices, is the LONDON METAL EXCHANGE. See USEFUL ADDRESSES.

Base rate Minimum rate at which banks are prepared to lend money, which acts as a benchmark for other interest rates, including personal loans and mortgages. Changes in base rate are influenced by the trend in the Minimum Lending Rate controlled by the government via the Bank of England as part of general economic policy. In turn, the base rate influences the trend in other interest rates. The cost of loans is often expressed as a percentage over base rate, varied according to the size of the borrowing and the risk involved.

'Managed' interest rates, like the fixed rates used for credit cards and mortgages for home purchase, are also influenced by base rate, but tend to change less often. A small variation in base rate may not affect 'managed' rates immediately, especially if it is viewed as only a temporary change; but eventually all interest rates are governed by the base rate, which represents the prime cost of borrowing money. Indeed in the United States it is called the prime (lending) rate.

Basis point The unit of an index. If an index rises from 150 to 160 it is said to have risen by 10 basis points – but of course this figure would be different if expressed in percentage terms.

Bear Someone who takes the view that something is going to decline in value or not to work out well; a pessimistic outlook. Originally, a stock market term believed to derive from the tradition that bear-hunters would make sure there was a market for the skins before they went out to shoot the bears. In other words, selling something they didn't yet possess – now known as 'going short'. An alternative view is that the term derived from the tactic of speculators selling when they were 'bare' of stock in the hope that they could buy back at a cheaper price,

thereby making a profit from the difference.

Bear selling is not confined to the stock market. It is a more common practice in commodity and financial futures, as well as in the forward currency markets, or indeed in any market where a fall in value is anticipated.

It is often claimed that in markets, like futures, where it is as easy to sell as to buy, 'bears' tend to make more money over the long term. Selling 'short' is slightly different in that it covers occasions where the seller does not possess what is being sold; whereas bear selling could mean disposing of a stock or possession in anticipation of its declining in value.

Over the years, the use of the term 'bear', or bearish, has developed into a much wider context to indicate a generally gloomy view that something will not live up to expectations. Politicians, for example, might take a bearish view of the economy over the next six months, or the chances of their party winning the next election; or a football fan may be a 'bear' of England's chances of winning the World Cup. The opposite of a 'BULL', who takes an optimistic view. Drawing of 'bears' and 'bulls' are often used to symbolize sellers and buyers.

Bearer bills, bonds, cheques, debentures, shares Documents which state that the holder (or bearer) is entitled to payment on presentation. This means that ownership can be transferred simply by passing on the document to someone, who then becomes the legal owner. This avoids a lot of the paperwork normally involved in transferring stock or money, but makes it risky since any thief would be able to cash them in without having to establish proof of ownership. See BONDS, DEBENTURE.

Bearer scrip A temporary document

issued after someone has paid the first instalment for a government bond or a new issue of company debentures.

Bear hug Notice to a company that a tender offer to buy it is under consideration. 'Strong bear hug' is when the offer is made public, putting pressure on the company, or 'teddy bear hug', by which the company indicates that it is in favour of being taken over, but only at a higher price.

Bear market Where values enter a downward phase. This can be over a long period or just temporarily. Normally used to describe stock markets, but also widely used for other areas like property, commodities or currencies.

Bear position Situation where someone has contracted to sell more stock than actually held in possession, and is, therefore, 'short' of the market.

Bear raid or campaign When dealers get together to force down the price of a stock by selling, in the hope of being able to buy it back at cheaper levels.

Bear squeeze Tactic by holders of stocks, futures or currencies to starve the market of supplies, thus forcing 'short' sellers to pay higher and higher prices in order to buy so that they can meet their commitment to deliver on a particular date.

Bear trap Setting up a bear squeeze.

Bed and Breakfast Stock Exchange term for a manoeuvre designed to save payment of capital gains tax. Holders of stocks sell one day in the afternoon, and buy back the same stock the following morning. This establishes a 'loss' or 'gain' on the sale which can be offset against tax

liabilities or use up the amount of profits that can be made each year free of capital gains tax (the annual exemption). Nowadays, bed and breakfasting is often used as a general term to describe simultaneous sales and purchases for tax relief purposes.

Beneficial interest When someone is not the official legal owner, but may have rights through a trust or private agreement to some or all of the benefits.

Beneficial loan A loan provided at a specially low interest rate. But in the case of a company loan, the employee might face having to pay tax on the amount of interest forgone.

Beneficial owner Person or persons who are the real owners of a stock or property even though it may be registered in someone else's name, such as a nominee, on their behalf. See NOMINEE.

Beneficiary Person or organization who stands to benefit, normally financially, from an insurance policy, trust or Will.

Benefit in kind Something extra, like free meals, use of car or house, or a holiday given instead of money to pay for services, usually to an employee. See FRINGE BENEFITS.

Benefit statements Legal requirement since 1987 for employers with pension schemes to provide statements to members showing how much they have earned in the scheme to date.

BES See BUSINESS EXPANSION SCHEME.

Best advice A requirement introduced by the Financial Services Act that anyone selling a financial product should recommend the most suitable product for the customer irrespective of what commissions might or might not be earned. For independent brokers and intermediaries, best advice means selecting the most suitable product available on the whole market. But for company salesmen it means choosing the most suitable product from the company range.

Best execution   Obtaining the most competitive market price for a buyer or seller, particularly on the stock markets and futures exchanges.

Beta shares   Second-line shares dealt in on the Stock Exchange. Under the system introduced by the Exchange in October 1986, the shares of companies traded were divided into several categories – Alpha, Beta, Gamma and Delta – based on the size, available stock and type of company. The Beta category includes the most actively traded shares after Alpha. Member firms dealing in the shares have to input into SEAQ (Stock Exchange Automated Quotes System) the prices at which they are prepared to buy or sell. But, unlike Alpha shares, the most recent price at which a transaction has been concluded does not need to be fed into the system. See STOCK EXCHANGE.

Betterment   Increase in the value of a property as a result of public improvements or commercial developments. Hence betterment levy, a charge imposed by government on the rise in the value of development land when sold, which was subsequently incorporated in the capital gains tax system.

Bid   Offer to buy something at a stated price. Originally used at auctions, but nowadays used widely to describe other financial transactions, such as TAKEOVER BID.

Bid basis or valuation   Term used to describe method of pricing used when sales of units in a unit trust or unit-linked fund exceed purchases, thus forcing the manager to sell holdings. This means that the price is lowered to reflect the amount managers could expect to receive if they sold the shares held in the fund. Moving to a bid basis discourages selling of the fund, and encourages buying, since the valuation of the units is at the lower end of the scale. But reducing the value of the units means that the fund's performance record is lowered; and it is therefore avoided, if at all possible. See UNIT TRUSTS.

Bid/offer spread   The difference between the price at which a share, unit trust or fund can be bought and sold. The bid price is the lower one, representing the price received by a seller, while the offer price is the higher, representing the price paid by a buyer. So if a buyer sells immediately, he loses the spread. In the case of unit trusts, the spread takes into account the initial charge, and other costs, as well as the spread in the value of the underlying shares held. With shares, the spread can vary considerably, depending on the level of trading activity. An actively traded share tends to have a low spread, reflecting the willingness of the market to deal. A wide spread means that the market-maker is more reluctant to take a risk in shares that may be difficult to sell.

Bid valuation   See BID BASIS.

Big Bang   Popular phrase coined to describe the changed system for Stock Exchange dealings introduced from 27 October 1986. Because the changes were so far-reaching they were compared with the astronomers' theory that the world was created as a result of a big bang (explosion) in space. What had not been anticipated was that the Big Bang changes would also quickly result in the abandonment of the Stock Exchange 'floor' as a trading centre, with all dealings now being conducted via screens and computer systems. The Big Bang changes, originally started by the Office of Fair Trading to stop the fixing of minimum commissions on dealings, also resulted in the disappearance of the whole jobbing system and the replacement of jobbers by market-makers. See STOCK EXCHANGE.

Big Board Popular name for the New York Stock Exchange, coined from the number of companies listed there and shown on a 'big board'.

Billion Now defined as a thousand million (1,000,000,000) on both sides of the Atlantic. Previously in Britain a billion was a million million (1,000,000,000,000), but it was decided to switch to the American version.

Bill of exchange A written order telling one person to pay a certain sum of money to a named person on demand or at some date in the future. Used mainly in foreign trade and as money market instruments. See MONEY MARKET.

Bill of lading A shipping document used in foreign trading. It is given by the shipper acknowledging receipt of the goods, describing their condition and promising to deliver them in the same condition to the recipient named in the document. It is normally accompanied by a bill of exchange drawn upon the purchaser to pay for the goods.

Bimetallism A monetary system based on having gold and silver as standard metals for the coinage, with a fixed rate of exchange between the two metals. The system was used in the United States and some parts of Europe during the nineteenth century, but became impossible to manage because of the change in world prices of the two metals. It became outdated when paper money replaced the use of metals as a standard basis for the coinage.

BIS See BANK FOR INTERNATIONAL SETTLEMENTS.

Black economy Popular term for undeclared earnings, on which no income tax, Valued Added Tax or National Insurance has been paid. Accurate assessments of the size of the black economy naturally are hard to come by, but it is estimated that several billions of pounds in tax revenue is lost by the government each year.

Blanket bond See BOND.

Blanket insurance Policy that covers several different risks, such as fire and theft, or several different properties.

Blanket mortgage New mortgage that replaces and continues several different existing mortgages.

Blind person's allowance Special government allowance available to anyone on the blind persons' register. In the case of married couples, only one partner has to be on the register for them to qualify for the allowance.

Block insurance Policy that covers several different kinds of risks, especially goods being transported.

Blue button Popular term for a trainee stockbroker who checks prices on the stock markets.

Blue chip A term used to describe investments that are viewed as being solid and secure. In fact the original phrase meant almost exactly the opposite. It was first coined in the United States to describe a particular type of share that was risky, since the blue chip used in gambling was the one with the highest value. Over the years, possibly because of mistaken association with 'blue blood' and 'chip off the old block', the meaning has changed to describe the safest and most reputable shares dealt on the stock market. Brokers seeking to reassure investors will advise dealing in blue chip companies, which are normally household name groups with substantial assets favoured by pension funds and financial institutions seeking safety. As a result, 'blue chip' is now used to describe any investment that is considered to be soundly based and secure with substantial backing.

Boilerhouse A derogatory term used to describe the activities of high-pressure sales operations, usually selling inferior or fraudulent financial products, ranging from speciality (strategic) metals to shares in non-existent companies.

Bona vacantia A property or asset with no known owner. Most frequently occurs with shares whose original owners have died and the heirs cannot be traced, or when a property remains in the hands of a liquidator when a company is dissolved. Eventually ownership of the property reverts to the government; land is compulsorily acquired by the local authority; and shares are returned to the company that issued them.

Bond Originally a formal document promising to repay a sum of money, acknowledging a debt or pledging to fulfil a commitment. In the financial markets, bonds are securities paying fixed rates of interest, normally issued by governments, local authorities or corporations which

guarantee repayment on the specified date.

But the term is also used in a more general sense to describe a wide range of investment products, ranging from guaranteed income bonds to investment bonds, property and broker bonds. There is, therefore, a considerable number of variously named bonds.

Active bond – A bond with a fixed rate of interest paid from the date when the bond is first offered for sale.

Administration bond – A bond which must be entered into by a person applying for letters of administration to administer the estate of someone who has died without leaving a Will. The bond states that the administrator will act according to the law, under the threat of losing double the value of the estate if failing to do so.

Annuity or perpetual bond – A bond which has no stated date for maturity, and therefore pays interest for ever. Most notable example is the Consols UK government security (gilt), which has no fixed repayment date.

Appeal bond – A bond pledging that the appellant will make sure all costs and damages are paid if the appeal is lost.

Assented or enfaced bond – A bond where the holder has agreed to a change in the conditions.

Assumed or endorsed bond – A bond, issued by one borrower, that is later taken over by someone else assuming the liability to pay.

Bearer bond – A bond which is not formally recorded in the name of the owner, but is simply payable to current holder or bearer. It is therefore a negotiable bond that can be easily passed from hand to hand. See NEGOTIABLE INSTRUMENT.

Blanket bond – An insurance contract protecting an employer from losses suffered as a result of dishonesty or failure to perform duties by any of the employees. Similar to fidelity or indemnity bonds (see below).

Callable or redeemable bond – Bond which can be repaid whenever the borrower wishes.

Clean bond – A government bond whose price needs no adjustment to allow for accumulated interest, since the interest has just been paid.

Common money bond – Promise to pay a sum of money.

Consolidated bond – Bond issued to combine several other issues of bonds into one.

Continued bond – Where the holder can claim payment later than the stated date of maturity.

Convertible bond – Bond, especially one issued by a government, that can be exchanged on the date of maturity for another bond instead of being repaid.

Coupon bond – A bond with a set of coupons, one of which is given up by the holder in exchange for the interest due on the date stated on the coupon. Often used with bearer bonds.

Currency bond – A bond which will be repaid in the currency of the country issuing it. However, a US currency bond can be repaid in the currency of any country.

Deferred bond – Pays interest at a low rate to start with, and gradually increases it to a full fixed rate by a specified date.

Dirty bond – Opposite of CLEAN bond in that the price has to be adjusted to allow for accumulated interest.

Discount bond – A bond sold at less than its face value at maturity.

Escalator bond – Dated loan stock where the rate of interest varies according to market conditions.

Extended bond – One of an issue of bonds where the holders, as a group, have agreed that the maturity (repayment) date be changed to a later date.

Fidelity or fiduciary bond – A bond which a trustee, or someone in a position of responsibility, bringing a lawsuit has to take out with an insurance company, and which promises to pay any damages or losses.

Gold bond – Bond where interest and repayment are payable in gold. Normally issued by governments, but sometimes also by gold mining companies and gold bullion dealers.

Guaranty bond – Special form of fidelity bond giving protection against loss arising from the failure of a named person to perform a stated duty.

Income bond – Issued primarily by life assurance companies as GUARANTEED INCOME BONDS, which provide the investor with a fixed income, paid at regular intervals, as well as guaranteeing the return of the original capital investment at the end of a specified term. See DEBENTURE, INCOME.

Indemnity bond – General description given to all bonds which provide payment in the event of losses caused by dishonesty or the failure of someone to perform certain duties. See BOND, FIDELITY OR FIDUCIARY.

Indexed or stabilized bond – A bond in which the rate of interest and the repayment sum are linked to the cost of living index, so that the bond maintains its value in line with inflation.

Interest bond – A bond offered instead of an interest payment, when the borrower is unable to pay the interest in cash.

Joint and several bond – A bond which is backed by two guarantors, who accept full responsibility for repayment if the borrower is unable to pay the debt.

Mortgage bond – See LOCAL AUTHORITY BONDS.

Municipal bond – One issued by local government authority; primarily a term used in the United States.

Option bond – Where the bond can be repaid when the borrower wishes to do so.

Participating or profit-sharing bond – Bond which not only pays interest at a fixed rate but also earns a share in the profits of the borrower's company.

Passive bond – One on which no interest is payable.

Penalty bond – Bond which states that a certain sum of money will be paid if a named party fails to perform a promised duty, such as failing to complete a building on time.

Performance bond – Insurance contract against the risk of a contractor failing to perform the contract.

Post obit. bond – Promise to repay a loan, with interest, on the death of a named person who is expected to leave money to the borrower.

Premium bond – See NATIONAL SAVINGS.

Property bond – Bond issued by a life assurance company, where the premiums are invested in a property fund. Also an investment fund which puts money into property rather than into stocks and shares.

Refunding bond – A new issue of bonds aimed at raising money to repay an earlier issue.

Registered bond – Where the holder's name is recorded by the issuer.

In the case of registered coupon bonds, the name of the holder is listed, but the coupons on which interest is paid can be cashed in by the bearer, who may not necessarily be the listed holder.

Surety or fiduciary bond – A formal agreement by a guarantor (often an insurance company) to pay a stated sum of money if a certain party fails to pay a debt, or perform a duty, by a specified date.

Town hall bond – See LOCAL AUTHORITY BONDS.

Transferable bond – A form of bearer bond where the ownership can be passed on without the change being recorded by the issuer.

Treasury bond (T-bond) – A bond issued by the US Treasury. Alternatively, describes any bond retained by the organization that issued it and kept in its treasury, because it has either not been sold or has been bought back.

Yearling bond – Bonds issued by local authorities, where the original capital is repaid after one year. See YEARLING.

Bonded goods Imported goods that are retained in a bonded warehouse, pending either payment of customs or excise duty, or re-export free of duty. Wine and spirits are held in bonded vaults. Some factories, which manufacture goods from imported raw materials for export, qualify as bonded warehouses. Bonded stores contain stores to be used on board ships that will not be liable to pay duty.

Bond washing Tactic widely used at one time in the government securities (gilts) and other bond markets by high rate taxpayers to reduce their liability to income tax due on dividends or interest.

The holder of a gilt or bond sells out just prior to the date for payment of the dividend or interest, when the market price is higher in anticipation of the payment, and buys back when the market price falls back to a lower level after the payment has been made. Thus a capital gain is made instead of receiving the income. Changes in the taxation laws to block this loophole made the practice no longer worth exploiting in a big way.

Bonus Additional payment. Bonuses on with-profit life assurance policies are paid in two main ways. Each year the insurance company values its assets and profits to decide whether it can afford to pay a bonus, usually called a reversionary bonus, to the policy-holders. Since the bonus depends on the prosperity of the company, it is not guaranteed to be paid. Once given, however, this annual, or reversionary, bonus is added to the value of the policy and cannot be taken away. At the end of the policy term, either on the death of the assured or the maturity (repayment) date having been reached, the insurance company may add another bonus (again depending on its financial prosperity), normally called the terminal bonus. See REVERSIONARY and TERMINAL BONUS.

Bonus shares New shares issued by a company to its existing shareholders, free of payment, as a way of turning some of the accumulated profits and reserves into capital. They are usually issued in the proportion of one bonus share for a stated number of shares already held. See SCRIP ISSUE.

Book or box Investments held to the account of a broker or manager for resale. Also a float of units kept by managers of unit trusts to balance sales with redemptions.

Book debts An amount owing to a business for goods already sold.

Book entry Entry made only to correct a mistake in an account. See CONTRA.

Book profit A profit which exists only on paper, such as the supposed increase in the value of asset over its original cost, but not yet realized for cash.

Book value The value of an asset in a business as shown in the accounts. This may not be the real value, since it is the custom to value stock at the original cost or current market value, whichever is the lower, and other assets at cost minus amounts written off for depreciation. See ASSETS (HIDDEN).

Borrowing A technical term used on the London Metal Exchange to describe the simultaneous purchase of a metal for delivery at a nearby date, matched by the sale of the same quantity of metal for delivery at a new and later date, thus effectively borrowing metal from the market for a limited period. The opposite of lending.

Boot strap A cash offer for the controlling interest in a company which is followed by a lower offer for the remaining shares.

Bottomry Mortgage of a ship. The money is borrowed to pay for repairs and other expenses to get the ship back to its home port, with the ship used as security against the loan.

Bounce Popular term for a bank refusing to pay out on a cheque, usually because the customer has insufficient funds to cover it. See BANK OVERDRAFT.

Bourse French word widely used,

especially in Europe, for a stock or commodity exchange or money market, although 'the Bourse' usually refers to the Paris Stock Exchange. Also used as a general description for international stock and futures exchanges.

Boutique Term used to describe a financial services company offering a range of specialist products or having an office in a shopping area which provides advice for investors walking in off the street. See SHARE SHOP.

Box See BOOK.

Break-up value Value of assets in a business if each asset is sold separately, as distinguished from the value of the business as a whole. As ASSET STRIPPERS were quick to realize, the break-up value of the profitable parts of a business, unencumbered by the less profitable or loss-making parts, can sometimes exceed the value of the whole group. Break-up originally referred to the sale of wrecked ships or other assets, which were no longer of practical use but whose component parts had some value.

Bretton Woods Place in the United States where a conference of 44 nations was held in 1944 to plan better co-operation in world trade and currency matters. This led to the founding of the International Monetary Fund (IMF) and the International Bank for Reconstruction and Development (better known as the World Bank). It also resulted in the Bretton Woods Agreement, aimed at stabilizing exchange rates between various currencies within agreed parameters, which has subsequently foundered.

Bridging finance Short-term funding for a company which is on the point of raising

additional capital either from investors or from the issue of shares.

Bridging loan A temporary loan, usually made by a bank, for a short period in order to help the borrower cover the gap in time between buying and selling, say, a house or a car. If the sale is assured, the bank will be more willing to lend and will charge a lower rate of interest than if the sale has not been finalized.

British funds Short name for fixed-interest stocks issued by the British government or the nationalized industries, guaranteed by the government.

Broken amount Stock market term for an irregular number of shares, which may be more difficult to sell than the normal amount offered for sale.

Broker A middleman. An agent paid for services rendered by a brokerage or commission, usually calculated as a percentage of the value of the business done but sometimes at a set fee. In theory a broker acts on behalf of a principal, either a buyer or seller, and cannot act in his own name. But there are many exceptions, notably commodity and some stockbroking companies, who are also market-makers. Brokers tend to specialize in certain areas: foreign exchange, insurance, and stocks. However, 'broker' has become a generic term to include COMMISSION HOUSES, FINANCIAL ADVISERS and INTERMEDIARIES.

Brokerage Payment received by a broker; usually in the form of commission, calculated as a percentage of the value of business done by the broker, but sometimes a fixed fee is paid in addition or instead. See COMMISSION.

Broker-dealer A new type of broker,

who is involved in the marketing of securities, as well as buying and selling them on behalf of customers.

Broker loan rate The interest rate charged by banks to brokers in the United States borrowing to cover the investment positions taken out by their clients.

Broker's bond An investment fund, managed by brokers on behalf of clients in return for commission or a set charge.

Broker's lien The right given by law to a broker to retain an insurance policy until the premium has been paid. This protects brokers who are liable to pay the premiums on the policy, whether or not they are paid by their clients.

Broking house A firm (partnership) or company that carries on the business of brokers.

BSS (Business Start-up Scheme) See BUSINESS EXPANSION SCHEME.

Bubble Derogatory slang term used to describe a market price upsurge that is thought likely to be only short-lived because it is unsoundly based. Dates back to the South Sea Bubble in 1720 when there was a spectacular collapse in the price of South Sea company shares. See SOUTH SEA BUBBLE.

Bucket shop Slang expression used to describe companies which are considered to be shady and dishonest. More specifically, brokers dealing in commodities, futures, stocks and shares who are not members of a recognized Exchange and are, therefore, trading out of a bucket. See BOILERHOUSE.

Budget An account of probable future income and expenditure over a specific period. Used as a guide in financial planning by governments, companies, organizations and individuals.

The British government's national budget is normally presented to the House of Commons each year in late March or early April, although on occasion there have been mini-Budgets at other times of the year to deal with a particular financial crisis. The Budget outlines the current state of Britain's financial position and prospects, in the view of the Chancellor of the Exchequer, and details any proposed changes in fiscal policy or taxation to be included in the Finance Bill that has subsequently to be approved by Parliament. The Budget is normally the main opportunity for the government to review its overall financial strategy and introduce the necessary legislation to implement it.

Budget account A special account, offered by banks and building societies, under which customers calculate their total bills for the year, divide the sum by twelve and pay that amount into the account each month, although the bills are paid whenever they fall due. This system smooths out the flow of money through the account and avoids the need to seek overdrafts during the peak payment periods.

Shops and department stores also offer budget accounts, whereby the customer contributes a fixed monthly sum and is able to buy and take immediate delivery of goods on credit up to an agreed ceiling, often twelve times the monthly payment.

Buffer stock A mechanism supposed to reduce price volatility, particularly in the value of raw materials. The buffer stock buys up surpluses during times of over-supply and sells the accumulated stock when there is a shortage. The scheme dates back to biblical times, when

Joseph accumulated grain in Egypt during seven years of plenty and helped avoid starvation during the following seven lean years when the harvest failed. In modern times, buffer stocks have been associated mainly with international commodity agreements concluded between the leading producing and consuming countries. The agreement sets a buffer stock price range, with a 'floor' and 'ceiling' within which it would like to contain prices. The buffer stock is a buyer when market prices sink to the lower half of the range, in order to try and prevent the price going through the floor; it is a seller when market prices rise to the upper half and threaten to reach the ceiling. There are, however, two major flaws. If the buffer stock price range is set too high, in the long term the buffer stock runs out of resources to deal with the over-production encouraged by the high price levels. In addition, a buffer stock is unable to control prices going through the ceiling once its surplus stocks have been sold off. See COMMODITY AGREEMENTS.

Buildings insurance Policies that insure buildings, as opposed to their contents, against damage from fire, floods, subsidence and weather. The sum insured should take into account the cost of rebuilding, rather than just the current market value of the property. In the case of leasehold property, the owner of the freehold is often responsible for insuring the whole building.

Building societies First formed during the Industrial Revolution in the early part of the nineteenth century by groups of workers combining their funds to buy land and build houses for themselves. Mutual societies were formed on a non-profit-making basis to pool resources and buy houses for each member in turn.

Many societies then expanded into providing a wider service to the general public by taking in savings, which were then lent to people wishing to buy houses. As they grew in size and stature, building societies became subject to government regulation to protect the public; they were granted certain privileges, which enabled them to be used as the main vehicle to expand home ownership and at one time gave them a virtual monopoly in providing mortgages. Since then, banks and other financial institutions have captured a larger share of the mortgage market, but the Building Societies Act 1986 allowed the societies freedom to move into many other areas of investment and savings, directly competing with banks.

Historically, building societies have relied on so-called retail savings by private investors to generate the funds required to provide mortgages, whereas banks use wholesale funds drawn from the international money markets. Now the lines have become blurred, with societies also obtaining a proportion of their funds from the wholesale money market.

Both banks and building societies are forced under government legislation to deduct composite-rate tax at an agreed level for any interest paid to UK residents or organizations. It is not deducted from interest paid on deposits held by overseas investors. Composite-rate tax, set slightly below the standard rate, is not reclaimable even if the investor is not liable to pay tax.

Traditionally, building societies have been non-profit mutual organizations, owned by the members with investment accounts; but the 1986 Act included powers that enabled societies to turn into public companies, and thus raise money from outside sources, if this is agreed by a majority of the members. See COMPOSITE-RATE TAX, FRIENDLY SOCIETIES and MORTGAGES.

Building Societies Association
Organization formed by the societies to
represent their interests. At one time, it
organized the fixing of a standard
mortgage rate for all its member societies.
But when that was abandoned, the main
function of the Association changed to
become an information unit and
representative of the building societies'
interests in discussions with the
government and other organizations. See
USEFUL ADDRESSES.

Building Societies Commission An
offshoot of the Treasury, set up in 1987 to
take over supervision of the building
societies from the Chief Registrar of
Friendly Societies. See OMBUDSMAN.

Building society ombudsman
Independent official appointed to run an
office that attempts to settle disputes
between building societies and their
customers. All societies have to be
members of the scheme, but the
ombudsman's powers are limited. See
OMBUDSMAN and USEFUL ADDRESSES.

Bull Someone who takes the view that
something is going to rise in value or work
out well; an optimistic outlook. Originally a
stock market term, used as the opposite of
BEAR and believed to derive from the
habit of bulls making a headlong charge
without bothering about obstacles in their
path. Bull speculators buy in anticipation of
values going up, hoping to make a profit by
buying cheap and selling out later at a
higher level; hence bull positions, which
can be achieved either by building up
stocks to hold or by making a forward or
futures buying contract. Bull, or bullish, is
no longer confined to the financial
markets; it also means taking a generally
optimistic view and expecting things to
improve. Someone may be bullish about
the prospects for the world economy or

England's chances of winning the Test
match against Australia. Figures of bulls
and bears are often used to symbolize
buyers and sellers respectively.

Bulldog Term used to describe
fixed-interest bonds denominated in
sterling but issued by foreign governments
and international agencies outside Britain.

Bullet A fixed interest security issued
with a single fixed maturity (repayment)
date.

Bullion Gold and silver, of standard
purity, in bulk form of ingots or bars; not
coins, jewellery or manufactured products.
Valued by its weight, not its appearance.

Bullion brokers or dealers
Organizations trading in gold, silver and
other precious metals. In London, when
trading in gold by individuals was forbidden
to damp down speculation, brokers dealing
in bullion had to be specially authorized by
the Bank of England to operate. These
restrictions were subsequently lifted, a
new London bullion association was
formed and its members authorized by the
Securities and Investment Board.
However, the original members of the
London bullion market still meet together
to decide the London daily fixing prices for
gold and silver. See FIXING.

Bullion market Worldwide market
dealing in gold and silver bars and ingots.

Bull market Where values are in
upward trend, either for a long period or
just temporarily. Normally used to
describe rising stock markets, but also
used widely for other areas such as
property, commodities or currencies.

Bursar A treasurer or trusted financial
official, especially of schools or colleges,

or a student receiving a bursary – an allowance or grant.

Business Expansion Scheme (BES) A scheme giving tax relief incentives to encourage investors to back higher risk business ventures, thus helping new companies, which might have difficulty in borrowing from banks or raising normal venture capital, to get off the ground and it is to be hoped create additional jobs. Originally called the Business Start-up Scheme (BSS) and then amended to the BES. The basic principle is to tempt high rate taxpayers in particular to invest in businesses they might normally consider to be too risky. In return for taking the risk, they receive relief on the sum invested at their top rate of tax. The scheme, however, is surrounded by all kinds of restrictions that are constantly being amended to stop loopholes being exploited. In the 1989 Budget ASSURED TENANCY SCHEMES were introduced with the different objective of relieving the shortage of rented accommodation.

Buy-out See MANAGEMENT BUY-OUT.

C

CACA See CERTIFIED ACCOUNTANT and USEFUL ADDRESSES.

Call A request for shareholders in a company to pay certain sums due on the shares that they already hold. This occurs when companies issue shares at below their par (nominal) value and then 'call' on holders to pay the difference or forfeit their shares. A similar system is used with new issues, notably the government privatization issues, where payments for the shares were divided into instalments. After the initial payment, calls are made for the rest of the money due.

Callable bond See BOND.

Call deposit Money left with a bank which can be withdrawn immediately (on call) without giving any notice.

Called-up capital The proportion of a company's issued share capital that has actually been taken up.

Call money Deposits placed on the money market available for withdrawal immediately.

Call option A contract giving the owner the right to buy a specified number or quantity of shares, commodities or futures, at a fixed price at any time on or before a given date.

CAMIFA Campaign for Independent Finance Advice. Organization set up, following the Financial Services Act 1986, by a group of insurance companies to promote independently owned brokers. It provides names of local independent advisers. See USEFUL ADDRESSES.

Candlemas See QUARTER DAY.

Cap A ceiling put to limit the rise in the rate of interest paid by a borrower, notably for mortgages. Also the initials for the European Community's Common Agricultural Policy.

Cap and collar Mortgages which set upper and lower limits to a range in which the interest rate can move, usually during a fixed period of time.

Capital The total financial resources available to a company, organization or individual. Money required to run a business or organization.

Capital allowances Deductions allowed by the Inland Revenue for the reduction in the value of assets.

Capital assets See ASSETS.

Capital bonds National Savings product introduced in 1989 that offers a guaranteed rate of interest annually, provided the Bonds are held for five years. Interest is paid gross, but there is a liability to pay income tax annually, so the investor faces paying tax in advance. See NATIONAL SAVINGS.

Capital conversion plan A tax avoidance scheme under which a lump-sum investment is gradually transferred into a life assurance policy, providing tax-free income. See QUALIFYING POLICY.

Capital gains tax (CGT) Introduced in two stages: on short-term gains in 1962, and then revised in 1965 to include long-term gains as well. The tax is aimed at profits or gains made from the rise in value of a capital asset, like a share or painting, as opposed to income. Previously, CGT was imposed at a single fixed rate, lower than the higher rates of income tax, so there was considerable incentive for higher rate taxpayers to convert income into capital gains wherever possible. However, in the 1988 Budget it was decided to equalize the capital gains tax rate with the income tax rate, with the introduction of higher rate capital gains tax payable if taxable income and capital gains exceed a specified level. An annual amount of tax-free capital gains can still be made before the tax starts to be imposed. This annual exemption, reduced in the 1988 Budget to offset other tax concessions, is adjusted in line with inflation, or with government policy, like other tax allowances. The main exemptions from CGT are owner-occupied private residences and government securities (gilts). Pension funds and charities are also exempt.

Additionally there is provision for taxpayers to reduce their liability to capital gains tax in line with the rate of inflation between the dates of purchase and sale. In 1983 the government accounced that as from April 1982, allowance would be made for inflation when calculating the taxable gain. The indexation allowance, as it is known, is based on movements in the Retail Price Index each month since March 1982 which represent the official inflation rate since then. The tax liability is calculated by assessing the gain made between the date of purchase and the date of the sale, after deducting the amount attributable to inflation during the period in question. In the 1988 Budget it was announced that gains made prior to March 1982 would be disregarded for capital gains tax purposes. See INDEXATION ALLOWANCE.

Capital stock The capital of a company provided by subscribers or converted into units from shares.

Capitalization Value of a company determined by the market price of its issued shares. A useful guide for investment purposes in assessing the size of a company.

Capitalization issue Method of creating additional share capital by the replacement of new shares for old or by share rationalization. See BONUS and SCRIP ISSUE.

Capitalize Take money out of the reserves of a company and turn it into capital by giving it to shareholders in the form of extra, or bonus, shares. Alternatively, sell an asset; calculate the value of an asset; or provide the money needed as capital for a business concern.

Capital market Name given to financial centres, for example London and New York, where money is raised for commercial and industrial companies, as well as central and local government and other organizations. The raising of capital is usually arranged by issuing houses, who are in touch with both institutional and private investors. The stock market then provides a trading market once the shares and loans have been issued.

Capital redemption policy A life assurance contract which pays out a sum of money on a specified date, whether the insured is alive or dead at the time.

Capital structure The different kind of shares, stocks and loans which, combined together, provide the capital of a company.

Capital sum The lump sum payable when an insurance or pension policy reaches its maturity (repayment) date.

Capital Taxes Office (CTO) Branch of the Inland Revenue dealing with transfers of capital that may be liable to inheritance tax.

Capital transfer tax (CTT) Introduced in 1975 to replace the system of estate, or death, duty. Subsequently replaced in 1987 by INHERITANCE TAX.

Capital units Device used by insurance companies to obtain their charges; it is applied in a way that confuses many investors. With unit-linked insurance policies, where the investor's money is put into units that should grow in value over the years, during the first few years the investment goes into the impressively named special capital, or initial, units. The special feature of capital units is that the insurance company deducts a prior charge on the units to cover its costs and profits. This charge is deducted, however well or badly the investment is performing. Inevitably this deduction tends to affect adversely the investment performance (increase in value) of capital units. See ACCUMULATION and INITIAL UNITS.

Capitation tax See POLL TAX.

Captive fund A venture capital fund owned and controlled by a larger group.

CAR See COMPOUND ANNUAL RETURN.

Carat The measure of the amount of actual gold in a gold alloy (a mixture of gold and other metals). Pure or fine gold is 24 carat; and 22 carat signifies the alloy as containing 11 parts gold out of the total 12 parts. Carat is also used to measure the weight of precious stones. One carat is equal to 3.17 troy grains or 200 milligrams.

Car insurance See COMPREHENSIVE and THIRD PARTY INSURANCE.

Carrot equity Term used to describe options offered to investors or managers in a new company to subscribe for further shares if the company reaches or fails to reach predetermined target levels.

Carrying Term used mainly in the futures markets to describe either BORROWING or LENDING operations, when a transaction is essentially carried forward to a date in the future. Also known as 'carries'.

Carrying charge The cost involved in taking actual delivery and then redelivering back to the same market at a future date.

Cartel Group of interested parties who combine to set prices and avoid competition, often by imposing export or production quotas and selling controls. Most famous cartels are the De Beers syndicate controlling the diamonds market and OPEC (Organization of Petroleum Exporting Countries) which seeks to set world oil prices.

Cash Money in the form of coins or notes, or cheques and other assets (like a bank draft), which can immediately be exchanged for coins or notes.

Cash agent An insurance agent who is not allowed credit by the insurance companies and who has to pay the premiums before the policies are issued.

Cash alternative In takeover bids, the bidding company will often offer shares in its own company as payment but give a cash alternative to those not wanting to take shares. The cash alternative normally has a lower, nominal value than the shares offered, since there is no element of risk (that the shares will decline in value) involved, and takeover companies generally prefer to pay with 'paper' (shares) rather than with hard cash, which they might have to borrow.

Cash bonus Payment on an insurance or investment policy paid in cash at the time it is earned or declared. Also, payment for a shareholder who has chosen to accept cash instead of bonus shares in a company seeking to capitalize some of its reserves or profits.

Cash card Plastic card, issued by banks and building societies, that can be used to obtain cash immediately, usually through cash dispenser machines.

Cash credit An arrangement made by banks and building societies under which customers can draw up to a previously agreed sum.

Cash discount Allowance, or reduction in price, offered in return for prompt or immediate payment.

Cash dispenser Machine from which customers of a bank or building society can obtain cash in banknotes up to a prescribed limit by inserting a card and using a personal identification number. See AUTOMATED TELLER MACHINES and PERSONAL IDENTIFICATION NUMBER.

Cash float Money set aside to meet PETTY CASH expenses. See IMPREST SYSTEM.

Cash flow The movement of funds through a business during a specified period, after taking into account capital expenditure, depreciation and any sums put into reserves. The resultant sum, after deducting the costs of running the business, shows the amount available for investment and is a measure of the company's financial strength. A strong cash flow means there are adequate funds available to run the business and invest in its expansion; a negative cash flow means the company may have to draw on its reserves in order to survive. Poor cash flows can often drive soundly based companies, with valuable fixed assets, into insolvency as a result of not having sufficient funds to pay their creditors, or to invest in future expansion.

Cash mountain Phrase used to describe the situation when a company has built up large surpluses of assets in the form of cash and is, therefore, 'cash rich'.

Cash on delivery (COD) A condition applied by a seller of goods warning that cash will have to be paid when they are received, or delivered.

Cash ratio Term used to compare the amount of cash held, normally by a bank, against the amount owed to customers or depositors. Cash held to meet the immediate demands of depositors earns no interest, so banks like to keep the cash ratio as small as possible.

Cash refund annuity Contract to pay, on death, the difference between the capital sum paid for the annuity and the actual payments made.

Cash settlement Deals where the purchase price is paid immediately, as compared with delaying until, for example, the end of the stock exchange account period. Purchases of new stock issues and government securities (gilts) normally require cash settlement.

Cash and carry A manoeuvre used, primarily in the futures markets, to take advantage of the situation when the cash price for immediate delivery is at a wide discount compared to the price for delivery sometime in the future. A guaranteed profit is made by buying at the lower cash price and simultaneously selling at the higher forward price. But from that profit has to be deducted the cost of carrying – loss of interest and any storage and insurance costs. Nevertheless, on occasions when the gap between the cash and futures prices is too wide, the guaranteed profit made can exceed the current rate of interest and make the cash and carry transaction worthwhile. In fact it is the possibility of cash and carry operations that restricts the gap between cash and prices for future delivery close to the current interest rate.

Catchpenny Cheap or worthless items presented in such a way as to 'catch' the attention of purchasers.

Cats Type of bond sold at a discount to its full value in return for paying less interest. See DEEP DISCOUNT and ZERO COUPON BONDS. Also stands for Computer Assisted Trading System, used to implement investment programmes run by computers.

Caught short Slang term for a situation in which a seller is trapped in a market having agreed to sell at a specified time and then finding the situation has changed, making the sale either unprofitable or difficult to complete. See SHORT.

Caveat A warning that someone (the 'caveator') has a prior interest and claims certain rights before action affecting that interest can be taken by someone else. Hence 'to enter a caveat' is to give notice that objection will be made if certain action is taken without prior consultation.

Caveat emptor Roughly translated from Latin as 'let the buyer beware', the phrase was used to describe the traditional practice that it was up to the buyer to find any faults in goods or property purchased or suffer the consequences. That has greatly changed with modern legislation like the Consumer Credit Act, the Trade Descriptions Act and the 1986 Financial Services Act. But the phrase remains in use as a general caution to buyers to be careful before committing themselves, or to justify sellers who may have failed to point out hidden faults or snags.

CD See CERTIFICATE OF DEPOSIT.

Central banks Banks, often government owned, which manage a country's financial affairs, issuing the currency, holding reserves, controlling the money supply and generally acting as the government's banker domestically and internationally. The Bank of England is Britain's central bank.

Certificate Document confirming proof of ownership. Normally has no value in itself, but is used when transferring ownership. However, BEARER BOND certificates have a value of their own.

Certificate of incorporation Document issued by the Registrar of Companies on formation of a new company to confirm that the provisions of the

Companies Act have been met and that the company has been incorporated. The company does not exist legally, and cannot start trading, until this certificate has been issued.

Certificate of inscription A document confirming that the holder's name and amount of stock owned has been registered with the Bank of England. Used when a stock certificate is not issued. See INSCRIBED STOCK.

Certificate of insurance Document issued by an insurance company, confirming that it has issued a policy covering certain stated risks and outlining the conditions of that policy. Motor vehicle certificates must be carried by drivers while using the roads to provide proof that the vehicle is insured according to the law. See COVER NOTE and THIRD PARTY INSURANCE.

Certificate of origin A document, used in international trade, stating which country the goods being bought and sold came from originally, so that import and export duties and restrictions can be assessed.

Certificates of Deposit (CDs) Documents issued by banks and financial institutions confirming that a specified sum of money is being held for a period of time, paying a fixed rate of interest. Widely used in the wholesale money market, they are normally for large amounts of money and pay a higher than average rate of interest. Payable to the bearer or to order, they can be bought and sold easily, with the seller not being penalized for early surrender.

Certification Marking on the transfer deed on the sale of shares to show that the certificate has been lodged with the company's registrars or with the stock

exchange. This is needed when the seller is not parting with the entire holding or when the shares are bought by more than one person. New certificates are then issued to cover the redistribution of the shares. See also SELF-CERTIFICATION.

Certified accountant A member of the Chartered Association of Certified Accountants, who are recognized by the Department of Trade and Industry as being properly qualified to audit the accounts of limited companies. They differ from chartered accountants, in that the Association of Certified Accountants does not insist on articles (working for a professional practice), and therefore draws the bulk of its membership from outside the accountancy industry; a large proportion of its members are drawn direct from industry, where applicants study accountancy while continuing full-time employment, although they are often given time off for their studies. See CHARTERED ACCOUNTANTS.

CF See COST AND FREIGHT.

CGT See CAPITAL GAINS TAX.

Champerty Legal term for the offence of someone interfering in legal actions that do not concern him, with the object of seeking to gain some share of any damages that might be granted.

Chargeable event A transaction which is potentially liable to payment of tax. Particularly important in INHERITANCE TAX planning. see POTENTIAL EXEMPT TRANSFER.

Charge account Arrangement between a supplier, normally a retail store, and a customer under which the latter is allowed to pay in full at the end of an agreed period for goods bought. See CREDIT ACCOUNT.

Charge cards Plastic cards, issued by a company, which can be used to pay for goods or services. They differ from credit cards in that with charge cards the holder is expected to pay in full on receipt of the statement detailing the total of the charges incurred or risk legal action and withdrawal of the card. Holders of charge cards normally have to pay a joining fee and an annual subscription in return for receiving free credit. Retail stores use charge cards to boost sales to customers, however, and normally issue them free. Some charge card companies nowadays do impose interest charges on unpaid accounts after a certain period. See CREDIT CARDS.

Chargee A person who has power in law to force someone to pay a debt which is charged, such as a mortgage.

Charges on assets Debts owing to creditors, who have the right to take possession of a company's assets if they are not paid when due. See FLOATING CHARGE.

Charging order An order made by a court of law, giving the creditor temporary possession of assets for so long as a debt is unpaid. If the debt remains unpaid after six months, the creditor obtains full possession of the assets to the value of the debt and any interest on it.

Charitable trust Fund set up specifically to finance charitable projects, such as relief of poverty or furthering educational or religious work. They are exempt from paying tax, but have normally to be registered and approved by the charity commissioners, a government organization. Some organizations offering special plans for paying private school fees use charitable trusts because of the tax advantages; but they have to give a proportion of the funds to charity and

must be registered for approval. See TAX EXEMPT FUNDS.

Charter Document by a state or government formally giving special rights and powers to a person or organization.

Chartered accountant A member of one of the institutes of chartered accountants in England and Wales, Scotland and Ireland, which are authorized to audit the accounts of limited companies. Unlike certified accountants, to qualify for membership of one of the institutes, chartered accountants must first serve a period articled to (working for) a practising accountant. As a result, chartered accountants tend to be drawn from within the profession. The qualifying examinations include a range of subjects, from auditing to taxation, law and management. When qualified, the initials FCA (Fellow) or ACA (Associate) may be used after a chartered accountant's name.

Charterer Person or organization agreeing to hire a ship or aircraft or part of the cargo or passenger space from its owners for a fixed period of time or for a stated number of voyages. Details of the contract are set out formally in a charter party document. The leading centre for arranging charter contracts is the BALTIC EXCHANGE.

Chartists Professional market analysts, sometimes called technical analysts, who use graphs of past price movements to try to predict the future trend in prices. The basic principle is that it is impossible to know all the hidden fundamental influences affecting the market and individual shares or commodities. But, it is claimed, all these influences will show up in the market price and can, therefore, be tracked by the chartist and put into context with the previous price history. A price that has doubled recently, for example, may be considered to have more chance of falling back than of going further ahead.

Pure chartists, relying solely on charts, have a saying: 'Don't confuse me with the facts.' However, many analysts combine fundamental developments – like a takeover bid – with charts to predict future price movements. The chartist's job is to interpret correctly the trends shown in the charts, taking into consideration many factors such as the volume of trading behind the different price variations. Because so many people follow charts, they are often self-fulfilling, with selling or buying being triggered off by the predictions made.

Chart point Term used by chartists to indicate a particular price level at which some movement in the market, either up or down, will be triggered.

Charts Graphs produced by chartists, either for their own use or for circulation or sale to customers, outlining past price movements of shares, commodities, currencies and financial futures. These charts may often include interpretative detail, such as upward and downward trend lines or the development of a recognized pattern like a 'head and shoulders' formation.

Chattel mortgage A loan whereby the borrower pledges personal possessions, instead of land or property, as security against repayment.

Cheque A bill of exchange payable on demand issued by a bank, normally in a book containing a number of cheques specifically identifying the account holder. They are not legal tender, but simply a common way of settling debts instead of using cash. Cheques, which in theory can be written on anything providing the bank

is prepared to honour it, can be 'open' or 'crossed' with two parallel lines. An open cheque is payable over the counter at a bank, while a crossed cheque can only be paid into an account. For extra safety, to try to ensure that the cheque cannot be cashed by the wrong person, words may be put into the crossing identifying the payee or restricting its use, such as 'non-negotiable' or 'account payee only'. Since cheques are expensive to process, requiring a lot of manual handling, banks are trying to replace them as much as possible by automated transfers and plastic cards. See ENDORSEMENT and RETURN TO DRAWER.

Cheque (guarantee) card Plastic card issued by banks to their customers guaranteeing that a cheque up to a stated amount will be honoured. Often confused with credit cards, partly because one card can often 'double' as both a credit and a cheque guarantee at the same time.

Chinese wall Expression coined during the 'big bang' in the City of London in October 1986 to describe artificial barriers, or unofficial agreements, between different parts of the same organization in order to prevent confidential or price-sensitive information being passed between the subsidiary companies of the big groups that were being formed to cope with the new trading conditions. This was to prevent a conflict of interest between subsidiaries serving different sectors of the financial or investment community. For example, a group including subsidiaries acting as market-makers, brokers and dealers, fund managers and takeover organizers would find it difficult to serve the interest of all clients independently if information received by one sector was available to the other subsidiaries. So, although owned by one group, the subsidiaries are supposed to be separated by Chinese (transparent) walls so that they can operate independently.

Christmas See QUARTER DAY.

Churning Derogatory term used to describe deliberate over-trading with the objective of generating more commission for the broker or dealer.

CIF See COST, INSURANCE FREIGHT.

Circular A document sent to shareholders in a company by directors when an important change in the nature of the business or in its share structure is proposed. See EXTRAORDINARY GENERAL MEETING.

Circulating assets See ASSETS, CURRENT.

City code General term to describe the principles and rules of conduct laid down by the Stock Exchange to regulate takeovers or mergers of quoted companies. See TAKEOVER BID.

Claims adjuster Person, or company, that acts on behalf of an insurance company in dealing with claims for payment made against the company. See ADJUSTER.

Clawback Money taken back, normally by the Inland Revenue, from taxpayers who have been granted certain tax reliefs which they are not entitled to receive. For example, the Revenue may claw back tax if a pension policy is surrendered early, breaking the conditions for the tax-free concessions given.

Clean bond See BOND.

Cleared funds Term used to describe

money which has passed through the clearing system and has, therefore, been transferred to the recipient.

Clearers See CLEARING BANKS.

Clearing A system used by banks and other financial institutions to put together all transactions, such as receipts and payments, and offset them against each other, leaving only the balances left over to be settled. This avoids each individual transaction having to be processed.

Clearing banks Banks which are members of the central clearing system. Commonly used to describe the big high street banks which deal primarily with retail customers through a network of branch offices, which are all members of the same clearing system.

Clearing house An organization set up to handle a clearing system. Apart from the banks' clearing system for cheques, there are also clearing houses for markets in shares or futures through which all transactions have to be channelled. Sales and purchases are offset against each other and the clearing house, which guarantees the contracts, usually makes members settle any outstanding balances at the end of each day or trading period.

Client account Special account set up by a broker, investment adviser or solicitor to handle clients' money separately. Specifically designed to protect clients against suffering from sharp practice, fraud or the holding company becoming insolvent. Any company handling investments on behalf of someone else now has to set up individual client accounts, which are kept separate from the company's overall day-to-day business. This provides a record of withdrawals and deposits made on behalf of the client and also makes it more difficult for creditors of the company to claim the clients' funds.

Clipped coin A coin that has had the edges cut off so that it is no longer legal tender and has reduced value as a piece of metal.

Close company A company in which the share capital is held or controlled by the directors or by fewer than six shareholders. In the 1989 Budget the old rules for apportioning retained profits as a tax liability for individuals was scrapped. Instead the top rate of corporation tax will be applied to Close Investment Companies which retain a substantial part of their profits – made from trading in land, shares or securities.

CNAR See COMPOUND NET ANNUAL RETURN.

Cold call An unsolicited approach by a salesperson on a prospective customer. Under the Financial Services Act, there are strict regulations governing cold calls, including the provision of a 'cooling-off' period during which customers have the right to change their minds without any loss of money.

Collar A combination of two interest rates used to provide protection against the cost of borrowing fluctuating too widely. A 'collar' mortgage, for example, limits the interest rate charged between an agreed floor and ceiling. See CAP AND COLLAR and STRADDLE.

Collateral Originally an American expression used to describe the security put up by a borrower of money to cover the lender if the debt is not repaid when due. With a mortgage (home loan), for example, the property provides the collateral or security for the lender. See SECURITY.

Collectibles Colloquial term used to describe alternative investments favoured by collectors, such as paintings, stamps or tin soldiers.

Collective goods Something owned by the public as a whole, like roads or parks, and not by private individuals or organizations.

Collective insurance Policy under which two or more companies cover the risks insured.

Collective investment scheme General term to describe schemes in which groups or investors are put together with a view to sharing any profits made, such as unit trusts. See UCITS.

Collusive tendering Illegal practice of companies, invited to bid or tender for business, getting together in secret first and deciding among themselves what offers to make.

Comex Acronym of Commodity Exchange of New York, containing futures markets for base and precious metals. See GOLD.

Commerce General term used to describe the exchange of goods and services by trading and business organizations. Originally referred to trading between buyers and sellers in different countries.

Commercial agency Organization which gives advice on the financial standing of individuals or companies, especially as to whether they can be trusted to repay any loans made.

Commercial banks Joint-stock or deposit banks which deal with the public. See CLEARING BANKS and JOINT STOCK BANKS.

Commercial Court Special court within the High Court which tries only commercial cases, with either a single judge or a specially selected jury.

Commercial credit An arrangement which provides for goods to be bought and sold without being paid for immediately, including HIRE PURCHASE. A commercial credit company makes loans to manufacturers and traders, using their book debts (money owed to them) as security.

Commercial paper Loans made by banks to finance buying of goods by companies. Also used to describe a variety of short-term negotiable instruments (transferring the right to receive payment), such as bills of exchange and promissory notes. 'Prime commercial paper' is promissory notes payable in four to twelve months, issued by large businesses and sold to investors via brokers and dealers. See PROMISSORY NOTES.

Commercial rate of interest Used to assess the value of capital if it had been lent. Normally calculated by referring to current rate at which banks will make secured loans.

Commission A method of paying employees, agents, brokers, financial advisers and intermediaries for selling goods and services, either instead of or in addition to a salary or fee. Particularly popular as a means of paying salesmen and representatives for their services. The rate of commission is normally based as a percentage of the value of the goods or service being sold, such as 10%, but can be a fixed flat rate, say £100 per sale. Term also used as an alternative to 'charges', as in banking commission for certain services or overriding commission charged by brokers arranging for a new issue of shares to be underwritten (guaranteed). The word is also used to describe an order or directive, as in to commission a painting. See INSURANCE.

Commission agent Official name for a bookmaker taking bets. Also in foreign trading it means someone who, in return for a commission, buys or sells goods and services in one country on behalf of a principal in another country.

Commissioner for oaths A solicitor officially appointed by the government to witness the swearing on oath, or affirmation (swearing without God's name), required for many legal documents.

Commissioner, Parliamentary See OMBUDSMAN.

Commissioners of customs and excise Officials appointed by the government to collect EXCISE TAX and VALUE ADDED TAX.

Commissioners of inland revenue Officials appointed by the government to collect INCOME TAX, CAPITAL GAINS TAX, INHERITANCE TAX and STAMP DUTY.

Commission house A company that specializes in handling, in return for commission, buying and selling orders solely on behalf of clients, as opposed to dealing and trading in its own right. A pure broker, relying on commission only – although the term is now more widely used to describe broking houses in general.

Commission merchant or salesman A middleman who holds no stocks but instead simply buys on credit sufficient to supply customers' immediate needs. Often sells by showing samples only.

Committee of inspection A panel of up to five people appointed by creditors, in the winding up of a company, either voluntarily or by court order. See WINDING UP.

Commodity Goods or services; tangible asset that has a market value. Generally used to describe raw materials, such as agricultural products, basic foodstuffs and metals that need processing before being sold to the consumer.

Commodity agreements Formal agreements between the governments of commodity producing and consuming countries to try and stabilize the price of a particular commodity within an agreed range. More acceptable than a cartel, since both sides – producers and consumers – are represented. However, commodity agreements have met with only partial success. See BUFFER STOCK.

Commodity brokers Agents for both buyers and sellers in the commodity markets and futures exchanges, in return for brokerage or commission. Unlike other brokers, they often act as dealers as well in buying, selling, holding stocks and trading on the futures markets on their own account. See FUTURES.

Commodity exchanges or markets Centres where commodity brokers, dealers and merchants meet, to negotiate the sale or purchase of specific and actual commodities, or alternatively to trade in commodity futures. See FUTURES.

Common money bond See BOND.

Common stock Term used in North America to describe ordinary shares or equities usually issued in bearer form.

Community charge See POLL TAX.

Commutation The right to receive cash in exchange for giving up receiving payments in the future. Particularly applicable to pension policy-holders who on retirement can choose, subject to certain Inland Revenue regulations, to take a tax-free lump sum instead of the whole or part of a pension. See PENSIONS.

Companies House Place where the central register is kept of all limited liability companies, both public and private, in the United Kingdom. The register, which is open for public inspection on payment of a fee, must be provided with all details of the company's shareholdings, names of directors, updated accounts and balance sheet. See USEFUL ADDRESSES.

Company See LIMITED.

Company cars Cars owned by a company but provided to employees, either for work on behalf of the company or for private use. Often used as additional incentive, especially for higher-paid employees or directors, since there are tax avoidance advantages. See BENEFITS IN KIND and PERKS.

Company doctor Popular term used to describe someone brought in to help rescue a company that has got into financial trouble.

Compensation Payment made to offset the whole, or part, of a loss of money, property or employment.

Compensation fund Reserve set up by members of an organization to provide protection for themselves and outside users against one member being unable to meet its financial obligations. The Securities and Investment Board in 1988 set up a common compensation fund to help those who suffer losses, through dishonesty or fraud, on financial products or services.

Complaints Under the Financial Services Act, a whole structure of regulatory organizations has been set up to regulate the activities of different financial sectors, and handle complaints. The Securities and Investment Board (SIB) is the umbrella organization which controls the subsidiary self-regulatory organizations: Association of Futures Brokers and Dealers (AFBD); Financial Intermediaries Managers and Brokers Regulatory Association (FIMBRA); Investment Management Regulatory Organization (IMRO); Life Assurance and Unit Trust Regulatory Organization (LAUTRO) and The Securities Association (TSA), incorporating the Stock Exchange. Each organization has its own complaints system.

There are also recognized professional bodies (RPBs), like the Law Society and the Institute of Chartered Accountants, who deal with complaints against their members. In addition there are the special ombudsmen for banking, building societies, insurance and unit trusts, who arbitrate in disputes. See OMBUDSMAN and USEFUL ADDRESSES.

Completion The date when a property formally changes ownership, usually about a month after the exchange of contracts. On completion, the balance of the purchase price is paid to the seller and the buyer is provided with the keys to the property.

Compliance Self-policing by a company to try and ensure that the rules and regulations, laid down by the Financial Services Act, are being obeyed properly. A full-time compliance officer is appointed by some bigger companies.

Composite insurance Companies that offer both life assurance and general insurance policies.

Composite-rate tax (CRT) Special tax deducted automatically from interest paid to those holders of interest-bearing accounts in banks and building societies who are UK residents. CRT is slightly lower than the standard rate of tax, in compensation for the fact that it cannot be reclaimed even by someone who is not liable to pay tax. Non-taxpayers, therefore, should put any savings into investments like NATIONAL SAVINGS or GILTS (government securities) where the interest is paid gross, without any tax being deducted at source. CRT is not payable by non-UK residents.

Compound net annual return (CNAR) Same as compound annual return, but basing figures on net interest paid after deducting tax.

Compound annual return (CAR) Amount of interest earned yearly, including the reinvestment of monthly, quarterly or half-yearly interest payments. The greater the frequency of interest payments, the higher the equivalent yearly rate becomes.

Compound interest Interest calculated on an accumulated balance, which includes both the original capital invested and the interest earned. For example, a £1,000 investment with a 10% annual compound rate would earn £100 during the first year, but 10% of £1,100 (£1,000 + £100) in the second year, and so on. This is important to bear in mind when borrowing money or calculating the return from investments, such as annuities.

Compound growth is measured by comparing the original capital with the total at the end of a period of time.

Comprehensive insurance Household and motor policies that provide the insured with protection against a wide range of additional risks, over and above damages that might be caused to a third party. With motor insurance, cover for damages to a third party is legally compulsory, but the additional protection provided by a comprehensive policy is voluntary.

COMPS See CONTRACTED OUT MONEY PURCHASE SCHEME.

Compulsory purchase annuity An annuity which is bought under a pension plan by the trustees for the pensioner. It can be taken out on a joint life basis, giving the surviving partner a reduced income for life. The disadvantage is that the pension income is liable for taxation as earned income.

Concert party Popular term used to describe the situation in which two or more shareholders get together secretly to try and take over control, or manipulate the price, of a company. By acting individually they seek to avoid regulations governing the disclosure of an interest in a company if a certain percentage of the total shares is held. See INSIDER DEALING OR TRADING.

Conference lines Groups of competing shipowners who get together and offer a standard rate for shipping of particular goods on specific routes.

Conglomerate Term used to describe a large company which owns subsidiaries operating a wide variety of different businesses. The theory is that the group is made more secure by spreading its interests or risk.

Consequential loss policy Insurance, normally against fire or theft, that provides compensation against additional losses in profits from the business having to suspend or halt trading.

Consideration Monetary value of a contract for either the purchase or sale of an investment, before commissions and charges have been deducted.

Also used to describe the agreement of one party to a contract promising to take some specific action or pay some money.

Consolidated accounts The accounts of a company, including all its subsidiary companies, put together into one set of figures. The results of the individual subsidiaries are totted up to produce a consolidated balance sheet and profit and loss account, for the whole group.

Consolidated bond See BOND.

Consolidated fund Portion of taxes retained by the Bank of England on behalf of the government to pay costs of the Civil Service, Armed Forces and other expenditures approved by parliament.

Consolidation of capital Description of the move by a limited company to raise the value of its nominal shares.

Consols Short for Government Consolidated Stock. One of the fixed-interest (gilt-edged) securities, which has been used by the government to raise money for a long time and historically favoured by investors. Consols have no final redemption (repayment) date, but are issued at various times at different rates of interest. Because there is no capital repayment to be taken into consideration, Consols provide a good guide to current interest rates available on the gilt-edged market. Traded in lots of £100, the purchase price of a lot is geared to the nominal quoted interest rate against the current market rate. So if a £100 lot of Consols 4% can be bought for £50 the investor is obtaining an interest rate of 8%. See GILTS.

Consumer Credit Act 1974 legislation, enforced mainly by the OFFICE OF FAIR TRADING, that seeks to protect consumers from being misled or swindled by money-lenders when hiring or buying goods or services.

Contango Term used in two different ways. On the Stock Exchange it is used to describe settlement of a sale or purchase being carried over from one account period to the next, with a compensating payment for the delay in paying up. In the commodity and futures markets, contango describes when the price for delivery at a date in the future is at a premium to the cash price for immediate delivery. This is the normal situation, since the price for future delivery should include the cost of storage, insurance and lost interest. But when there is a shortage of immediately available supplies, the cash price can be at a premium, or in a BACKWARDATION.

Contemptuous damages Very small, nominal sum, awarded by a court when the claimant has suffered little loss and it is considered that the case should never have been brought.

Contingency insurance An accident policy that covers a variety of risks, from rain ruining the financial return of an event

to a breach of trust or missing documents. See INSURANCE.

Contingency reserve or account Fund set up to cover a loss that might be suffered if a particular event occurred. See INSURANCE.

Contingent assets See ASSETS.

Continuation day First day of a Stock Exchange account period.

Continued bond See bond.

Contra An entry made in an account to balance (and thereby cancel) an earlier entry. Often used by banks to correct mistakes. Contra credit is an entry made in a cash book to record cash taken from or deposited in a bank account.

Contract An agreement between two or more parties which is legally enforceable.
    Also used to describe the underlying units of trading in markets.

Contract bond See BOND, PERFORMANCE.

Contracted-out money purchase scheme Pension plan in which contributors have left (contracted out of) the State Earnings Related Pensions Scheme (SERPS) and rely on the returns earned from investing the contributions. See MONEY PURCHASE SCHEME and PENSIONS.

Contracting in/contracting out Options open either to participate in the government pension scheme (SERPS) or to contract out and make private pension arrangements instead. It is, of course, possible to do both, although the 1986 Pensions Act encouraged employees to contract out of the government scheme. See PENSIONS.

Contribution 'holidays' Popular term for when companies decide to stop making payments to their pension scheme for a period because it is overfunded and the reserves might exceed the maximum limits set by the government and thus become liable for tax.

Contributory pension Scheme in which the employee, as well as the employer, pays contributions.

Convertible bond See BOND.

Convertible currency One that can be freely exchanged for other currencies at the rates of exchange quoted in the currency markets.

Convertibles A cross between a share and a fixed interest security. A type of loan stock (normally issued by companies to raise extra capital by offering a fixed rate of income) but including the right to convert it to a specified number of ordinary or preference shares at some stated time in the future.

Also refers to stock issued by the government, which gives the holder the right to convert to a new stock instead of obtaining repayment. See LOAN STOCK.

Conveyancing Transfer of the title or ownership of land or property. Normally handled by solicitors, but can be done by REGISTERED LICENSED CONVEYANCERS.

Cooling-off period Time given in which investors or buyers of assurance policies or unit trusts may change their mind and cancel the whole transaction without suffering any loss of money. See COLD CALL.

Copyright Legal right of reproducing literary, musical or artistic work and preventing anyone else from doing so. Normally lasts for the life of the person who creates the work and for 50 years after their death. But can be assigned in writing to someone else.

Corner Manoeuvre to obtain control of the price of an article, commodity, stock or share by buying up the available supplies, thus creating an artificial shortage and forcing buyers to pay inflated prices to those who have cornered the market.

Corporation stocks Loan stocks issued by local authorities, which normally offer a higher rate of fixed interest than the equivalent national government stock. See LOCAL AUTHORITY BONDS.

Corporation tax Tax on the profits of business corporations, but not applicable to partnerships. There are two different rates, with 'small' companies – defined in the 1989 Budget as those with profits of less than £150,000 a year – paying a lower rate.

Corset Popular term used to describe controls imposed by the government on the amount of money that can be lent by banks to their customers.

Cost and freight (CF) Value of goods, including cost of delivery.

Cost insurance freight (CIF) Value of goods, including cost of insurance and delivery.

Cost price The bare cost of production, without any profit added. Alternatively, refers to the price paid by a merchant for goods to be resold.

Countersign Provide an additional signature on a document to give further authority. Often used for cheques drawn on accounts held by a company or organization.

Coupon A slip of paper (or warrant) attached to a bond or share certificate that is presented for payment of the interest or dividend on the due date.

Term also used on the Stock Exchange to describe the rate of interest paid on a fixed-interest stock, like government securities. See GILTS.

Coupon bond See BOND.

Covenant Agreement in the form of a deed binding the parties to perform some duty (positive) or alternatively not to do something (negative). Deeds of covenant are used to make regular payments at annual or more frequent intervals, which in some cases – contributions to registered charities – qualify for tax relief. In the 1988 Budget, the tax relief on non-charitable covenants was scrapped.

Cover Protection against a possible loss, as with insurance cover. Also, in the options market, the underlying stock provides cover against a CALL OPTION; or a risk in the currency or commodities markets is avoided by taking cover in the forward or futures market. See also DIVIDEND COVER.

Cover note An acknowledgement in writing that a certain insurance contract exists. A temporary document for use only until the policy has been drawn up and issued. In motor car insurance, a cover note acts as a temporary certificate of insurance up to the date specified.

Crawling peg Popular name for the system whereby governments adjust the value of their country's currency in line with the change in its value on the foreign exchange market.

Credit Opposite of cash. Having the resources, or borrowing power, to pay for goods or services without paying cash.

Credit account Arrangement, often with a shop or store, by which the customer can buy up to a specified amount and pay at an agreed later date.

Credit agency Organization that, for a fee, supplies information about the financial status of a company or individual.

Credit card Plastic card, issued by banks and other financial organizations, which enables card-holders to obtain goods or services without immediate payment. The payments due are grouped together, normally in a monthly account, which has to be paid within a specified period or incur high interest rates. Unlike CHARGE CARDS, there is normally no joining or annual fee for credit cards. However, the period of free credit granted is limited, and delayed payments are penalized by high interest rates. Some cards are now offering the alternative of paying an annual fee in return for paying a lower rate of interest.

Credit insurance Policy taken out to cover the risk of a borrower not being able to repay a loan for specific reasons such as accident, illness or sudden loss of employment.

Credit limit The maximum amount of credit allowed by a lender or supplier. The limit applies to both the total value and the time allowed for payment.

Credit policy Insurance which provides compensation for sellers of goods when the buyer becomes insolvent and unable to pay.

Credit rating The estimated financial worth of a person or company on which the amount of credit to be granted is based.

Credit scoring A mathematics-based system, using computers to assess the risk involved in lending money and providing goods or services on credit to a particular person or organization. The scoring system is based on financial resources and other factors influencing the ability or otherwise of the borrower to pay up.

Credit transfer Method of payment under which anyone can pay money into a clearing bank for the credit of any customers within the system. See BANK GIRO SYSTEM and DIRECT DEBIT.

Crossed cheque Cheque with two parallel lines drawn (or printed) across as a security measure. Payment of a crossed cheque can only be made into a bank and cannot be exchanged for cash across the counter. No words are required for a general crossing but specific instructions restricting payment to a particular recipient can be given by writing between the lines 'account payee' or 'not negotiable'. A crossed cheque may be uncrossed (or opened) by writing the words 'pay cash' against the crossing and initialling it.

Crossed warrant Similar to a cheque and payable to a bank, it is normally used for withdrawing large amounts from National Savings. Can be made out to a third party, if required.

Cross rate Rate of exchange between two currencies measured by comparing them with a third currency.

CRT See COMPOSITE RATE TAX.

CTO See CAPITAL TAXES OFFICE.

CTT See CAPITAL TRANSFER TAX.

CUM dividend Cum is Latin for 'with', so a share quoted cum dividend carries the right to a recently declared dividend. The same applies to 'cum rights', 'cum scrip' and any other benefits. See EX DIVIDEND.

Cumulative preference shares Holders have the right to receive any outstanding dividend payments and take precedence over dividends for holders of ordinary shares.

Currency Any kind of money that is in general use as cash, such as coins and banknotes. Or the money of a particular country. In Britain, foreign currency refers to any currency but sterling. See EXCHANGE RATES.

Currency bond See BOND.

Currency markets Generic term applied to international trading on different currencies by banks, financial institutions and investors, which set the different rates of exchange for currencies.
  Also refers to currency futures markets, used to speculate on, or take protection against, the rise or fall in the value of a currency. See FUTURES.

Current account Normal, standard account with a bank providing a cheque book and other banking services. There are usually no charges if the account is not overdrawn. Most banks now offer current accounts with interest paid on any surplus balances held in credit, but high charges for overdrafts.

Current assets See ASSETS.

Current capital See WORKING CAPITAL.

Current cost accounting Method of showing a company's accounts to include the effects of inflation using a formula laid down by the official accountancy organizations.

Current ratio Comparison between a company's current assets and current liabilities used to assess its financial strength.

Current yield The annual return, before tax, on an investment at its current price compared with the interest or dividend paid. With fixed interest stocks that have a known repayment date, the annual return is calculated on the interest only. See YIELD.

Customer agreement Form, or letter, signed by clients of investment advisers, brokers and managers specifying in advance the terms and conditions for managing funds, dealing in stocks and shares, and receiving instructions. Under the rules laid down under the Financial Services Act 1986, such an agreement has to be signed unless the client wants to transact execution only business – merely an instruction to buy or sell without receiving any advice.

D

Daisy chain Popular term used to describe a series of trading transactions where the same item is bought and sold a number of times. Legitimately used in some markets, for example oil trading, to reduce the cost of holding expensive cargoes. But also used by market manipulators to create artificial trading activity and supply shortages in order to boost prices. See RAMP.

Damages at large Where the court is left to decide what sum of money is fair and reasonable to meet a successful claim for damages.

Dated security Loan or debenture with a stated date for repayment.

Dawn raid Stock market term used when a buyer seeks to acquire a large block of shares in one fell swoop, normally at the start of trading in the morning before other dealers are aware of what is happening. The purpose is to build up a strategic shareholding, possibly as a preliminary to a takeover bid.

Day order Instruction to buy or sell at a given price on one particular day. If not carried out, the instruction is cancelled automatically at the end of the day.

Dead capital Money either uninvested or in some investment providing poor returns.

Dead loan Temporary borrowing that has not been repaid on the due date.

Dead rent Rent paid on unused land or buildings, or, in the case of mining, the fixed rent paid whatever the scale of production.

Dead security Assets like mines which have stopped working and therefore have little value.

Dealing General term used to describe buying and selling, or other business transactions. Dealers tend to act in their own names as principals, as compared with brokers who deal on behalf of third parties.

Dealing for new time Stock Exchange term. During the final two days of an account period, shares can be bought for payment at the end of the next account. However, there is normally an extra charge to cover the delay in payment.

Death duties See INHERITANCE TAX.

Death grant Sum paid by the government to help cover some of the funeral costs.

Death in service benefits Amounts paid, normally by a pension scheme, when an employee dies while still working for the company. Many pension schemes include special arrangements to try and ensure that payments to dependent relatives are made quickly.

Death Valley curve Colourful phrase used to describe that difficult time just after a new company is formed when capital is being used up and little or no income is coming in.

Debenture A fixed-interest bond or stock issued by a company or organization, normally backed by the assets. It ranks ahead of ordinary shares for payment if the company is liquidated or wound up, and debenture interest must be paid before dividends are declared. In the case of a single loan, the debenture deed is held by trustees on behalf of the holders. A company is required to maintain a register (list) of debenture-holders, but often debenture stock is issued, since it is easier to transfer either in whole or in part.

The issue of debentures by a company or organization is especially suitable where finance is required for only a limited period since they can be easily redeemed, with individual debentures being repaid in the order in which they were issued. In some cases, instead of receiving money, debenture-holders are given certain rights or privileges, such as centre court seats at Wimbledon.

There are several different types of debenture.

Bearer debenture – Payable to the bearer, with ownership being transferred simply by handing it over, with the change of owner having to be registered. Opposite of normal registered debenture.

Fixed debenture – Where the loan is backed by one particular asset, such as a building or machine. Opposite of floating debenture, where the loan is backed by all the borrower's assets.

Floating debenture – See Fixed debenture, above.

Guaranteed debenture – Where the payment of interest is guaranteed by a third party.

Income debenture – Where payment of interest and capital can be made out only to the borrower's income or profits.

Irredeemable or perpetual debenture – Where there is no arrangement for repayment of the sum, unless the borrower goes into liquidation.

Opposite of redeemable debenture, which may be redeemed (repaid) by the borrower either at a fixed date or any time, subject to the conditions of the loan.

Mortgage or secured debenture – Promises to repay a certain sum borrowed with interest and gives the debenture-holder the right to receive payment if necessary from specified funds or from the sale of some or all of the borrower's property. Opposite of naked or unsecured debenture, which simply acknowledges a debt, without any security for repayment.

Naked debenture – See Mortgage debenture, above.

Perpetual debenture – See Irredeemable debenture, above.

Prior-lien debenture – A debenture, issued with the agreement of existing debenture-holders, that carries first claim to payment of interest and capital.

Redeemable debenture – See Irredeemable debenture, above.

Registered debenture – See Bearer debenture, above.

Secured debenture – See Mortgage debenture, above.

Unsecured debenture – See Mortgage debenture, above.

Debenture capital See LOAN STOCK.

Debenture stock Usually not redeemable, since it represents only part of one large debt (the debenture). However, debenture stock holders have the right to be paid debenture interest, before any dividends are paid on the share capital.

Debenture trust Formed by a company to hold assets that provide the financial security for an issue of debenture stock.

Debit Technically the entry on the left-hand (debtor) side of an account, showing debts owed by a company or organization. Generally, any deduction made to cover a charge or sum owed. Opposite of CREDIT.

Debit balance The amount owed by someone after adding up all payments and receipts due.

Debit card Plastic card used to make prompt payments, or to withdraw cash, as an alternative to a cheque. Fits in better with automation of banking services than cheques, but can often also double as a cheque guarantee card. Similar in some uses to a CREDIT CARD, except that no credit is given and payments are made from the holder's account automatically, so there is less risk involved for the issuer.

Debit note Reminder or notification of a sum owing. Similar to invoice, but normally used to cover extra charges or to correct mistakes, such as undercharging for goods or services. Also used by insurance companies to show the premium to be paid on a new policy.

Debt Something, usually money, owed either in repayment of a loan or for goods or services provided.

Debtor A person owing money to someone. Opposite of creditor.

Debt ratio Measure of the extent to which assets have been financed by

borrowings, repayable in both the short and long term. Provides an indication of the company's financial strength or otherwise. See GEARING.

Debt servicing Payment of interest on a debt.

Debt to equity ratio The borrowings of a company divided by the shareholders fund, to show how much would be available to shareholders if the company went out of business.

Decimal currency System of notes and coins based on units of ten, as contrasted with the duodecimal system using units of twelve. Britain switched to decimal currency in 1971. See METRIC SYSTEM.

Decimalization The conversion of a system of counting or measurement to one based on the number ten, or multiples of ten, which is claimed to be the easiest figure to divide and multiply by.

Declaration insurance Policy where the insured declares at agreed regular intervals the value of the risks covered, so that the premiums can be adjusted.

Declaration of solvency Used when a company is planning a voluntary winding-up, it signifies that all debts will be paid in full within twelve months. See INSOLVENCY and WINDING UP.

Declinature Official term for the rejection by an insurance company of a proposal for insurance.

Decreasing term assurance Where the sum assured reduces by a stated amount until it reaches zero at the end of a specified period. Used to cover a reducing debt outstanding, especially home loans, in which case it is also called MORTGAGE PROTECTION POLICY.

Deed A legal agreement or contract in the form of a written document, which has to be formally executed by signing, sealing and delivering (handing over).

Deed of arrangement or assignment Formal agreement made by a debtor (borrower) with creditors (lenders) for settlement of debts. The debtor gives ownership of his/her property to a trustee to be sold and the money divided among the creditors. At the same time the creditors agree to accept payment of a reduced sum instead of the full amount of the debt.

Deed of covenant Legal document used to implement a COVENANT.

Deed of inspectorship Used to hand over to the creditors a business which is insolvent (unable to pay its debts when they become due) and threatened with bankruptcy (unable to pay debts in full). The creditors then appoint inspectors to try to save the business.

Deep discount bond A fixed interest bond, with a low or even zero rate of interest, sold at a substantial discount to its redemption (repayment) value. With little or no interest paid, the investor receives instead a guaranteed profit between the sale and redemption value in the form of a capital gain. Several different variations exist, using the same basic idea to reduce tax liabilities by limiting payments of income. See ZERO (COUPON) BONDS.

Default Failure to pay a debt in time or to fulfil a duty.

Defective title Ownership of land or

property not properly registered, and therefore vulnerable to a claim by another owner.

Deferred account Agreement under which an insured person is permitted to pay premiums by instalments.

Deferred annuity An annuity that becomes due to start payments only at a specified date in the future. See ANNUITY.

Deferred assets See ASSETS.

Deferred bond See BOND.

Deferred credits or income Sums received for goods or services to be supplied at a future date. They are, therefore, listed on the liabilities side of a company's balance sheet since they represent a form of debt. See LIABILITIES.

Deferred delivery Agreement by a buyer of shares that extra time will be given for the broker to obtain the shares ordered.

Deferred interest certificate Document given by a company to holders of loan stock, such as debentures, when the payment of the interest due is postponed. See SCRIP and WARRANT.

Deferred payment Agreement to pay for something by instalments over a stated period. Often made between a buyer and a finance house, or directly between a retailer and a customer. Subject to the regulations laid down in the Consumer Credit Act. See CONSUMER CREDIT ACT and HIRE PURCHASE.

Deferred pension Employee leaving a company pension scheme before the retirement age specified is entitled to a deferred or preserved pension, payable only when the retirement date is reached. How the size of the payment is calculated depends on the scheme, for example whether it is a money purchase or final salary plan. See PENSIONS.

Deferred shares A special type of share on which dividends are paid only after holders of other shares (such as preference and ordinary) have received payment. Often owned by founders, promoters or managers who receive a large proportion of the remaining profits once the ordinary shareholders have been paid. Another type of deferred share receives little or no dividend at first and only later receives the same rate as do ordinary shareholders. See FOUNDERS' SHARES.

Deferred taxation Term used in company accounts to refer to amounts set aside to meet some future tax liability.

Deficit An amount that is lacking to fulfil a need. Opposite of surplus. Deficit financing is deliberate policy by a government to borrow money in order to make up for a shortfall in monies received. Balance of payments deficit happens when the value of imports exceeds the value of exports. Budget deficit is when income is insufficient to cover expenditure.

Deflation Decline in the supply of money available as the result of a deliberate economic policy by the government to reduce demand and stop prices rising. See DISINFLATION and INFLATION.

Deflator A statistical device used to adjust past movements in prices or values in order to take account of inflation.

Defunct company A company that has ceased to operate and has been struck off

the official Register of Companies. The company's name is then transferred to the Register of Defunct Companies, known as the 'dead book'.

Degressive tax Rate of tax that declines on incomes below or above certain levels.

Del credere agent An agent who is employed to sell goods or services on behalf of a principal on condition that he, the agent, bears the risk of non-payment by customers.

Delta One of the four categories of shares on the London Stock Exchange brought in when a new system of trading was introduced after the Big Bang in October 1986. Delta shares are those least actively traded, compared with the other three categories – ALPHA, BETA and GAMMA. As inactive shares dealt in by only a few market-makers, they are not quoted on the Stock Exchange Automated Quotation System (SEAQ) screens, so their prices have to be obtained either from a broker or from the STOCK EXCHANGE *Official List* of prices, published on each trading day.

In the options market, Delta is used as a technical term to describe how the price of an option compares with the value of the investment or asset into which it can be converted.

Demise Legal term for letting property or granting a lease on buildings and land. Alternatively, for hiring out a ship on charter.

Demonetize Put an end to the use of a note or coin as legal tender. In Britain, the farthing was demonetized in 1961, the half-penny in 1969, and the half-crown in 1970.

Demonstrative legacy Inheritance

money that must come from one specified fund in an estate.

Demurrage Money paid if a building or shipping contract is not completed on the agreed date. Normally it is paid for each day completion is delayed or ships are kept waiting.

Dependant (relative) allowance Special tax relief given to people supporting dependants, particularly relatives. But it was scrapped in the 1988 BUDGET. See INVALID CARE ALLOWANCE.

Deposit Sum of money given as part payment, or first instalment, for something to be bought in future. Also money or its equivalent left with a person or organization, particularly a bank, for safe-keeping, as security, or to earn interest.

Deposit account An interest-earning account, normally with a bank or building society, used to keep money not immediately required. Normally, the depositor has to give notice of withdrawal for a specified period to avoid loss of interest and is not allowed to use the account for paying bills or writing cheques. For UK residents, composite rate tax (CRT) is automatically deducted from any interest earned.

Deposit based pensions Pension plans, mainly offered by banks or building societies, where the pension earned is based on the contributions put into an interest-bearing deposit account, so there is little or no rise in the value of the capital, apart from the interest accumulated over the years by re-investment. See PENSIONS.

Deposit currency That part of money held by banks which is on current account and can be used to meet cheque withdrawals.

Depository Person or organization in whose care money and other possessions have been left for safe-keeping. Authorized depositories are those permitted by the Bank of England to hold foreign securities in Britain on behalf of the owners. Usually banks, brokers or solicitors.

Deposit premium Partial payment on an insurance policy while it is being drawn up. Or any premium that is adjusted periodically.

Deposit protection fund Scheme set up by the Bank of England that pays compensation if any bank or licensed deposit taker collapses and is unable to pay money owing.

Deposit receipt Written acknowledgement, normally by a bank, that a certain sum of money is held, repayable at a specified date. Has to be presented when the depositor wants to withdraw the money, and is not transferable. See CERTIFICATE OF DEPOSIT.

Depreciate Lose value gradually over a period of time.

Depreciation Rate at which the value of assets gradually declines because of wear and tear, or through becoming out of date. This is viewed for taxation purposes as one of the costs of running a business or organization and is charged against the profits.

Designated Investment Exchange (DIE) Overseas stock markets, which have been approved by the Securities and Investments Board as being suitable to handle business from the UK without having to comply with all the rules and regulations surrounding British markets. A good example is the New York Stock Exchange, which has its own domestic rules and regulations.

Designated territories Overseas countries which have been authorized by the UK Department of Trade to sell insurance and collective investment products (such as unit trusts) in Britain because they have rules and regulations that provide the UK investor with equivalent protection to that given by domestic regulations. Good examples are the Channel Islands and Isle of Man, whose offshore funds can be promoted freely in Britain because they are designated countries or territories subject to approval by the Securities and Investment Board.

Devaluation Mainly used to describe a fall in the value of one currency against the others in foreign exchange markets. Used by governments to make imports more expensive and exports cheaper and more competitive, to help improve a country's balance of payments.

Dictum meum pactum Latin for verbal contract: 'My word is my bond'. Traditional boast of stockbrokers and others in the City of London as governing their code of conduct. But not heard so often since the Financial Services Act and the introduction of stricter rules and regulations to protect investors.

DIE See DESIGNATED INVESTMENT EXCHANGE.

Differential prices Practice of charging different prices for the same products or services.

Differential rent Higher-than-usual rent because it includes special extras, like a better view. See FERTILITY RENT.

Dilapidations Old-fashioned term to describe the liability of a tenant to pay any costs involved in restoring buildings, when they are returned to the landlord, to the same condition as when the original lease was granted.

Diminishing balance method Way of calculating DEPRECIATION in company accounts by reducing the value of an asset by a certain percentage over a stated number of years.

Direct debit Arrangement used to make regular payments on a stated date to a third party from a bank account on behalf of the customer. This can be for specified or variable amounts and for different time-periods, according to the instructions (or mandate) given. Differs from a STANDING ORDER in that with a direct debit the receiver is responsible for organizing the deduction, although the bank will repay the customer if it allows an incorrect payment to be made. A system favoured by the banks and large organizations, since it is much easier to automate than standing orders and is therefore better for making more frequent payments of varying amounts.

Dirty bond See BOND.

Disablement or disability benefit Allowance paid by the government under the National Insurance Scheme to people temporarily disabled.

Disablement or disability pension Government allowance paid to people permanently disabled because of an injury received at work.

Disbursements Payments of cash to

meet out-of-pocket expenses, normally by a professional person (usually a solicitor), on behalf of clients and which can be claimed back later.

Discharge A combined form of receipt and acknowledgement that an insurance claim has been paid in full or payment of a debt has been met, so that nothing is owing. See BANKRUPT.

Disclaimer Legal term formally giving up rights and duties.

Discount A deduction in the cost or price of something, often offered for immediate payment or as incentive to purchase at a particular time or to buy a certain quantity. On the stock exchange, used to describe shares trading at a price below the company's value or assets. In insurance, discounts are offered to allow for the special nature of risk or risks covered. See NO-CLAIMS BONUS (DISCOUNT).

Discount bond See BOND and DEEP DISCOUNT BOND.

Discounted cash flow A way of assessing whether a new capital investment is worth making. The extra income from the investment is discounted (reduced) using the current interest rate on the money used.

Discount houses or banks Businesses which act as wholesalers for money and operate in the discount market in London. They provide a regular flow of cash funds, particularly to the clearing banks, by bills of exchange and other financial instruments with a short-term repayment date, at a discount below their redemption value. The discount rate paid by the houses of discount brokers is calculated on the time between the date of purchase and the date of repayment, taking into account

the current interest rate if the money advanced was invested elsewhere. See ACCEPTING HOUSES.

Discounting back A method of assessing the present-day value of a sum to be paid at some time in the future by working out what sum would be needed to earn the required amount if invested at current interest rates.

Discount store Retailer who offers deductions from the list prices, particularly of durable goods, in order to boost sales turnover.

Discretion Freedom given to act on someone's behalf, normally within certain limits.

Discretionary order Instruction by a client to a broker or financial adviser giving freedom to decide what to buy with a specified sum of money. See BEST ADVICE.

Discretionary service Offer to act on someone's behalf, either free of charge or for a specified payment. Particularly used by banks, brokers, financial advisers and intermediaries to take investment decisions on behalf of clients with either limited resources or little knowledge of financial affairs and the stock market. Can be dangerous, especially if the broker or adviser is given too much freedom. See CHURNING.

Discretionary trust A trust where the trustees have absolute discretion as to how much of the income is distributed to the beneficiaries. See TRUSTS.

Discriminatory tax Special tax levied on some industries in order to make it easier for other industries to compete.

Disinflation Measures taken by a government to reduce, or reverse, the rate of inflation. Opposite of INFLATION.

Disposable income The amount of a person's earnings left over after all the compulsory deductions (like income tax, National Insurance and pension contributions) have been made.

Dissolution See WINDING UP.

Distraint Action open to creditors in certain circumstances when a debt is not paid on the due date. The creditor is allowed to enter the debtor's premises and take property or assets, and these are held until the debt is paid.

Distributable reserves Accumulated past profits of a company that can be paid out, subject to certain rules and regulations.

Distributions Payments made to unit trust holders out of income. They are paid net of standard rate tax, but this can be reclaimed by non-taxpayers.

Distributor funds Offshore funds, which have qualified for distributor status under the UK Inland Revenue regulations. To block a tax loophole, in 1983 the Inland Revenue declared that any returns from investment in offshore funds would be taxed at income tax rates unless the fund qualified for distributor status by distributing at least 85% of its accumulated income annually to the holders. See ROLL-UP FUNDS.

Dividends Payments made by a company to shareholders as a regard for their investment in buying the shares. The payment of dividends is voluntary, depending on the profitability of the company, both present and expected.

However, many investors buy or sell according to the rate of dividend, so most companies try to maintain a steady rise in dividend income even if profits are not rising, in order to try and prevent the share price from falling. Dividends are paid with standard rate tax already deducted to UK residents and are added on to a person's total earnings for tax purposes; but non-taxpayers can reclaim the tax deducted. Companies often pay dividends in instalments throughout the year in the form of INTERIM and final dividends.

Dividend cover The number of times by which the dividend paid is covered by the company's total profits after tax. Used as a measure of a company's financial strength. If the dividend is only just covered by the earnings, there is a possibility that the dividend may have to be cut or omitted altogether if the earnings decline. On the other hand, if the dividend is covered too many times, it suggests that the company may not be investing in the future or is cash rich and attractive as a takeover victim.

Dividend mandate An authority provided by a shareholder specifying to whom and where the dividend should be paid.

Dividend per share (DPS) The total dividends paid, divided by the number of shares, in order to calculate and compare the dividend payments by companies. See EARNINGS PER SHARE.

Dividend restraint A policy, imposed by the government, to limit the sums of money paid out by companies to shareholders, thus encouraging further capital investment from the retained profits.

Dividend stripping A slang term used to describe the activities of those financiers who take over a company primarily to sell its assets and then distribute the cash reserves in the form of dividends to themselves as chief shareholders. See ASSET STRIPPING.

Dividend waiver A decision, normally by the leading shareholder in a company, not to take payment of a dividend, in order to maintain the company's cash resources.

Dividend warrant A document, similar to a cheque, authorizing payment of a dividend to the recipient, but also giving details on a voucher of the tax deducted from the dividend, which the non-taxpayer can send to the tax authorities in order to reclaim the tax.

Dividend yield A measurement of the return (profit) on an investment and the financial strength of a company. Companies normally declare the dividend as a percentage on the nominal value of the shares, which may be very different from the current market price. The ratio of the dividend to the market price is known as the dividend yield. It is calculated by multiplying the gross (before tax) dividend by 100 and then dividing it by the current market share price.

Dollar Anglicization of the 'thaler', originally a silver coin widely circulated in Europe. The dollar is best known as the unit of currency of the United States, but is also used as the currency in many other countries – Australian dollar, etc. See RESERVE CURRENCY.

Dollar area The area of the world where the US dollar is used as the standard currency.

Dollar stocks US or Canadian companies quoted on the London or European stock exchanges.

Domicile Legal term, important for tax purposes, defining the country if a person has a permanent home or intends to return to it at some stage from overseas. Different from residence, in that it is possible to be domiciled in only one country at any time while resident in more than one.

Domicile of choice The country to which a person goes to live and intends to stay, but where he was not born.

Domicile of origin Country in which a person is born.

Donation A gift, normally of money, to provide financial support.

Donor A person or organization who gives an asset, money or a power of attorney to a third party.

Doomsday price The price of a share on 5 April 1965 when CAPITAL GAINS TAX was introduced. No longer important following the change in 1988 for calculating INDEXATION ALLOWANCE and could now more properly be applied to the value of shares on 31 March 1982.

Dormant company One that is involved in activities or transactions not requiring entries in its account books or records. It is, therefore, exempted from providing group accounts or appointing auditors. The directors must, however, file with the annual accounts a statement that the dormant conditions remain.

Double endowment An insurance policy under which the sum insured will be doubled if the policy-holder lives to the end of a specified period.

Double-entry Basic form of book-keeping for companies and organizations, under which the accounts are divided into two sides: credit and debit. All transactions are entered twice, once in the credit side (as the giver) and once in the debit side (as the receiver). The total of all credits and all debits should equal each other at any time, otherwise a mistake has been made and this can be quickly spotted and corrected.

Double insurance   Arrangement to insure against a risk with two or more policies. However, the combined total value of the sums insured must not exceed the value of the loss incurred. If this happens, one insurer company will claim contributions from the other(s) so that the policy-holder receives only the value of the loss. See INSURANCE.

Double option   An option giving the owner the right to be a buyer or seller at predetermined dates. See OPTION.

Double taxation relief   Arrangement to stop people paying tax in two or more countries on the same income. The government in one country makes allowance for the fact that tax has already been paid in another country and gives whole, or partial, exemption from payment. Many countries now have formal double taxation agreements with other countries. The agreements are also used to trace those avoiding tax, since information about earnings is swapped and a check made to see whether any tax has been paid on them.

Double top/bottom   Term used by chartists to describe a particular development on charts tracing price movements, which very often precedes a definite change in the market trend.

Douceur   Eighteenth-century term for a bribe.

Dow-Jones Index   Best-known measurement of the movement of prices on the New York Stock Exchange, compiled by a financial news service, Dow Jones, which also publishes the *Wall Street Journal*. There are a number of different indices of American stock market price movements but the best known is the Dow-Jones Industrial Average, which records the change in share prices of the leading industrial companies. The London market equivalent is the *Financial Times* (FT) Index.

DPS   See DIVIDEND PER SHARE.

Draft   See BANK DRAFT.

Drawback   Repayment of customs duty paid on goods or materials when they are subsequently exported.

Drawer   Someone who signs a cheque or bill of exchange ordering another party (the drawee) to pay out the sum specified.

Drawing account   A current bank account, from which money can be taken out.

Drawing rights   Original rights given to members of the International Monetary Fund (IMF) to buy specified amounts of foreign currencies, from a reserve collected and managed by the Fund, to help settle temporary balance-of-payments deficits with other countries. This was developed, and extended, in 1968 to become a new international reserve currency system, called Special Drawing Rights (SDRs). See INTERNATIONAL MONETARY FUND and RESERVE CURRENCY.

Drop dead fee   A commission paid to lenders by bidders when the planned acquisition or takeover fails and the money earmarked to be borrowed for the acquisition is, therefore, not used.

Drop lock An agreement which allows a variable rate loan package (like a mortgage) to be changed into a fixed-interest loan.

Dual capacity Investment companies which act as both brokers and market-makers in stocks and shares. This was not permitted until the change in the trading system on the London Stock Exchange in October 1986, which scrapped the previous arrangement under which all dealings had to be placed through jobbers via stockbrokers who were separately owned. See BIG BANG and CHINESE WALLS.

Ducat Gold and silver coins formerly used as currency in several European countries, from the thirteenth to the eighteenth century.

Dud cheque One that is not honoured by the paying bank, normally because insufficient funds are available. See BOUNCE.

Due date Term used to describe the time when the repayment of a loan or payment of a premium has to be made.

Dues Subscription or other charges to be paid.

Dummy shareholder Someone who deals in shares on behalf of a third party to hide the identity of the real buyer or seller.

Dumping Term used in international trade to describe goods or services being sold in another country at below the cost of production, or with a very small profit margin, in order to undercut domestic competition and establish a foothold or monopoly in the market.

Dutch auction Situation in which the seller (auctioneer) starts offering at a high price and gradually lowers it until a buyer is forthcoming. Opposite to a normal auction, where the bidding starts low and builds up. Sometimes called a 'Chinese auction', it is often adopted when selling goods or services for charity.

Dutch bargain Popular term for a deal in which one side gets all the advantages.

Duty Government tax imposed on imports or home-produced goods. See EXCISE TAX.

E

Early leaver Someone who leaves a pension scheme before retirement age.

Early surrender value Amount an endowment or life assurance policy is worth if it is cashed in before reaching the maturity date. Since charges and costs are deducted in the early years of the policy, the early surrender value is often below the total sum of premiums paid. See PAID-UP POLICIES.

Earned income That part of an income, for taxation purposes, obtained as the result of working either for an employer or as self-employed. Special relief from taxation used to be given on earned income only, but this has been replaced by the personal allowance given to everybody. Income for the employee, however, is subject to a different type of tax (schedule E, normally deducted straight from salaries under the PAYE – Pay As You Earn – system), while schedule D taxation, which allows more types of expenses to be deducted, is applied to self-employed income. See PAYE.

Earnest money First payment given by buyers to provide proof that they intend to honour a contract to buy.

Earnings-related Contributions made to a pension scheme based on the salary level of the employee member. See FINAL SALARY and PENSIONS.

Earnings per share Guide to the value of a share. It is calculated by dividing a company's net (after tax) profit as shown in its last accounts by the number of shares issued. The current market price of the company is then divided by the earnings per share to estimate the PRICE-EARNINGS RATIO.

Earnings rule System scrapped in the 1989 Budget under which the state pension was reduced according to salary received during the five years after the official retirement age if the pensioner continued to work.

Earnings yield Proportion of total profits available for distribution to share and stockholders, compared with the current market price of the share or stock.

Easement Legal term for a right. An example of a positive easement is: one person may have a right of way (permission to cross), another person's land. A negative easement might be the right to stop someone blocking the view.

Econometrics Branch of economics which uses mathematics and statistical models, usually on computers, to analyse information and predict likely future trends.

ECU See EUROPEAN CURRENCY UNIT.

Educational trust Special trust set up to invest lump-sum payments for covering school fees. It has charitable status and therefore does not have to pay tax so long as it is used solely for educational purposes.

EFTPOS See ELECTRONIC FUNDS TRANSFER AT POINT OF SALE.

EIRIS (Ethical Investment Research Information Services) See ETHICAL INVESTMENT and USEFUL ADDRESSES.

Electronic funds transfer at point of sale (EFTPOS) System of paying for goods and service using a plastic card, instead of a cheque, normally at a retail shop or garage. The amount spent is deducted directly from the customer's account.

Electronic Random Number Indicator Equipment (Ernie) The machine used to select PREMIUM BONDS prizewinners. See NATIONAL SAVINGS.

Embezzlement Legal term for the crime when a trusted employee dishonestly uses money intended for the employer.

Emergency reserves Money held by a company or organization on deposit, to provide for some unexpected emergency.

Emergency tax code Used to deduct tax under the PAYE (Pay As You Earn) system when the employer does not have full details of the employee's allowances.

Emoluments Old-fashioned term used to describe earnings in the form of fees received by professions, public officials and directors who are not employed by the company on a full-time basis. ·

Employee Retirement Security Act (ERISA) Law in the United States controlling the operation of personal pension plans, which provides general guidelines for the management for pension funds.

Employee share ownership plans (ESOPs) Scheme, pioneered in the United States, for distributing shares in a company to its employees. A special trust is set up by the company to acquire its shares for distribution to its employees over a period of up to seven years. The trust, which must have a majority of independent trustees, acts as a 'market maker' in the shares for the employees' benefit. The 1989 Budget gave a boost to ESOPs by proposing that companies should be given relief from corporation tax on payments made into an ESOP trust, providing that certain conditions are met. It was part of a general package to encourage employee share-owning schemes, which receive special tax privileges. It will, for example, be possible for ESOP trusts to distribute shares via the approved profit-sharing scheme and in this way allow employees to take advantage of the tax-free concessions available. See PROFIT-RELATED PAY.

Employee share schemes Special tax concessions are given to various schemes that have to be approved by the Inland Revenue, encouraging employees to own shares in the company they work for. Under the approved profit-sharing scheme employers can give employees shares tax-free each year up to a maximum amount, which is adjusted from time to time.

In addition there is the approved savings-related share option scheme under which employees make monthly savings, up to a maximum sum, which are held in an interest-bearing account. At the end of five years employees have the option of buying shares in the company at the market price quoted at the time five years before when they first started contributions, thus making a guaranteed tax-free profit if the share value has risen in that period. Alternatively in the unlikely event of the shares having fallen in price, the employees can take out the savings, plus accumulated interest, tax-free.

Employers' liability policy See INSURANCE.

EMS See EUROPEAN MONETARY SYSTEM.

Endorsed Bond See BOND, ASSUMED.

Endorsement Signature on the back of a cheque or bill of exchange signifying a change of ownership to the new holder. Also used to authorize changes to terms or conditions in an assurance policy.

Endowment insurance Policy where the insured is entitled to a guaranteed fixed sum at a specified maturity (repayment) date in the future, or at death if earlier. As there is a guaranteed payment, endowment policies are often used as security for loans, especially mortgages.

Endowment mortgage When repayment of a loan to buy a property is linked to an endowment life assurance policy guaranteeing a fixed sum to be paid at a particular date. The borrower pays interest only on the mortgage loan, and premiums on the endowment policy, which are used to repay the capital part of the mortgage loan when the policy matures or if the borrower dies.

There are several types of endowment mortgage: the old fashioned NON-PROFIT version where the assurance policy pays only a guaranteed sum to repay the mortgage; a WITH-PROFITS version, where the insurance policy pays out a

guaranteed sum plus any accumulated surplus profits resulting from investing the premium money. Most popular version these days is the low-cost policy, where the premiums are lower because the guaranteed sum payable is smaller. However, the sum needed to repay the mortgage is made up by bonuses given annually and when the policy matures. With the LOW START version, the policy premiums are reduced at the beginning, but then are increased later to make up for the early shortfall in payments. See INSURANCE and MORTGAGES.

Enduring power of attorney Special type of power of attorney to help protect the assets of people who may become mentally incapable of managing their own financial affairs. It is often granted by older people to relatives or to solicitors, so that their affairs can be managed if they do become mentally incapable without going through all the expense and time required in applying to the Court of Protection to appoint a receiver. However, Enduring Powers of Attorney have to be approved by the Court of Protection before they can be implemented.

Enfaced bond See BOND, ASSENTED.

Enterprise allowance Government grant given weekly for a year to unemployed who start up their own business.

Enterprise zones Selected areas where special incentives and tax concessions are given to enourage industry and building development. See PROPERTY ENTERPRISE TRUSTS.

EPP See EXECUTIVE PENSION PLAN.

Equalization System introduced by unit trusts to reduce investors' liability to income tax. When units are purchased the initial income earned is refunded as a capital payment until holders receive their first distribution of income.

Equalization of estates Division of family assets between husband and wife to obtain the maximum reliefs available from INHERITANCE TAX.

Equitable assets See ASSETS.

Equitable mortgage Normal form of home loan where the borrower gives the lender the title-deeds of the property as security, but the lender has to apply to a court of law before gaining possession of the property, should the debt not be paid.

Equities Alternative name for shares in a limited liability company, normally traded on a stock market, as opposed to fixed-interest or property investments. So called because shareholders have a right to a proportion of the equity capital in a company. Term more generally used to describe investments in companies.

Equity (capital) Strictly, the residue of capital left in a company and owned by shareholders after all prior charges have been deducted. But more frequently used to describe someone's stockmarket investments, money or property.

Equity dilution Where the stake held by existing shareholders is reduced by the issue of new shares carrying equal rights. See PARI PASSU.

Equity linked Investment, insurance or pension policy that involves buying stocks or shares.

Equity of redemption Right of a

mortgagor (borrower) to reclaim property on repayment of money borrowed.

Ernie See ELECTRONIC RANDOM NUMBER INDICATOR EQUIPMENT.

ERISA See EMPLOYEE RETIREMENT SECURITY ACT.

Escalating annuity or family income policy Where the payment increases by a fixed percentage each year.

Escalation clause Condition often included in a contract, which may take some time to complete, to allow for an increase in costs as a result of inflation or other factors.

Escalator bond See BOND.

Escrow Legal term for assets, often a sum of money held by an independent third party as a form of guarantee that a contract is completed.

ESOP See EMPLOYEE SHARE OWNERSHIP PLANS.

Estate duty Tax on the transfer of assets on someone's death, now replaced by INHERITANCE TAX.

Estimated (initial) yield The expected return from an investment fund, such as a unit trust, from dividends or interest. See YIELD.

Ethical investment Funds that will not put money into certain areas that are considered to be politically or socially undesirable. Examples include companies with a record of treating employees badly, or links with South Africa. Also those producing alcohol, armaments and tobacco, fur traders and companies causing pollution or spoiling the environment. Some guidelines are provided by EIRIS (Ethical Investment Research Information Services), but the policy of investment funds of this type varied according to the managers.

Eurobonds International long-term interest bonds offered outside the domestic market of the issuer. Originally resulted from the desire of US groups to raise money in Europe, but subsequently extended by any company wishing to raise funds outside its own country. They are denominated in a variety of currencies. The interest paid is free of any local withholding tax and they are issued in bearer form, making it easier to transfer ownership.

The three most common types of Eurobonds, issued by syndicates of banks, are STRAIGHTS or BULLETS with a fixed interest and fixed maturity (repayment) date. FLOATING RATE NOTES (FRNs) offer a variable interest rate, tied to an international rate, like London Inter Bank Offer Rate (LIBOR), and CONVERTIBLES which can be converted to ordinary shares.

Eurocheques Special cheques, issued together with a special encashment plastic card, that can be used to pay for goods in participating stores, and withdraw cash from banks all over Europe. An alternative form of TRAVELLERS' CHEQUES.

Euro-currencies General term for bank balances held in Europe in a particular currency apart from domestic currency of the country where the money is held. They are therefore subject to fewer rules and regulations than currencies in domestic markets.

Euro-dollars Dollar balances in US banks, held in the names of European persons or companies. They are used to finance international trade without ever being withdrawn, and at one time were viewed as the closest thing to an international currency, until the US dollar started to lose value against other currencies.

Euro-markets General name given to the trading of Eurobonds, Euro-currencies and Euro-dollars.

European currency unit (ECU) Currency established by the European Community; made up from a weighted average of the currencies in the European Monetary System (EMS) and sterling. Deposits and securities can now be denominated in ECUs, and this has become an internationally accepted form of currency and is the mutually agreed unit for settlement of balances between member countries of the Community, as well as the common denominator for deciding price support levels. See GREEN CURRENCIES.

European Monetary System (EMS) Set up in 1979 by member countries of the European Community to stabilize exchange rates among themselves, using the European Currency Unit as the common denominator for judging the value of individual currencies within the EMS. See SNAKE.

Evergreen fund Venture capital fund which provides support for new companies providing a continuous source of finance to sponsor their development on a longer-term basis.

Ex From the Latin 'without', used as the opposite of CUM.

Ex all Without any of the benefits soon due on a bond, share or stock.

Ex bonus, Ex distribution, Ex repayment, Ex rights, Ex scrip, Ex warrant All cases where the price of the stock does not include the right to take up a recent offer of extra allocations.

Ex cap(italization) Without the capitalization shares about to be issued.

Excepted perils Insurance term for risks not covered in a policy for transporting goods and for which the carriers are not liable. See ACT OF GOD.

Exceptional items Term used in company accounts to distinguish a payment, or receipt, which has nothing to do with the company's normal business and which, therefore, should not be included in the profit and loss account. For this reason, they are listed separately. See EXTRAORDINARY ITEMS.

Excess The amount in an insurance claim that the policy-holders have agreed to pay on their own behalf. The amount varies from policy to policy, but normally the holder can obtain a reduction in the premiums by agreeing to a higher excess figure.

Exchange Used in many ways, apart from its literal meaning of accepting one thing for another. Exchange can be used to describe a trading centre, such as the COMMODITY or STOCK EXCHANGES. It also applies to currencies and money dealing. See BILL OF EXCHANGE, EXCHANGE RATE and FOREIGN EXCHANGE MARKET.

Exchange contracts Technical term for completing a transaction, notably buying a house. When contracts have been exchanged, both parties are legally bound to complete the transaction. See COMPLETION.

Exchange control Government regulation to prevent or limit the movement of money to other countries, as a means of preventing an outflow of capital or to underpin the domestic currency. Abolished by Britain in 1979, but still used in many countries, especially in those developing or Communist countries with weak economies or currencies.

Exchange equalization account Fund run by the Bank of England, on behalf of the government, primarily to manipulate the value of sterling by buying or selling on the foreign exchange markets in accordance with the government's wishes. An important part of the controls used to regulate the economy and Britain's role in international trade.

Exchange rate Value of different currencies; the amount which one currency will buy of another currency at a particular time. The rates are either fixed by a government, comparing its currency with a leading currency such as the US dollar, or alternatively are established by dealings on the foreign exchange market. Governments are often forced to change fixed rates if the value of the currency in question is established at a different level on the foreign exchange market. See FLOATING EXHANGE RATE.

Exchequer Department of the Treasury in charge of the country's revenue and expenditure, controlled by the Chancellor of the Exchequer on behalf of the government. See BUDGET.

Exchequer account Run by the Bank of England to receive all government revenues, forming the CONSOLIDATED FUND, and to pay out all government expenditure authorized by Parliament. Each week the Treasury gives details of revenue and expenditure in a public statement called the exchequer return.

Exchequer stock Government-fixed interest security (gilt), used to raise funds from investors. See GILTS.

Excise tax The duty or tax charged by the government on certain domestically produced goods such as beer, spirits, wine and tobacco. Collected by the Customs and Excise department on behalf of the government.

Exclusions Risks not covered in an insurance policy. See ACT OF GOD.

Ex coupon Without the interest soon due for payment on a bond.

Ex dividend, Ex interest Where the buyer is not entitled to the next distribution of profits or income. Shares go ex-div on a specified date, normally the first day of the stock exchange account period, while government stocks go ex-dividend 36 days before the next payment of income is due. Often abbreviated to XD or XIN.

Executed trust Trust set up in a will giving specific instructions on how the property transferred to it on death should be dealt with.

Executory trust is similar in specifying the property to be transferred on death, but gives the trustees only guidelines on how it should be used.

Execution only service Where a dealer or broker offers only to buy or sell stocks or shares, without offering any advice or information thus reducing the cost.

Executive director A director of a company who is also a working employee, normally with a particular responsibility.

Executive pension plan (EPP) Special pension scheme devised particularly to provide extra rewards for directors and senior executives of a company. See PENSIONS.

Executor Legal term for a person named in a Will to carry out the wishes of the deceased in distributing the estate.

Exemplary damages Extra damages awarded by a court as a penalty for the original loss being made worse by the actions of the person who caused the loss.

Exempt funds Investment funds that do not have to pay tax, such as those for charities and pensions.

Exempt gilts Government securities issued to attract investment from non-taxpayers like charities, pension funds and overseas investors. They pay gross dividends, instead of deducting standard-rate tax at source. See NATIONAL SAVINGS.

Exercise notice Formal notification by holders of an option that they wish to buy or sell underlying stock or commodity at the EXERCISE PRICE. See OPTIONS.

Exercise price The price at which an option to buy (call) or sell (put) can be exercised. The option is normally only exercised if it means that the owner of an option can make a profit, and that depends on how the exercise price compares with the current market value of the shares, stock or commodity.

Ex gratia Literally translated from the Latin, means 'as a matter of favour'. Used to describe payments, especially by insurance companies, where no legal obligation to pay is admitted but where there may be a moral obligation or desire to seek a compromise against a possible claim.

Ex growth Stock exchange term used to describe a company which is considered to have limited scope (or none) for further expansion at least in the near future, so the share price is unlikely to rise much.

Expense account Amount of money permitted to be spent on running or promoting a business, without adding to its assets.

Expense ratio Relation between the cost of running a business compared with the turnover or total sales. Alternatively, a comparison between an insurance company's outgoings and its income from premiums.

Expiry date The last day on which an option to buy or sell can be exercised. Alternatively, the last day protection against a risk is given by an insurance policy.

Express transfers Fast way of sending money abroad. Instructions to credit an overseas account, or to pay cash to a specified person, from funds held in Britain are transmitted by telex or cable. See TELEGRAPHIC TRANSFERS.

Expropriation Legal term for a government's right to take away a person's property. Alternatively, used to describe the cancellation of a number of units in a unit trust fund. When a unit trust holder sells, the fund manager has the choice either of buying the units or of cancelling them and paying out from the sale of stock held by the fund.

Extended bond See BOND.

Extended credit When a borrower is allowed longer than usual, or at a later date than previously agreed, to pay up.

Extended warranty When the guarantee on goods or service is given for a longer period than normal, often as a sales inducement.

Extraordinary General Meeting (EGM) Special meeting called to obtain the views of investors in companies or funds about a major decision that could radically affect their interests. A shareholders' EGM is required when a company wishes to make a major purchase or disposal, or alter its capital structure. An EGM for investors in funds/unit trusts is called if charges are to be raised beyond the level allowed on the trust deed or if there is to be a significant change in its investment strategy or merger with another fund.

Extraordinary items A one-off profit or loss in a company's account not related to its normal overall trading activities. See EXCEPTIONAL ITEMS.

Extraordinary reserves Money set aside to cover a possible expense or loss that might result from a development outside the company's or organization's normal course of business.

Extrinsic value Value that exists for an indirect reason; for example, a cheap pen may have great extrinsic value if used by a famous author to write books. See INTRINSIC VALUE.

F

Face value Value shown on a banknote or coin, but not necessarily its true market value. Gold coins, for example, have a face value well below the value of the metal content, and this also applies to other forms of coins with a rarity value. Shares also have a face, or nominal, value normally well below the market price on the stock exchange.

Factor Particular type of agent employed to sell goods on behalf of a principal in return for commission, known as factorage.

Factoring Arrangement under which a special type of finance house takes over from a supplier of goods or services the right to collect payment from approved customers at some future date. The supplier receives payment immediately, with a fee deducted to cover the factor's charges for taking over responsibility for collecting payments.

Fair rent Rent fixed by a rent officer for accommodation where the tenant is protected against eviction. The assessment is based on the age, size and state of the property and does not take into account current market values locally, so it is fixed at a much lower level than similar property on the market.

Fall-back price See RESERVE PRICE.

Family credit Government grant to help families with low incomes.

Family income policy Insurance taken out by a parent to produce a tax-free income should he/she die before the children have finished full-time education. With an ESCALATING FAMILY INCOME POLICY, the payments made increase by a fixed amount each year.

Farthing Old British coin, now out of circulation, that was worth 1/4 of the old penny (1/960 of the pound), prior to decimalization.

Federal Reserve System Group of twelve regional banks in the United States, under the control of the Federal Reserve Board in Washington, which regulates the country's finances on behalf of the government. The local Federal Reserve banks act as bankers to the banks in their region, issuing banknotes and coins, discounting bills and making loans, including being a lender of last resort.

Fee A payment, charge or commission for professional advice or some special service.

Fertility rent Extra amount paid for land which gives above-average crop yield.

Fictitious assets See ASSETS.

Fictitious payee Use of an obviously fictitious name on a cheque, so that payment is made to the borrower.

Fidelity insurance Special policy that

provides protection against dishonesty or breach of contract. See INSURANCE.

Fiduciary Legal description of person, for example a trustee, given a position of special confidence on behalf of a third party.

Fiduciary bond See BOND, FIDELITY; BOND, SURETY.

Fiduciary loan Loan made entirely on trust, without any security being provided.

Fifo See FIRST IN, FIRST OUT.

FIMBRA See FINANCIAL INTERMEDIARIES, MANAGERS, BROKERS REGULATORY ASSOCIATION and USEFUL ADDRESSES.

Final earnings/salary pension scheme Type of company pension plan under which the pension is based on a percentage of the final salary of the employee at retirement age, or when leaving the scheme. The advantage of this type of scheme is that the employee is guaranteed a pension whatever might happen to the scheme's investments. The disadvantage is that early leavers often receive much reduced benefits, since the most important period of contributions is during the few years prior to retirement and the transfer value may not be great. This was one factor that influenced the government to introduce far-reaching changes in the pensions industry, extending the entitlement of personal pensions to everyone, under the 1986 Pensions Act, which came into effect in 1988. See PENSIONS.

Finance Act An annual Act of Parliament, mainly designed to put into effect the various proposals announced by the Chancellor of the Exchequer in the annual Budget. However, during the passage of the Act through Parliament for approval, there are often amendments to the Budget proposals.

Finance company/house General term covering companies, merchant banks, industrial banks and the subsidiaries of clearing banks specializing in hire purchase transactions. Retailers and distributors offering hire purchase facilities usually use a finance house, which takes over the responsibility for collecting instalments in return for a commission. The finance houses obtain funds from clearing banks and investors, either directly or by issuing Bills of Exchange, and have their interest lending rate, which tends to fluctuate in line with bank base rate. Their operation is supervised by the Finance Houses Association.

Financial adviser Either a merchant bank called in by a company to provide help during a takeover battle. Alternatively refers to an independent broker or intermediary who gives advice on investments, savings and other financial matters. Since 1988 the latter must be authorized by FIMBRA and comply with its rules and regulations, in accordance with the Financial Services Act. They must also make it plain whether they are truly independent or are 'tied' into selling the financial products of a particular group or organization. It is a criminal offence to offer services as an independent financial adviser and not be a member of FIMBRA or one of the self-regulatory organizations.

Financial futures Futures markets that trade contracts based on financial indices, instruments or currencies, as opposed to traditional commodity markets. See FUTURES and LIFFE.

Financial Intermediaries, Managers and Brokers Regulatory Association (FIMBRA) One of the self-regulatory organizations set up under the Financial Services Act 1986 to improve investor protection, under the umbrella of the Securities and Investments Board. FIMBRA is the biggest of the self-regulatory organizations in membership terms, since it includes all brokers and investment advisers selling financial products and services direct to the public. See SELF-REGULATORY ORGANIZATIONS and USEFUL ADDRESSES.

Financial Times (FT) index Most widely accepted guide to price movements on the London stock market. The *Financial Times*, a daily newspaper specializing in business and financial matters, produces several different indices to record movements on the stock market. Best known is the Industrial Ordinary Share Index, also known as the 30 share index since it is based on the price movements of 30 leading shares considered to represent the whole of British industry. The FT All-Share (FTA) Index, produced in conjunction with the Institute of Actuaries and the Faculty of Actuaries, is an all-share index divided into a number of sub-groups covering companies in various sectors. The *FT* also produces a 500-share index, a long gilt yield index and a world index covering the international stock markets. The FT-SE 100 (share) index is produced in co-operation with the stock exchange and forms the basic contract for the FT-SE 100 Index ('footsie') futures market on the London International Financial Futures Exchange (LIFFE). See INDEX.

Financial year An accounting period, normally of twelve months – but not necessarily so, since it covers the period of the accounts. Companies can choose when to start their own trading year, although often a calendar year is used as the accounting period. See FISCAL YEAR.

Financier A person who arranges sources of money, like a banker, or who supports a particular deal or venture with his/her own money.

Fineness Measure of the standard of purity in gold and silver. Gold of correct fineness is called 'fine gold'.

Fine paper Cheques, Bills of Exchange or promissory notes accepted or endorsed by banks and finance houses with a good reputation.

Fire loss adjuster Expert with a special knowledge of assessing damage caused by fire and settling insurance claims to cover losses. See CLAIMS ADJUSTER.

Fire office A company that provides insurance coverage against fire and similar risks to property.

Firm sale Either a fixed or an agreed price; or a sale that is settled and not conditional on anything.

First in, first out (Fifo) Method of valuing stock using the cost of the oldest items held, on the grounds that those received first were also sold first.

First loss An insurance policy that covers only the first part of a loss, when the insurance company is not prepared to take on an open-ended commitment to cover all possible losses.

Fiscal drag The 'gap', benefiting the government, between the setting of allowances and tax relief rates and their adjustment for inflation.

Fiscal policy Strategy used by government in raising and spending money.

Fiscal year A government's financial year, in Britain from 6 April in one year to 5 April of the next year. The twelve-month period used for calculation of taxes and expenditure usually dealt with in the annual Budget.

Fixed assets See ASSETS, CAPITAL.

Fixed cost Payment that has to be made and does not vary with the volume of goods produced or services provided.

Fixed debenture See DEBENTURE.

Fixed income An income that does not increase in line with the cost of living or over a period, such as an annuity or pension payment, or rent from a property let on a long lease.

Fixed interest security Bonds, certificates or stock that pay a set amount of interest, usually at specified times for a predetermined period. See GILTS and LOAN STOCK.

Fixed liabilities Debts which do not have to be repaid for some time, such as a mortgage.

Fixed offer price Normally used when launching a fund in which the units are offered at a single figure for a limited period of time; however, the managers have discretion to change the price if there is a significant change in market conditions, either up or down. Fixed price offers are sometimes also used to boost sales of an existing unit trust.

Fixed rate loans/mortgage Where the rate of interest to be charged is set at a specified figure for an agreed length of time. Most lenders are reluctant to offer fixed rates for a long period because of the volatility of interest rates in recent years, although it is possible to obtain money at a fixed rate for long periods ahead on the wholesale money market.

Fixed-sum debenture Given to a bank as security against all money owed by the borrower for the present and the future.

Fixed trust Investment fund that can put money only in a specified range of investments.

Fixing Term used to describe a method of settling price levels at a particular time by negotiation between interested parties. The members of the bullion market in London meet each trading day to 'fix' the price of gold and silver. There are two gold 'fixings' daily, one at the end of morning trading and one in the afternoon. Daily fixings are also issued for platinum and silver price quotations.

Flag Term used by followers of charts to describe a short-term price movement that may signal a further strong move in the same direction.

Flat rate or yield The rate of interest paid, calculated as a percentage of the amount invested. Repayment of a loan, such as mortgage, with payments averaged out to be the same amount by dividing the total loan by the number of payments.

Flat-rate tariff Method of charging for something at a fixed rate.

Fleece Rob someone of all their money.

Flexible policies See UNIVERSAL (LIFE) PLANS.

Flexible trust An investment fund in which the managers have powers to sell and buy any shares, normally within certain specified limits.

Float Start a company, or prepare for a company to be quoted on a stock market. See FLOTATION.

Floating assets See ASSETS, CURRENT.

Floating or working capital Stock of money needed by a business to carry on day-to-day production or trading. The sum left after deducting current liabilities from current assets.

Floating charge When creditors have the right to receive payment from any asset held by a limited company, should it fail to pay debts when due.

Floating currency When the value of a currency is allowed to rise or fall according to supply and demand in the foreign exchange markets.

Floating debenture See DEBENTURE, FIXED.

Floating debt A loan that may have to be repaid at short notice.

Floating exchange rate See FLOATING CURRENCY.

Floating insurance An insurance that covers property in more than one place, or covers more than one employee.

Floating money Cash held only temporarily by bankers.

Floating rate notes (FRNs) Loan stock in a company which pays interest that varies according to movements in the market rate. May well be linked to the London Inter Bank Offered Rate (LIBOR).

Floor or floor price The lowest level below which a controlled market is not allowed to fall. See BUFFER STOCK and COMMODITY AGREEMENTS.

Floor trader A broker or dealer trading on an exchange on behalf of his/her company or clients. Originally, it referred specifically to those on the actual 'floor' of the exchange, but is now generally used to describe someone undertaking the deals with other members of the exchange rather than dealing directly with clients.

Florin Ancient gold coin, originally from Florence, that became part of British currency system in the fourteenth century. Currently alternative name in Britain for 10p coin (1/10 of a pound) and in Holland for the guilder.

Flotation Raising capital for a new company, or one being quoted on the stock exchange for the first time, either by special deals (private placing) or by offering shares to the general public, based on a prospectus. Often used to describe the situation where a private company decides to 'float off' capital by offering shares to investors and becoming a public company. See PRIVATIZATION.

Flotsam Legal term for cargo goods floating at sea after a shipwreck. In British waters, they become the property of the government if not claimed within one year and a day. See JETSAM.

Fluff Deliberately give a customer the wrong change, in the expectation that it will not be noticed.

Flutter A small bet or commercial venture.

FOB See FREE ON BOARD.

Fob off Sell an article of poor quality by pretending it is good.

Footsie Popular nickname for the FT-SE 100 Share index.

Force majeure Term of French origin, literally translated as 'superior force'. Used to describe a special clause in a contract that allows the contract to be suspended if something occurs that is beyond the control of the parties to the contract, such as a war, accident or strike by workers. For example, a mining company might declare force majeure on deliveries of metal promised to its customers if the mine's production is hit by an accident, machine failure or a strike.

Foreclosure Right of a mortgagee (lender) to obtain a court order against a mortgagor (borrower) for failing to repay a debt by the due date; possibly leading, if the debt is not paid, to the mortgagee being given permission to sell the property.

Foreign currency or exchange (FX) The currency of any other country but one's own.

Foreign exchange market Trading carried out by groups of dealers and brokers, representing banks and other financial institutions, in the currencies of different countries, which decides the rates of exchange between the different currencies. The SPOT MARKET deals with transactions made immediately, while the FORWARD MARKET covers transactions to be completed at some specified date in the future. See EXCHANGE RATE.

Forfeited share One that has been

given up, because the shareholder to whom it was originally allocated has paid only part of its value, and has failed to pay the balance of the cost.

Forfeiture Lose right to some property as a punishment for a crime or wrong-doing such as failing to fulfil a duty or pay a debt.

Formation expenses Money advanced by promoters of a new company before it is incorporated and can start trading, such as legal and accounting fees, or stamp duty and registration charges. These expenses are due to be repaid once the company starts trading.

For the account Stock market term for dealings to be settled on the next account settlement date.

Forward discount See FORWARD PREMIUM.

Forward exchange contract Purchase or sale of foreign currency for delivery at a date in the future, usually undertaken as protection against possible changes in currency values.

Forward market Dealings that are made for settlement at some specified date in the future rather than immediately (on the spot). Particularly applies to trading in the commodities, currency (foreign exchange) and money markets. Differs from FUTURES in that forward trading is concerned with dealing in the actual commodity or currency, whereas futures are 'paper' contracts used for speculation or as protection against the risk of losses incurred in forward trading as a result of the price or rate changing unexpectedly.

Forward premium When the cost of

something, bought or sold for delivery at a future date, is higher than the price for immediate (spot) delivery. Opposite of forward discount.

Founders' shares Class of share sometimes issued to the founders of a company; they receive dividend payments only after other shareholders have been paid an agreed amount. See DEFERRED SHARES.

FOX See FUTURES AND OPTIONS EXCHANGE and USEFUL ADDRESSES.

Fractional certificate A share certificate for a part of a share, often resulting from a merger of two companies, involving them in an exchange of shares in unequal proportions.

Fractional currency Coins which are a fraction of the standard unit of currency.

Franchise Right given to sell goods or operate a service on behalf of a third party, normally in return for a percentage of the profits or turnover. A method used by manufacturers, and new businesses, to obtain wider distribution for their goods or services through using independently run outlets.

Franked income Investment income received by a company on which tax equivalent to the basic rate has already been paid at source; for example, dividends paid by UK companies from which standard rate tax has been deducted, so the income can be passed on to investors in unit and investment trusts with no further tax deduction.

Freehold Legal right to hold land as the absolute owner. The freehold of a property can be bought or sold, with the owner often being known as the freeholder or landlord.

Free insurance When no further premiums are due on an insurance policy.

Free market Popular term used to describe the situation when buying and selling is carried out free of outside interference. The free market value is, therefore, judged to reflect the true cost based on supply and demand. Hence the reference to 'free market forces', as opposed to controls applied by governments or companies. In fact, free markets are often residual markets in which only a proportion of the total trading takes place. For example, metal producers sell the bulk of their output direct to consumers, but often at a price fixed by the free market, which deals only in the residual supplies left over.

Free on board (FOB) Term used when an exporter agrees to pay all the costs of getting goods sold on to the ship taking them to the buyer. As opposed to CIF (cost, insurance, freight) where the seller also pays the costs of transporting the goods to the buyer's premises.

Free pay Girobank scheme for paying for goods advertised in the media.

Free reserves Money or assets of an insurance company that are not committed to paying possible future claims.

Free standing additional voluntary contributions (FSAVC) Extra pension scheme taken out separately to supplement a company scheme but with another pension provider, independent of the company scheme (hence free standing). See PENSIONS.

Freight rates Cost of carrying goods from one place to another. See BALTIC EXCHANGE.

Friendly societies Organizations, mutually owned by the members who originally paid subscriptions to provide economic help if any of them, or their families, fell on hard times. Founded at the same time as the BUILDING SOCIETIES during the Industrial Revolution in Britain by workers to provide economic support, by clubbing together to buy land or houses and provide protection for their members hit by sickness and unemployment. Some trade unions started as friendly societies.

Societies approved by the Registrar of Friendly Societies have certain tax advantages but these are restricted to small investments only. There are several types of friendly society, offering a varied range of products and services. Basically, however, they tend to cater primarily for people with low incomes, interested in savings or insurance and not investing in the stock market directly.

Fringe benefits Extra rewards given to employees over and above their normal wage or salary. Can include pensions, subsidized meals, company cars and many other perks.

For investors, fringe benefits are extra rewards given in addition to dividend payments. See PERKS.

Front-end load Charge made on investment product or insurance policy to cover the costs of making the offer to investors. It often includes the commission paid to brokers selling the product or policy. The front-end load (or initial charge) is deducted from the sum invested. For example, a 5% front-load charge would mean that out of every £100 paid only £95 would actually be invested. In the case of unit trusts this is done via the BID/OFFER SPREAD, the gap between the buying and selling prices of the units. See NO LOAD FUNDS.

Frozen assets See ASSETS.

Frozen credits Balances in bank accounts which, normally by government order, cannot be transferred to their owners.

FRNs See FLOATING RATE NOTES.

FTA See FINANCIAL TIMES.

FT-SE 100 See FINANCIAL TIMES.

Full-bodied currency One entirely of gold or silver.

Full-cost price One which includes the cost of production and a satisfactory profit margin.

Full listing Companies which qualify to have their shares quoted and traded on the main stock market in London as opposed to the USM (Unlisted Securities Market) or Third Market. See STOCK EXCHANGE.

Fully paid shares Where the full nominal value of the shares issued in a company has been paid up.

Fund Stock of money put aside for a specific purpose, such as charity, investment or pension. General term used to describe pool of money invested on behalf of its owners and controlled by fund managers.

Fundamental analysis Research into the underlying value of an investment by examining the basic influences affecting the business or market, rather than just relying on following former price movements as chartists do.

Funding Replacing a short-term debt with the issue of long-term or perpetual bonds, or supplying a sum of money to cover the debt.

Fund manager Someone who manages an investment fund.

Fund of funds A unit trust or fund that invests in other funds.

Funeral expenses Local authority grant available to help meet the cost of death: undertaker's fee and simple burial or cremation.

Funk money Savings or investments that are moved around in response to fears of what might happen to them, normally because of political developments.

Futures Contracts dealt on an exchange or market for the delivery or purchase of something at a specified date in the future. The prime purpose of futures markets is to provide protection against unpredictable price movements and therefore to make forward trading, for delivery at a future date, safer against possibly crippling losses. This is done by establishing opposite transactions (sale and purchase) in the forward and futures market that cancel each other out, whatever may happen to the price in the meantime. A loss resulting from a purchase in the forward trading market, as a result of the price falling by the time delivery date arrives, is compensated for by the matching gain made by the sale in the futures market which can be cancelled at a profit as a result of the price fall. For example, the purchase of, say, 1,000 tons of cocoa for delivery in six months would be matched by the sale of 1,000 tons of cocoa at the same time on the futures market. When the cocoa is physically delivered, the sale on the futures market is cancelled by making a purchase. If in the meantime the price of cocoa bought six months ago has fallen, resulting in a loss to the buyer, this is offset by the profit made from the sale in the futures market. If the price of cocoa has gone up instead of down, then the profit made on the physical forward purchase will be cancelled by the loss on the futures sale. This is known as 'hedging'.

On most futures exchanges, all the transactions are channelled through a central clearing system or house, which matches together all the purchases and sales made each day and guarantees the contract. Futures markets are not basically intended as centres for trading the underlying physical contract or financial instrument. But in order to ensure that they stay in line with the trend in the physical market and provide proper hedging, there is normally an option to deliver or take delivery (or make a cash settlement) against a futures contract.

Futures contracts were originated by commodity dealers and merchants, seeking protection from the risks involved in trading raw materials whose prices could fluctuate widely. In more recent times, futures markets have been developed to cover financial instruments, like bonds, certificates, currencies and shares, whose value can also move violently and unpredictably.

However, the markets are also used to establish the price of something at a future date, in line with the expected balance of supply and demand. A bumper harvest, for example, might depress the price of wheat in the months after the crop becomes available, even though there might currently be a shortage of supplies. The constant changes in future price expectations provide opportunities for speculation as to whether the market has guessed right at any particular time. Speculating in futures can, however, be highly dangerous, since trading is done on margin. This means that only a percentage of the total sum involved has to be paid initially, with the balance due on the delivery date. Margin trading magnifies not only the potential gains but also the potential losses. The requests for additional money to maintain the margin at the original percentage of the total transaction can be very high indeed if the market suddenly moves the 'wrong' way for the speculator.

The biggest centres for international futures markets are in Chicago, New York and London, but they are now operating at local centres throughout the world.

In London, all firms operating on the futures markets on behalf of others, or offering advice on futures trading, must be approved members of the Association of Futures Brokers and Dealers (AFBD), one of the self-regulatory organizations set up under the umbrella of the Securities and Investment Board to provide protection for investors. See REGULATION.

Futures and Options Exchange (FOX) Centre in London for several of the 'soft' (non-metal) futures markets, owned by the LONDON COMMODITY EXCHANGE.

Futures funds Collective investment funds that buy and sell in the futures markets to try and make a profit for shareholders in the fund. Because they deal on margin, futures funds are high risk, able to make above-average returns – but also liable to suffer above-average losses.

FX See FOREIGN CURRENCY OR EXCHANGE.

G

Gamma shares One of the four categories of shares (the others are ALPHA, BETA and DELTA) dealt in on the London Stock Exchange under the new trading system adopted there after the BIG BANG in October 1986. Gamma shares are rarely traded. Market-makers in the shares are required to display gamma share prices on the Stock Exchange Automated Quotes System (SEAQ), but the prices quoted on the screens are not regarded as binding, merely as providing some indication.

Garnishee Legal term for an order sent to persons owing money to someone, to pay the money into court or to a third-party creditor. Used to prevent debtors spending money for themselves instead of paying their creditors.

GATT See GENERAL AGREEMENT ON TARIFFS AND TRADE.

Gazumping Popular term to describe the situation in which the seller of a property, having agreed to sell to one person, suddenly decides to take a better offer from someone else. A buyer with ready cash is often in a position to gazump someone who has to raise capital, since the seller is not legally committed until after contracts have been exchanged.

GDP See GROSS DOMESTIC PRODUCT.

Gearing Comparison between the amount of a company's loan capital (borrowed at a fixed rate of interest) and its ordinary share capital. Gearing is high when there is a large proportion of fixed-interest capital to ordinary share capital, and low in the reverse situation. High gearing means that a larger percentage of the profits has to be set aside to pay the fixed interest, so dividends are likely to be more variable, whereas companies with a low gearing tend to have a fairly constant and predictable rate of profit.

Alternatively, gearing is also used to describe the borrowing of money at a fixed rate of interest to invest in something that, it is hoped, will produce a bigger yield and therefore a profit.

General Agreement on Tariffs and Trade (GATT) An international agreement signed in 1947 by over 40 countries to try to limit the imposition of duties and quotas in trading between each country.

General creditor A lender who has no special preference or security for repayment, and therefore comes well down the list of those to be repaid in cases of bankruptcy.

General crossing When a cheque is crossed either without any words or simply with 'and company', written between the two parallel lines drawn across it. See CROSSED CHEQUE.

General extension rate Additional rate of interest, paid on most issues of National Savings Certificates which have reached

their maturity (repayment) date but have
not been cashed in. The rate is varied in
accordance with government policy –
whether or not the government wants to
encourage savers to retain or sell the
original certificates. See NATIONAL
SAVINGS.

General management trust See
FLEXIBLE TRUST.

General reserve Fund built up by a
company or organization out of
undistributed profits, to help cover the
increasing cost of running a business.

Gentleman's agreement An
agreement that is informal, but not legally
binding.

Geometric mean Statistical average,
particularly suitable in compiling indices of
a number of prices, since it smoothes out
large fluctuation in prices within the index.

Gifts inter vivos Gifts between living
persons, which may be liable to
inheritance tax if the donor dies.

Gilts (Gilt-edged securities)
Fixed-interest stocks issued or guaranteed
by the British government, primarily used
to raise money from investors for
government spending. They are issued in
units of £100 and often have a specified
repayment date and rate of interest
payable annually. For example, Treasury
10% 2000 pays £10 per £100 unit annually
and is repayable in the year 2000. Some
gilts, like Consols and War Loan, have no
repayment date but simply pay interest at
the stated rate.

Gilts are traded on the London stock
market, and the prices are calculated on
the current interest levels and the various
dates of repayments. Although
theoretically they are risk-free

investments (since it is assumed the
government will always honour any debt),
the variation in prices at which the stock
can be purchased means that investors can
suffer losses as a result of buying a gilt at a
higher price than the level at which it is
subsequently sold.

To add to the confusion – and mystique
– of the market, changes in price
movements are measured in terms of 1/32
of a £ and multiples of that basic unit (1/16,
1/8, 1/4 and 1/2) so to outsiders there may
often seem to be only minimal variation in
value.

Gilts, also known as British funds, are
categorized according to their dates of
repayment as 'shorts' (with lives of up to
five years), 'mediums' (five to fifteen
years) and 'longs' (over fifteen years).
Those with low coupons (interest rates)
tend to be available at lower prices, unless
they are near the maturity date, when
they can be redeemed at £100. Those with
high coupons are normally more
expensive, but vary according to the
repayment date.

The price of undated gilts reflects the
trend in interest rates. Consol 4%, for
example, priced at £50 would give a yield
of 8%, since the interest rate quoted is
based on £100 units.

Index-linked gilts were introduced in
1982 to try and counter investors'
nervousness about inflation and possibly
tying up money for a lengthy period.
These carry interest yields and
redemption values that are adjusted every
six months in line with the change in the
Retail Price Index, measuring inflation.
Gilts are primarily used by the
government to raise money to be repaid
over longer periods, since it can raise
short-term money by taxes or by
borrowing on the money markets. In
recent years the government has become
a net buyer of gilts as part of a new policy
to reduce its debts, and the interest

payable. Normally, however, the primary gilts market is fuelled by sales of new stock issues or large quantities of existing securities. The traditional method is for the Bank of England to invite tenders from the approved gilt market-making companies on the Stock Exchange to bid for new stock, with a minimum price set at or slightly above the current market levels for similar stock. The Bank allots stock at the highest price acceptable to all the bidders, and any stock left over is used as TAP STOCK which is available from the Bank to sell to market-makers whenever it is wanted. The Bank can influence the trend of the market by the price it sets for tap stocks. A new system of selling gilts by auction was introduced in May 1987. No minimum price is set; but the market-makers, bidding in competition, set prices in accordance with their views on interest rate trends.

Gilts provide a large proportion of the turnover on the London stock market, and the number of approved (by the Bank of England) market-makers was substantially increased after BIG BANG in October 1986 as one of the series of changes introduced at that time in the exchange's trading system.

Gilts are normally dealt in large quantities by institutional investors, such as pension funds, who want a proportion of their portfolio in safe, fixed-interest stocks. However, gilts are also available to private investors from stock market brokers, investment advisers and banks. A limited number of gilts, on the National Savings register, can be bought via Post Offices, normally at lower commission charges than from a broker or a bank.

Most private investment portfolios have traditionally included a proportion of gilts, which provide a safe, assured flow of income without the risks attached to investing in the more volatile company shares. Apart from the security of the investment, gilts have an additional appeal to private investors in that no capital gains tax is payable, and tax is not deducted at source from the interest, so they are particularly suitable for non-taxpayers. See REDEMPTION YIELD.

Gilt trusts Funds that invest in the gilt market on behalf of others. These funds have a disadvantage in that the profits made from the increase in the value of the units are subject to capital gains tax, whereas this tax is not paid on profits made from direct investment in gilts. Nevertheless, promoters of these funds claim that the lower commissions they pay for larger deals in gilts, and the extra profits made by a professional management in the highly complex gilts market, more than make up for the tax disadvantage.

Ginnie Mae Popular term in the United States for the US Government National Mortgage Association and the certificates for home loans issued by the Association.

Giro System operated in most European countries and in Japan for transferring money from one bank account to another, or to persons with no account. The word 'giro' stems from the Greek word 'guros' meaning a circle, ring, revolution or circuit. This describes the distinguishing feature of Giro banking systems which involve the rapid transmission and circulation of money to and from a single centre. Probably the earliest known Giro system was used by the ancient Egyptians for storing grain. See BANK GIRO SYSTEM and NATIONAL GIRO BANK.

Give as you earn Scheme, approved by the Inland Revenue, by which charitable donations can be deducted from employees' salaries and automatically qualify for tax relief. The tax-free limit was doubled in the 1989 Budget. Also known as PAYROLL GIVING.

GMP See GUARANTEED MINIMUM PENSION.

Gnomes (of Zurich) Popular phrase describing bankers, especially those in Switzerland, with a reputation for secrecy and influence.

GNP See GROSS NATIONAL PRODUCT.

Going concern Business that is trading steadily and profitably. As such, it is likely to fetch a premium price, above the value of its assets, if sold.

Going public Obtaining an official stock exchange quotation for a company by selling shares to outside investors, thereby obtaining extra capital resources. See FLOTATION.

Going rate Current market value or interest rate.

Gold Precious metal that is a traditional symbol of wealth, since it has been used to support currencies and measure their value throughout history. Because of its acceptability worldwide, many investors still prefer to own gold instead of 'paper' money, which can be devalued by currency rate changes and inflation. Although the price of gold varies daily, according to supply and demand, it is considered to have an intrinsic value particularly useful in times of crisis, high inflation and uncertainty. It is also easily transportable, and is therefore often viewed as the ultimate currency that can be exchanged for goods and services anywhere. See GOLD STANDARD.

Gold bond See BOND.

Gold bullion Gold in the form of bars and ingots, used for trading in the international bullion market, of specific quality and therefore valued by its weight as a precious metal and not by its value as a coin. Also provides the unit of trading for most gold futures contracts.

Gold card Plastic card, which offers its holder more benefits than the ordinary credit or charge card. Works on the simple principle that wealthier people are likely to be better credit risks and can therefore be given more facilities for borrowing. To qualify for a gold card, holders normally need to have a high income and/or reasonable financial resources. In return they are offered increased facilities, including the ability to spend more on credit, obtain guaranteed overdrafts at competitive interest rates, and special insurance and travel concessions. Yet more prestigious is the PLATINUM CARD, which is for even wealthier individuals.

Gold coins Specially produced coins to attract investment from the smaller investor, who may not be able to afford the larger bars and ingots traded on the bullion market. Gold coins are more profitable for gold mine producers to sell, since an additional premium is charged above the bullion price to cover the cost of minting the coins, plus a profit margin. Gold coins contain a small proportion of other metals to help them retain their shape and design, but their quoted weight is based on the gold content: thus a one ounce coin contains one ounce of gold. The price of the coin is based on the bullion price, plus a premium that varies according to the size of the coin and the demand for it. The gold content of a small (say 1/10th ounce) coin is proportionately more expensive since the premium charged for minting is the same as for larger coins. For many years the South

African-produced Krugerrand was the most popular gold coin, but production in it has ceased, and a range of alternative coins is available, mainly from gold-producing countries: Canadian Mapleleaf, American Eagle, Australian Nugget and Chinese Panda. The UK has produced the Britannia coin, using gold bought on the world market, and a range of old sovereigns are still available.

Golden handcuffs Popular term for financial inducements offered by companies for key employees not to leave. The benefits given are often provided only after a period of time, thus persuading the employee to stay until then.

Golden handshake Popular term for payment made by companies to compensate, or encourage, employees leaving their employ.

Golden parachutes A provision in the employment contracts of top executives in a company for them to be paid sums of money, often equal to several years' salaries, in the event of the company being taken over and the new owner deciding to dispense with their services.

Golden shares Special shares in a company, carrying extra voting powers. Used by the government in privatizing state-owned organizations as a means of retaining control, to ensure that the new private company will not agree to something against the public interest or government policy.

Gold futures Markets that deal in futures, trading with gold as the basic contract. See COMEX and FUTURES.

Gold reserves Stocks of gold kept by countries, to be used as a last resort to pay their international debts to other countries, whose currency they may not possess.

Gold standard Monetary system widely used internationally under which the value of the standard unit of a country's currency was fixed by law to a weight of gold of a stated fineness (standard of purity). Gold was chosen as a common denominator to back up the value of currencies because of its acceptability worldwide as a symbol and store of wealth. The system enabled the rates of exchange between the various gold-standard countries to remain constant, which helped international trade; but it limited the power of governments to control the supply of money in fighting inflation and unemployment, and for that reason was finally abandoned. For some time international governments, led by the United States, used reserves of gold to keep the price controlled so as to provide stable gold backing for their currencies. However, this too was abandoned when increasing demand for gold from speculators threatened to exhaust the reserves.

The price is now allowed to move freely, although the central banks still hold some of their monetary reserves in the form of gold, mainly for the purpose of making international payments and intervening on occasions in the market.

Goods-in-transit policy Insurance that covers damage or loss of goods from the moment they are loaded on to a vehicle until they are unloaded at the end of the journey.

Goodwill Value of a business over and above the value of its tangible or realizable assets. The custom built up by an established business, enabling it to earn more profit than a similar or new business, and therefore benefit a purchaser who pays extra for the right to use the established name and connections of that company.

Government loan scheme To help small businesses, the government will guarantee 70% of loans, up to a maximum figure, but an additional rate of interest is charged.

Government securities Fixed-interest stock issued by governments. See GILTS.

Graduated pension Scheme, originally operated by the UK government between 1961 and 1975, which provided extra benefits on top of the basic state pension in return for extra contributions. However, it was not protected against inflation, so the additional benefits declined in real value. In 1978 it was replaced by the State Earnings Related Pension Scheme (SERPS), which pays pensions on a scale based on earnings prior to retirement. See PENSIONS.

Granny bonds Popular name for special certificates issued by National Savings whose value is increased in line with inflation, as measured by the Retail Price Index. When originally introduced in 1975, the certificates were intended primarily to help protect pensioners against the ravages of inflation and they could be bought only by those who had reached retirement age – hence 'granny'. Subsequently, as inflation fears subsided, the restriction on sales was abandoned and they can now be bought by everyone. See NATIONAL SAVINGS.

Gratis Free of cost, available without payment.

Gratuity Tip, or sum of money given to an employee in reward for long service.

Grease A bribe. Money that is paid in

advance to secure services, possibly dishonestly.

Greenback Slang term used for the US dollar, which is usually printed on one side in green.

Green currencies Artificial rates of exchange used by the European Community to equalize farm support prices under the Common Agricultural Policy.

Greenmail A term used mainly in the United States to describe the situation where a company is forced by a hostile or unwanted takeover bidder to buy back its shares, at a price above the market, to avoid being taken over. As the dollar is known as the 'greenback', this form of blackmail was rechristened.

Green pound See GREEN CURRENCIES.

Grey knight A rival bidder to take over a company, whose intentions are unclear and who is therefore feared by both the company and the original bidder.

Grey market Dealings in stocks and shares before they have actually been issued, prior to flotation. Market-makers set prices in anticipation of the shares and stock becoming available, based on the issue value and the likely demand. This provides a good indication of the likely price-level obtainable on the market when the issue actually takes place and may decide whether an investor applies for an allotment or not.

Gross A quantity, sum of money, or yield, before any deductions, such as tax and expenses, have been made. Thus gross dividend, gross income, gross interest, gross investment, gross profits and GROSS YIELD.

Gross Domestic Product (GDP) Part of a country's Gross National Product (wealth earned) that remains after deducting its net income from overseas. Thus a measure of total earnings as a result of domestic production only.

Gross equivalent A notional figure, taking into account a net amount, plus any deductions made, so that it can be compared with other gross figures which might have different deductions. Used to compare company profits, dividends and interest yields.

Grossing up The calculation that converts a net figure into its gross equivalent, before deductions for tax have been made.

Gross National Product (GNP) The total wealth earned or brought into existence by a country during a particular year. A measure of the country's economic performance and prosperity, it takes into account earnings from overseas, as well as allowing for depreciation and any reduction in the stock of capital goods.

Gross value Annual value of a property, based on the rent that tenants would be expected to pay, if they paid the rates and taxes, and the landlord paid the repairs and insurance. The rateable value of the property, on which the local authority bases its rates, is the gross value, which can be varied if there are changes that might raise or lower the rent payable.

Gross yield The percentage return on a capital investment or deposit before any deductions are made. A useful way of comparing the return of an investment,

disregarding the individual circumstances of investors or the special liabilities of the company concerned. See NET YIELD, REDEMPTION YIELD.

Ground rent The amount paid by the occupier or leaseholder of a property to the ground landlord (owner of the property which has been leased for a fixed period of years).

Group insurance Insurance under a single policy covering a group of people, such as employees of a company, members of a pension scheme or organization. See INSURANCE.

Group of Ten Wealthier industrialized countries which have agreed to lend money to the International Monetary Fund (IMF). Also known as the Paris Club.

Growth stocks or shares Market term for shares of companies which are expected to grow in size faster than other equivalent companies; they are often small or medium-sized companies considered to have better chance of expansion, or companies in sectors that are expanding. Growth stocks often pay low dividends in order to finance their expansion, but make a big capital gain for the investors as the market price of their shares rises in value.

Guaranteed annuity An annuity that is paid for a specified number of years, whether or not the recipient has died. Alternatively, an annuity that is paid until the money used to purchase it has all been repaid.

Guaranteed debenture See DEBENTURE.

Guaranteed growth bond
Single-premium insurance bond that

guarantees repayment of a capital sum after a specified number of years.

Guaranteed income bond

Single-premium insurance bond paying a fixed amount of income annually and returning the original sum invested at the end of a specified period. Of special interest to investors during periods of high interest rates, since they can be used to lock in the high rate over a period of years.

Guaranteed investment bond

Single-premium insurance policy that guarantees repayment of the original capital investment at the end of a specified period, usually between three and ten years.

Guaranteed minimum pension (GMP)

Minimum pension that must be paid to someone leaving (contracting out of) the State Earnings Related Pension Scheme (SERPS).

Guaranteed prices Certain minimum prices that farmers receive for their products.

Guaranteed stocks Stocks issued by state-owned industries that are guaranteed for repayment by the government. They are therefore a form of GILTS.

Guaranteed sum assured The payment under a life assurance policy guaranteed to be paid if the policy-holder dies. It may be increased in the case of a with-profits or unit-linked policy.

Guarantor Person or organization who makes an agreement with a banker or other creditor to repay the debt of a third party if the debt is not repaid when due.

Guaranty bond See BOND.

Guardian's allowance Tax-free government grant paid to those bringing up orphans or children without parental care.

Guide price The level fixed by the European Community under the Common Agricultural Policy as being a fair average price for certain farm products.

Guinea Former British coin, first issued in the seventeenth century, made from gold obtained from Guinea. Replaced by the sovereign in 1812; but it continued to be used as a unit (worth 21 shillings) for charging for professional services and some luxury goods.

H

Half-commission man Someone who introduces business to a broker and in return receives half the commission earned.

Halfpenny Small British coin, made of bronze, now out of circulation, worth half as much as the old penny, prior to decimalization in 1971.

Hallmark An official mark or marks that must by law be stamped on gold, platinum and silver articles to show that the metal has been assayed (tested) and is of the right quality.

Hammered Until 1970, was used to describe the formal procedure adopted when a member of the stock exchange was unable to pay his debts. The announcement was accompanied by a series of hammer-blows, to warn other members of the name of the defaulter, who had to stop trading until the debts were paid.

Hancock An annuity (fixed sum paid at regular intervals) taken out by a company on behalf of a former employee to provide an income in retirement. The level of benefits is restricted to the employee's final salary level, and the capital used to buy the annuity is deductible as a company expense against corporation tax. The term 'Hancock' came from the name of the person who took the case to the House of Lords to gain approval.

Hard currency Term used to describe a currency, usually from one of the main industrialized countries, which it is always possible to buy or sell on the foreign exchange markets, and which therefore always has a known value. Opposite of SOFT CURRENCY, which is of dubious value and often difficult to sell.

Hard money Coins, as opposed to notes.

Head lease The original lease when a property is sub-let.

Health insurance Provided either by the government through the National Health Service or privately by special insurance policies against ill-health. See MEDICAL (EXPENSES) POLICY and PRIVATE MEDICAL INSURANCE.

Hedge To obtain protection against a possible risk of losses. Simply, this can involve taking some profits already made or buying currency in advance for delivery at a future date in order to ensure that it is bought at the rate at which an export or import order was struck. Other alternatives include back-to-back loans, options or using the futures markets. See FUTURES.

Heirloom Artefact, such as a painting, that has been owned by members of the same family and passed down from generation to generation.

Hereditament Legal term for property, land and buildings.

Heritable bond Scottish term for a

bond, for which the security of the loan is a transfer of land.

Hidden assets See ASSETS.

Hidden reserve Resources not shown on a company balance sheet, either because assets are undervalued or liabilities overvalued.

Hidden tax An indirect tax included in the price of goods or services that the buyers do not realize they are paying.

High coupon Fixed-interest security that pays a high rate of interest. See GILTS.

Higher rate tax Premium rate of income or capital gains taxes paid by private investors whose taxable annual income is above a certain level or who make capital gains above a specified level. In the 1988 Budget, a higher rate of capital gains tax was introduced similar to that of income tax. This higher rate is payable if the combined taxable income and gains exceed a specified level.

High interest cheque accounts (HICA) Deposit accounts with banks and building societies that offer higher than usual interest rates and a cheque book, as well as other limited banking services, like payment of direct debits.

High yielders Stocks and shares that provide an above-average rate of income, and normally therefore give less capital growth in value.

Hire purchase Method of paying for something by making regular payments over a period of time, although taking immediate delivery. A form of consumer credit to enable buyers to purchase goods they might not otherwise have been able to raise sufficient cash to afford. It is normally a rather expensive way of

borrowing money from finance houses that specialize in the business. However, the Consumer Credit Act 1974 gives considerable protection to buyers against overcommitting themselves and being forced to return the goods.

Hire-purchase price The cost of an article bought under a hire purchase agreement, taking into account the cash price plus interest and all the other charges.

Historical cost The original cost of something, as opposed to its current saleable or replacement value.

Historic(al) cost accounting The traditional method of book-keeping, under which all values, either assets or liabilities, are taken at the original amount spent. Of course, this does not take into account the impact of inflation, as with CURRENT COST ACCOUNTING.

Hock Slang for pledging or pawning an asset to raise money.

Holding company A company formed specially to retain at least more than half of the share capital of one or more companies, which then become its subsidiaries. Sometimes known as a parent or shell company, it has to present consolidated accounts on behalf of the whole group.

Holdings Short for shareholdings, or investments owned.

Hold-over relief Tax concession allowing the payment of CAPITAL GAINS TAX on gifts by individuals and trusts to be deferred. However, the 1989 Budget proposed sweeping changes severely restricting hold-over relief to only a few specified categories of gifts that would not normally be liable to inheritance tax.

Home income plans Special schemes to enable older people to receive an income for life by borrowing against the value of their home. The money borrowed is normally used to purchase an annuity; but these plans tend to be worthwhile only for people well above retirement age, since otherwise the annuity payments are too low and may barely exceed the interest rates payable. Also often used to describe plans where loans are offered using a charge on the home as security or collateral.

Home loan A mortgage specifically provided to buyers of a property, especially owner-occupiers. A government home loan scheme for first-time buyers only was introduced in 1978; but it has made little impact, since it is highly complicated and restricted. It offers a small tax-free bonus and a small interest-free loan for five years to first-time buyers who have been saving under the scheme through a building society or bank for at least two years. However, the scheme is also limited to low-price houses. The government annually adjusts the qualifying price ceilings, based on regions, in line with inflation.

Homeowner's or household policy Comprehensive insurance that covers private property and the contents against a range of risks.

Home reversion plan Method of raising capital on a house in which the owner still wants to live. The owner sells a reversionary interest in the house to a buyer, or organizer of the plan, but retains the right to live there, rent free, for the rest of his life and that of his spouse. The price received depends on the age and life-expectancy of the house-owner.

Honorarium payment for professional services, such as to a lawyer or accountant.

Hospital cash plans See MEDICAL (EXPENSES) POLICY and PRIVATE MEDICAL INSURANCE.

Hot money Stolen or counterfeit money; but also used to describe funds that are transferred quickly from one place to another in search of the highest interest rates.

House (home) contents insurance Policy covering possessions and fixtures and fittings, but not the building. With indemnity cover, claims are paid on the basis of the original value, less wear and tear. Under a new-for-old terms policy, however, a sum is paid to cover the cost of replacement. An all-risks clause may be included to cover certain items outside the house as well, for example articles in the car or taken abroad.

Household insurance policy Policy covering both buildings and contents of the home.

Housekeeper allowance A tax relief, previously available to widows or widowers who had someone living in their home as a housekeeper, which was scrapped in the 1988 Budget.

Hushmail Where a company will buy, normally from a key executive, shares at a premium price in return for not revealing some secret or sensitive information.

Hush money Bribe paid to someone for not divulging some information.

Hyperinflation When inflation rate is very high indeed.

I

ICCH International Commodities Clearing House. See CLEARING HOUSE and USEFUL ADDRESSES.

Idle balances Money held in a bank account earning no interest.

IFA See INDEPENDENT FINANCIAL ADVISER.

Illiquid assets See ASSETS.

IMF See INTERNATIONAL MONETARY FUND.

Immediate annuity An assurance contract that provides, in return for a single premium, regular payments starting immediately. See ANNUITY.

Impact day First day on which the terms of a new or rights issue of shares or stock is made known to the public and when dealings normally start on the stock market.

Impaired capital Part of the subscribed capital of a company that is not backed by assets and which therefore has no support if the company goes bankrupt.

Impaired lives Term used by insurance companies to describe applicants applying for assurance cover who have serious medical problems and who therefore pay higher premiums for any policies taken out.

Imperial system Traditional system of weights and measures used throughout the British Empire and former colonies. It is being phased out and replaced by the metric system. An imperial ton, also known as long ton, is equal to 2,240 lb weight, while a metric ton (tonne) is 2,200 lb and a short ton 2,000 lb.

Impersonal accounts Book-keeping term for entries in accounts recording capital assets, expenses and income, not those for debtors and creditors.

Implicit cost Unrecorded or hidden extra cost, such as free services performed by the owner of a company in managing it.

Implicit rent Amount of rent that the owner of a property or land could get if it was lent to a tenant.

Implied terms Legal term to describe something assumed to be included in a contract although not physically written into it.

Import duty Tax on goods entering the country, imposed either to raise money or to protect the domestic industry against foreign competition. See TARIFF.

Import surcharge An extra tax on imports, in addition to the normal duty. Often used as a temporary method of discouraging imports.

Impost A customs duty on imported goods.

Impound Seize and keep something as security against an unpaid debt.

Impressed stamps Official stamps required for certain documents.

Imprest system Method used to run the petty cash arrangements in an office. The cashier is given a fixed sum of money (CASH FLOAT) which is considered sufficient to meet expected expenses over a certain period. A record of expenditure is kept, and at the end of the period the cashier receives a sum equal to that expenditure, thus returning the cash float to its original size.

Impute Assume a probable or theoretical value on something, where the actual value is not known.

IMRO See INVESTMENT MANAGEMENT REGULATORY ORGANIZATION and USEFUL ADDRESSES.

Inchoate instrument An incomplete or unfinished instruction to pay money that has been signed by the drawer with the details to be filled in by someone else; for example, a cheque that has been signed but otherwise not completed.

Incidental expenses Sums that have to be spent from time to time but not regularly.

Inclusive charge Price or cost that includes other costs which might normally be paid separately.

Income Money received either as a result of working for someone, providing a service, or as the return on an investment in the form of dividends or interest.

Income and expenditure account An account prepared by a non-trading organization owning assets to show not only the cash position but also any changes in the capital position. Equivalent to the profit and loss account for a trading organization or company.

Income bond Single premium insurance policy that provides a guaranteed income.
  Alternatively, NATIONAL SAVINGS product for investors requiring a monthly income.

Income debenture See DEBENTURE.

Income distribution Term used to describe the payment of income by unit trusts or other funds to investors.

Income in kind Payment that is received not in the form of money but in goods and services, like rent-free accommodation or free use of an office or car. See PERKS.

Income multiple The formula used by mortgage-lenders to calculate how big a home loan they are prepared to advance, based on the borrower's annual income. An income multiple of three would mean that the mortgage supplier is prepared to lend a sum equal to three times the borrower's annual income.

Income stock A stock paying a fixed rate of interest, or a share that is likely to pay regular dividends.

Income support Extra allowance given to pensioners, the unemployed, single parents and those unable to work because of illness whose income is below a set figure. Previously called Supplementary Benefit.

Income tax The tax on personal incomes that provides a large proportion of the money required by the government for paying for public services. The rates are set annually in the Finance Act, after being announced in the Budget; income tax is assessed and collected by the Inland Revenue.

Income tax allowances Deductions from income, such as personal allowance, that can be claimed to reduce the amount liable for taxation. See TAXABLE INCOME.

Income tax code Employees paying tax direct from their salary under the PAY AS YOU EARN (PAYE) system are allocated a code number, which takes into account allowances to be deducted which the employee is entitled to claim. The number is then used by the employer to assess the amount of tax to be taken out of the salary payment and remitted to the Inland Revenue.

Income tax schedules The different classes of tax into which incomes are divided for assessment by the Inland Revenue. Best known is Schedule E, covering income from employment. See TAX SCHEDULES.

Income units Units in a fund that distribute dividends to investors; as opposed to accumulation units, when the dividends are automatically re-invested.

Inconvertible currency One which cannot be freely exchanged for other currencies, often because it is of dubious value, making it difficult or impossible to find a buyer.

Incorporate Form and register a company. When this has been done, the Register of Companies issues a Certificate of Incorporation.

Incorporeal possession Ownership of a legal right, such as a patent or copyright.

Increasing annuity A life-insurance annuity policy which provides for an increase in payments at a stated rate and over specified periods. It is intended to help the recipient of the annuity keep up with the rise in the cost of living.

Increment The amount by which a person's salary increases, often following an agreed scale. Also used to describe a salary or payment for a service provided.

Incremental or marginal cost The additional cost of increasing the output of goods or services.

Incumbrance Charge or liability on a property such as a mortgage.

Indebtedness A sum owed. The borrowings of a company as at a particular date within 28 days of a prospectus being issued.

Indemnify Pay money to make good a loss or settle a claim. Alternatively, provide security against a possible future loss.

Indemnity Insurance which guarantees that the insured should be in the same position after a loss as immediately before it – neither richer nor poorer.

Indemnity bond See BOND.

Indenture Originally a form of deed that was torn in two as a protection against forgery, since the tears had to match. More recently, refers to a contract binding workers for a specified period of time, to repay the cost of training and provision of tools.

Independent financial adviser Broker or intermediary who sells the whole range of financial products and is not tied to a particular group. Has to be authorized by FIMBRA (Financial Intermediaries, Managers and Brokers Regulatory Association) and abide by its rules and regulations.

Independent taxation See MARRIED COUPLE'S ALLOWANCE and TAX REFORM.

Index Method of measuring price movements by combining a number of constituents and averaging them into a single figure. Normal approach is to compare the value of the constituents chosen with a value, selected at a specified starting time, which is taken as 100. The value of the index then fluctuates from the 100 starting figure to reflect the rises or falls of the constituents contained. The constituents can be weighted by mathematical means according to their importance. Indexes (or indices) have a wide variety of uses, ranging from tracking price movmements in the commodity, currency and stock markets, to measuring industrial production or inflation. See RETAIL PRICE INDEX and SHARE INDEX OR INDICES.

Indexation A way of adjusting payments or allowances in line with inflation or general rises and falls in prices. Used for pensions, tax allowances and investments.

Indexation allowance Special tax allowance aimed at discounting the effect of inflation in assessing a capital gain for tax purposes. Introduced in 1982 it allows the taxpayer to strip out any 'paper' profits which are purely attributable to the effects of inflation. In some cases this might even turn a capital 'gain' into a loss in real terms if the rate of inflation was higher in percentage terms during the period between buying and selling than the profit made. Thus if the rate of inflation was

10%, and the 'gain' 8%, this would qualify as a loss of 2% when assessing liability for capital gains tax. In the 1988 Budget the system was changed so that all assets bought before March 1982 could be valued at their market price in March 1982, if this was higher than the original cost. The Inland Revenue each month issues figures tracking inflation, based on the movements in the Retail Price Index, since March 1982, so that taxpayers can calculate their indexation allowance.

Indexed bond See BOND.

Indexed-income bonds Bond issued by National Savings which offers a monthly income, guaranteed for ten years against inflation and other changes in interest rates. However, the value of the capital is not index-linked and therefore diminishes. In the first year the income is paid at the starting interest rate. On subsequent anniversaries of the purchase date, the income is recalculated for the next year in line with the Retail Price Index. See NATIONAL SAVINGS.

Indexed pension Where payments are increased in line with the rise in the cost of living so as to try to protect the pensioner against loss in value suffered as a result of inflation.

Index fund A fund that links its performance to an index by investing in all or a substantial proportion of the companies used to make up the index, thereby ensuring that the return for the investor is tied to the performance of the market index. Favoured by cautious investors such as pension funds, which do not wish to take the risks involved in trying to outperform the general market trend by selecting specific shares. Also used for some unit trusts where investors want to follow a particular market without being involved in the extra risk of trying to outperform it.

Index-linked (savings) certificates Offered by National Savings to investors wishing to protect themselves against inflation. Each year the value is increased in line with the Retail Price Index. Interest is calculated on the revised value. Originally known as 'Granny Bonds'; when first introduced, they could be bought only by people of retirement age, a restriction subsequently lifted. See NATIONAL SAVINGS.

Index-linked gilts Special government securities introduced in 1982 for investors nervous about the impact of inflation on fixed-interest stocks. Both the interest and the capital repayment are guaranteed to rise or fall in line with the Retail Price Index and are adjusted accordingly every six months. See GILTS.

Index-linked policies Assurance contracts in which the amount payable on the maturity date is constantly revised to maintain the real value of the sum assured in line with inflation.

Index-linking Tying a payment or receipt with the movement of an index; especially applied to pension schemes.

Indicators See MONEY SUPPLY.

Indirect exchange A comparison of the value of two currencies, not against each other but with a third currency. See CROSS RATE.

Indirect taxation Tax not paid direct to the Inland Revenue; instead, like Value Added Tax (VAT) and customs duty, it is added to the value of goods and services and collected by the suppliers for remission to the government.

Alternatively, used to describe artificial price support levels, as with the Common Agricultural Policy, which put up the cost of products to the consumer although no direct tax is involved.

Industrial disablement benefit Government benefit that can be claimed by anyone who has become disabled as a result of an injury at work or an industrial disease.

Industrial life assurance Policies designed for industrial workers with low incomes. The premiums are collected in small amounts on a regular basis; but the cost of doing this means that the benefits paid are then poor in comparison with other types of insurance policies.

Inflation The rise in the general cost of living and prices, resulting in a reduction in the value of money. Measured in Britain by a sample of goods and services known as the Retail Price Index (RPI). The rate of inflation is the annualized rise in the RPI, which is published monthly.

Inflation accounting Accounting system which seeks to allow for the effect of inflation by taking into account the current market price for stocks and fixed assets.

Inflationary gap Government spending that is not covered by taxes or borrowing from the public and is instead met by borrowing from banks or by issuing more paper money.

Inflationary spiral When inflation becomes worse and worse, with higher prices triggering off demands for higher wages, so causing even higher prices.

Inheritance tax The latest form of duty payable on death, introduced in the 1986

Budget to replace capital transfer tax. It was further simplified in the 1988 Budget to become a single flat rate of tax payable on assets at death by anyone (not a spouse) if the estate is valued above a minimum tax-free exemption level. Also payable on gifts valued above the annual tax-free exemption limits made during the donor's lifetime if he or she dies within seven years. However, the tax liability rate starts to reduce from the full rate three years after the gift is made. See POTENTIALLY EXEMPT TRANSFERS.

Inheritance trusts Schemes to reduce the amount of capital transfer tax (CTT) payable, and one of the reasons why CTT was replaced by Inheritance Tax. New schemes are no longer applicable, but those started prior to March 1986 continue to operate.

Initial allowances Deductions allowed by the Inland Revenue for the depreciation of capital from profits of the company under Schedule D. Also used to describe the basic, personal allowances from income tax. See CAPITAL ALLOWANCES.

Initial units Special type of units, used in life assurance investment plans and pension policies, from which the company deducts extra charges to cover the administration and commission costs. Also known as CAPITAL UNITS.

Initial yield Percentage figure given when a unit trust is first launched to estimate the return (income) that the investor is likely to receive in the first year. It is calculated by assessing the income that would have been received on the stocks held in the initial portfolio during the past year, after deducting charges. A low initial yield means that the fund is concentrating on stocks, paying low dividends and hoping to rise in capital value

as a result of an increase in its market price.

Inland Revenue The government department responsible for the assessment and collection of direct taxes on income, capital gains and stamp duties. The Customs and Excise is responsible for collecting indirect taxes, like Value Added Tax (VAT).

Inner Reserve See HIDDEN RESERVE.

Input tax Tax, charged by a supplier of goods and services, which can be set against payment of VALUE ADDED TAX.

Inscribed stock Form of government security for which no stock certificates are issued. Instead, the owner's name is inscribed in a register or record book and a certificate of inscription issued. Not much used these days because of the difficulties involved in transferring ownership.

Insider dealing or trading Buying or selling stocks or shares, using information that is confidential and unknown to other investors, for example by directors or employees with prior knowledge of a takeover bid for a company. It is now a criminal offence for any individual or organization to take financial advantage of privileged information by insider trading.

Insolvency Unable to pay debts when they become due, even though they can be paid at a later date. To be distinguished from bankruptcy, which applies when the debts are unlikely to be paid in full at any time. A rich man can be insolvent if his assets cannot be realized for cash in time to pay his debts on the due date. Technically, a business is insolvent if its liabilities are greater than its assets and its debts cannot be met within twelve months. The Insolvency Act 1985

introduced new measures for dealing with
insolvent individuals or organizations.

Inspector of Taxes Inland Revenue
official, responsible for assessing and
collecting direct taxes.

Instant access Popular term for savings
or investment accounts which allow
depositors to withdraw money immediately
without losing interest. The rate of interest
on an instant access account tends to be
lower than those which require a period of
notice before withdrawals.

Institutions/institutional investors
Collective term for professional managers
who invest on behalf of others. They
include insurance companies, pension
funds, investment houses, banks and unit
trusts. Because of the large size of money
handled, they are a powerful force in the
stock markets, owning a large proportion
of government stocks and company
shares.

Insurable interest Policy taken out to
protect someone's interest in a property
or the outcome of a specific event. A
proved insurable interest exists between
husband and wife, but in other cases the
proposer must show that a financial loss
will be suffered.

Insurance Payment of a sum of money
(premium) into a 'pool' in order to secure
protection against a possible risk or loss.
'Insurance' refers to events that may or
may not happen, such as an accident, fire
or theft, as opposed to 'assurance', which
covers events which will definitely happen
sooner or later, such as death or
retirement. There are many different
types of insurance policies, including those
which are primarily investment or savings
schemes (endowment policies) with life
cover included as an extra.

Insurance agent Person who
introduces business to an insurance
company in return for a commission.
Alternatively, an insurance company
employee who looks after a group of
policy holders.

Insurance broker Intermediary or
financial adviser with a special knowledge
of insurance, who sells insurance products
normally in return for commission but
sometimes for a fee. Some are tied to
selling the products of a particular
insurance group; but it must be made
abundantly clear that in reality they are
company representatives, offering a
restricted range of products from one
company. Independent insurance brokers
have to be members of the Financial
Advisers, Managers and Brokers
Regulatory Association (FIMBRA) and
abide by its rules and regulations.

Insurance ombudsman Appointed by
the insurance industry in 1981 with the
task of investigating complaints from the
public against insurance companies, most
of which are members of the scheme. See
OMBUDSMAN and USEFUL ADDRESSES.

Insurance premium Payment made
under an insurance policy to buy the risk
protection required.

Intangible assets See ASSETS.

Intellectual property Another name for
INTANGIBLE ASSETS.

Inter bank The international market in
currencies and wholesale money operated
by banks and other financial institutions.
Inter-bank rates are the wholesale cost of
money at which major banks will lend
money to one another. Smaller banks and
financial corporations often pay percentage
points above the inter-bank rate for their
borrowings. See LONDON INTERBANK
OFFERED RATE and MONEY MARKET.

Interchangeable bond One that carries the right to be exchanged for another bond.

Interest The price paid for borrowing money. The rate varies according to the amount involved and the length and terms of the loan.

Alternatively used to describe the return on capital invested, particularly stock, or rights of ownership in a business or property.

Interest bond See BOND.

Interest only mortgages See MORTGAGE.

Interest rate The figure, expressed in percentage terms usually on an annual or monthly basis, that a borrower has agreed to pay on a loan. See ANNUAL PERCENTAGE RATE OF CHARGE.

Interim accounts Those prepared by a company to cover results during part of the full accounting period. Often unaudited, they are used mainly to show the progress being made and keep shareholders informed.

Interim bond Certificate given to prove ownership while the bond document is being prepared.

Interim dividend A partial dividend payment that may be announced before the full profits for the year are known and the final dividend decided. Interim dividends are normally declared half-yearly or quarterly, and have to be formally approved before the final dividend is announced.

Intermediary Broker or financial adviser who provides investment advice and financial products, in return for commission or a fee. An independent intermediary, not linked to any one company, must be a member of Financial Advisers, Managers and Brokers Regulatory Association (FIMBRA) and abide by its rules and regulations.

International Bank for Reconstruction and Development See WORLD BANK.

International Monetary Fund (IMF) Organization set up in 1944 at the Bretton Woods Conference as a specialized agency of the United Nations, to encourage co-operation among countries in monetary affairs and international trade. Each member country deposits an amount, based on its national income, of its own currency and gold, which can then be lent to other member countries with balance-of-payment problems and in need of financial help. It is essentially a collective bank, through which the member countries use their own currency to finance borrowings of other countries' currencies. Each member was allocated drawing rights on the Fund's reserves, and this was later supplemented by the creation of special drawing rights (SDRs) which act as a type of international reserve currency, since it is backed by all the members.

International money order Method of making payments through a post office in Britain to someone overseas.

Intervention price The point under the European Community's Common Agricultural Policy at which surplus supplies are bought up for storage in order to prevent the market falling further.

Inter vivos trust Trust which becomes operative during the lifetime of its creator instead of waiting until after his or her death.

Intestate Die without making a Will, and thus possibly leaving a lot of problems to the inheritors; for example, a spouse (husband or wife) may receive only a proportion of the estate if there are other relations entitled to benefit.

In-the-money option An option whose exercise price is at a level where it could be exercised in the market at a guaranteed profit. It therefore commands a bigger premium than out-of-the-money options. See OPTIONS.

In the red Slang expression to describe owing money. Based on the traditional habit of banks of entering debits and overdrafts in red ink.

Intrinsic value The basic worth contained in the substance from which an article is produced, rather than the market value of the article. Metal products, gold coins for example, often have a greater intrinsic value than their stated price. It is the intrinsic value of metals and other raw materials which makes them attractive as an investment when inflation or currency-rate changes are undermining the value of 'paper money'.

Invalid care allowance Government grant available to those who cannot work because they have to look after a disabled person.

Invalidity allowance and benefit Government grants for those unable to work because of ill-health.

Inventory Detailed list, for example of the contents of a furnished flat or house, given to a tenant by the owner. Also used to describe stock held by companies or the process of valuing stock.

Investment Generic term used to describe something in which money, or its equivalent, is used to produce an income, profit or savings. Can range from a property to a share, fixed-interest stock or a bank or building society account. See ALTERNATIVE INVESTMENTS.

Investment account National Savings product for savings particularly suitable for non-taxpayers, since it pays interest gross, with no tax deducted at source. Also general term for interest-bearing bank or building society account.

Investment allowances See CAPITAL ALLOWANCES.

Investment bank(er) Financial organization which, alone or within a group, buys new issues of stocks and shares in bulk for sale in smaller quantities to investors. It sometimes also arranges mergers and takeovers, as well as acting as financial adviser to companies in a similar way to merchant banks.

Investment bill Bill of exchange bought at a discount to the repayment price, with the objective of holding it until the repayment date and thereby making a capital profit.

Investment bond A single-premium insurance policy in which the money is invested in units of a range of sub-funds. The units can subsequently be switched between the sub-funds free or at a low cost. The policy-holder is entitled to withdraw a proportion of the original premium each year to provide 'tax-free' income, although this is taken into account when the bond finally matures, and the gain is top sliced to assess any tax that may be payable. The fund is liable to pay capital gains tax, and is thus at a disadvantage in comparison with unit trusts. In reality the income withdrawals are not 'tax free'; payment of the tax is merely deferred to a later date. See TOP SLICING.

Investment club Informal voluntary groups of investors who get together to pool their money in order to gain the advantages of dealing on the stock market in larger quantities, spreading the risk, paying reduced commission charges and receiving a better service from stockbrokers. There is no set formula, so their operation may vary considerably, and they face strong competition from unit trusts, investment bonds and trusts with professional management.

Investment income Money earned from investments.

Investment-linked policy Life insurance policy under which part of the premiums is used to buy units in an investment fund.

Investment Management Regulatory Organization (IMRO) One of the self-regulatory organizations, under the umbrella of the Securities and Investment Board, set up under the Financial Services Act 1986 to improve protection for investors. As its title implies, IMRO regulates the activities of investment companies, how they can operate and what they are permitted to do. It has close links with the Life Assurance and Unit Trust Organization (LAUTRO) in particular. See SELF-REGULATORY ORGANIZATIONS and USEFUL ADDRESSES.

Investment referee Official, appointed jointly by two self regulatory organizations, IMRO and FIMBRA, to deal with complaints against their member companies. Unlike an Ombudsman, the

Referee is an arbitrator, whose decisions are binding on both parties – the complainant and the accused. See COMPLAINTS and OMBUDSMAN.

Investment trust Company which buys shares in other companies or investments in order to earn profits for its shareholders. A collective investment vehicle that is an alternative to unit trusts. The shares of investment trusts are quoted on the stock exchange and are therefore normally cheaper to buy than unit trusts, since only stockbroker's commission is payable and the gap between buying and selling prices (bid/offer spread) is much narrower. However, like any share, the price depends on supply and demand in the market and does not always move in line with the value of the investments held by trust. Very often the share price is at a discount to the amount that could in theory be earned by selling all its assets; and for this reason they are vulnerable to being taken over. As companies, they are closed-end funds (they cannot be enlarged simply by the issue of extra units, unlike unit trusts).

Investment trusts – which were originally devised in Scotland for the benefit of small investors but subsequently came to be dominated by large investors seeking to move into specialized sectors – have freedom to deal not only in shares but also in other investments and can 'gear up' by borrowing money if necessary. Many of them deal in specific sectors, like the Far Eastern markets or technology, and often provide good returns. They are, however, restricted by the rules and regulations of the stock exchange and, since they do not pay commission to intermediaries, are not so widely marketed or promoted. However, investment trust savings schemes are very cheap to enter and a good way for private investors to deal in shares indirectly. They are mainly sold by stockbrokers or the investment trust groups themselves direct to the public.

Invisible assets See INTANGIBLE ASSETS.

Invisible earnings Earnings from industries providing services, like banking, insurance and shipping, which are not included in a country's normal balance of payments comparing imports and exports. So, for example, while on paper a country like Britain might have a deficit balance with imports exceeding exports, the contribution from invisible earnings may more than make up the deficit.

Invoice discounting The practice by some companies of selling their debts to be collected at a discount to their total value.

IPE International Petroleum Exchange. The London futures markets for oil and oil products and a member of the Futures and Options Exchange (FOX). See FUTURES and USEFUL ADDRESSES.

Irredeemables Fixed-interest stocks, bonds and debentures which have no redemption (repayment) date stated. See BOND, DEBENTURE.

Irrevocable (letter of) credit Used in foreign trading to describe a borrowing facility that cannot be changed or cancelled once it has been opened.

Issue broker A firm of stockbrokers which supports companies making new issues of shares to financial institutions or the general public.

Issue by tender A method of offering new shares or loan stock by asking applicants to state a price they are willing to bid. The highest bidders receive the allotment of shares or stock available. A minimum price, below which bids will not be accepted, is normally set.

Issued capital Total amount of capital actually provided by shareholders in a company in return for shares or stock.

Issue of securities The offer of new shares or loan stock in a company that is either traded on the stock market or is a private company which intends to 'go public' (have its share dealt on the stock market).

Issue price The initial cost of shares or stock, offered to the public and quoted in the prospectus. Or the price fixed by the issue broker when offering shares or stock to financial institutions. Alternatively, with an issue by tender, the issue price is the highest price bid and accepted.

Issuing house Financial institution, often a merchant bank, that specializes in raising money for companies by finding buyers for issues of new shares or other forms of stock. Sometimes the issuing house takes up some or all of the stock being offered and then sells it to investors, thus ensuring that the capital is raised for the company, whatever reception the issue may receive from investors. This is called underwriting.

IT See INHERITANCE TAX.

J

Jetsam Goods thrown overboard (jettisoned) from a ship to lighten the load, or those washed ashore after a wreck. See FLOTSAM.

Job Verb used to describe buying and selling by professional traders (known as jobbers) on the commodity, foreign exchange and stock markets. Also refers to general short-term trading, making sales and purchases that are quickly completed: jobbing the market.

Jobbers Professional traders who make a market in shares; in other words, buy and sell on their own account. They used to handle all the shares traded on the stock exchange prior to the change of the trading system in October 1986 (see BIG BANG), when they were replaced by MARKET-MAKERS.

Jobber's turn Profit made by a jobber or market-maker – the difference between the price at which stocks or commodities are bought and the selling price.

Joint account A bank account held in the name of two or more people, often husband and wife, who can all use the account either jointly or separately. Also an account held by a joint venture business; or stock exchange term for shares owned by two or more persons or firms.

Joint and several bond See BOND.

Joint annuity An assurance policy of the lives of two persons that provides for the payment of an annuity that continues for the lifetime of the person living longer.

Joint life and survivorship annuity Similar to a JOINT ANNUITY, except that the payments are reduced from the time the first person dies.

Joint life endowment An insurance policy on the lives of two people, it pays the sum insured on the death of the first to die if this occurs before the maturity (repayment) date of the policy is reached. There are also joint life first death and joint life last survivor policies.

Joint-stock banks Largest section of the banking industry, made up of banks owned by many shareholders and serving the general public. See CLEARING BANKS.

Joint stock company Business organization which has its capital divided into many small units of stock or shares of low face-value so that they are owned by both large and small investors. Joint stock companies can be formed by royal charter; by Act of Parliament, as happened with the early railway companies; or by registration, like a limited company, under the Companies Act.

Joint tenancy or ownership Owning of land or property by two or more persons, who are co-owners or joint tenants. Each has rights in the whole of the property and is entitled to a share of any money obtained from selling it.

Joint venture Partnership, often temporary, in launching a new company or business activity.

Joint whole-life policy An assurance policy on the lives of two people, it pays the sum insured on the death of the first to die.

Judgment or appeal bond A guarantee that has to be given by the appellant in a court case that all costs and damages will be paid even if the case is lost.

Judgment creditor Someone who has obtained a court order for payment of a debt. Hence, judgment debt is one that a court has ordered to be paid.

Judgment note Special type of promissory note that gives the holder power to have a court order declared against someone refusing to pay a debt without actually having to go to court.

Junior capital See EQUITY (CAPITAL).

Junior insurance Policy on a parent's life for a period until a child is eighteen years old or over, when a lump sum is payable.

Junior issue Shares or debentures that rank after securities when it comes to receiving dividends, rights issues or repayment of capital if a company is wound up.

Junior markets London stock market term for the UNLISTED SECURITIES MARKET and THIRD MARKET for companies that are not listed on the main market. See STOCK EXCHANGE.

Junk bonds Term used originally in the United States to describe high interest stock offered by companies with a low credit rating, and therefore considered to be of higher risk from an investor's point of view. Often used by companies to raise money to help finance a bid for a larger company. As an inducement to supply the financial resources needed to support the takeover bid, investors are offered not only a high return for their money but also the possibility of the bonds increasing in value if the takeover bid proves successful.

K

Kaffirs Traditional slang name for shares in South African companies, particularly mining companies, dealt on the London stock market.

Kangaroos London stock market term for shares in Australian companies, especially those in mining, property or tobacco.

Keelage Charges paid while a ship is in harbour or a port.

Kennedy round Series of meetings initiated by US President, John F. Kennedy, in 1963 to improve international trade by renegotiating the terms of GATT (General Agreement on Tariffs and Trade).

Kerb broker Broker who is not a member of an exchange.

Kerb trading An unofficial market. Term derived from the habit of dealers and merchants of continuing to trade, once official dealings had finished, in the street outside the market or exchange. This practice was later formalized by allowing the dealers to remain on the exchange after the official closing hour, to continue trading there and to avoid blocking the pavements (kerbs) outside. Pre-kerb and late-kerb dealings refer to any trading that takes place before and after the official market opening times.

Key-man insurance Special policy taken out by companies to insure against the risk of important (key) employees dying or suffering from ill-health. The sum assured is based on the potential loss of profits to the company.

Key money Extra premium, over and above the rent, that sometimes has to be paid by the new tenant of a house or flat. It is normally paid to the owner, or agent, before a key is supplied and is, therefore, simply an additional charge to acquire the tenancy. In some cases it is refundable, by the old tenant simply charging the new tenant for passing over the keys.

Key reversal A term used by followers of charts to describe a point at which prices have reached either a low or peak level.

Kickback Slang term, from the United States, to describe a bribe paid in order to secure a favour or part of the profits made.

Killer bees Stock market term for investment bankers or financial advisers who help companies fend off unwelcome takeover bids.

King's shilling Traditional term for joining the armed forces, deriving from the shilling coin that used to be given by the British army to new recruits in the nineteenth century when a king was on the throne.

Kite Slang term for issuing a worthless cheque or bill of exchange to try and appear affluent. Hence 'kite flying': paying in a worthless cheque to a bank and using it as credit to draw out money or to write another cheque to pay a bill.

Knock-down price Officially the cost of something bought at auction, but more generally used to describe a low, or reduced, price or bargain.

Knock-for-knock An agreement among insurance companies, primarily motor insurers, that they each will pay its own policy-holders' claims in order to avoid the trouble and expense of making claims against one another. This may be acceptable for the insurance company, especially when there is difficulty in establishing who was to blame for an accident; but there are complications for policy-holders, who might thereby lose their no-claims bonus.

Knock-out agreement Secret (illegal) pact between dealers at an auction not to bid against each other, so that as a result prices are kept artificially low.

Kondratieff wave Theory propounded by a Soviet economist, Nikolai Kondratieff, that the economies of capitalist countries, and therefore the stock markets, are prone to major cycles lasting 50–60 years. He claimed to have predicted the 1929–30 crash, based on the previous crash in 1870.

Krugerrand Gold coin that was produced in South Africa for investors unable to afford, or forbidden to buy, gold bullion. It also provided an extra source of profit for gold producers. Production ceased in 1986 as a result of bans on import of the coin being introduced by several countries in protest against the South African racial laws and political system. However, millions of krugerrands are still in circulation, held by investors who wanted to invest in gold; so there is still an active trading market, even though a series of rival gold coins has been introduced by other countries to replace the krugerrand. See GOLD COINS.

L

Lady Day See QUARTER DAY.

Lame Duck Stock exchange term for a member who will soon be banned from trading because of an inability to pay debts.

Lammas See QUARTER DAY.

Land bank Bank set up specially to provide loans for farmers to develop the land, especially longer-term loans.

Land Charges Registry Government office responsible for recording all charges, such as a mortgage, on land whose title is not (yet) registered with the Land Registry.

Landlord Owner of a property who allows a tenant to use the land or house in return for a rent or payment of some kind. Also used to describe the owner of a FREEHOLD.

Land Registry Government department responsible for recording details concerning the ownership of property in England and Wales. When a property changes hands, it is registered with the Land Registry to record the new ownership and establish a proper title. A fee is charged, based on a percentage of the sale price.

Lands tribunal A special court with power to decide what compensation should be paid to the owners of land taken over for public use.

Land tax Tax formerly charged on the ownership of land, but now abolished.

LAPR See LIFE ASSURANCE PREMIUM RELIEF.

Last in, last out (Lilo) Accounting method used to value stocks based on the cost of the latest purchases. In times of rising prices, this method reduces a company's stated profits as compared with the alternative FIRST IN, FIRST OUT (Fifo) system.

Last survivor policy Assurance on the lives of two people paid out only when the second one dies.

Laundering Slang term for channelling money, often obtained illegally, through various bank accounts or markets with the purpose of disguising the origin of the funds. A crook, for example, might use stolen money to buy shares, property or gold and then sell these purchases to obtain an apparently legitimate source of money.

LAUTRO See LIFE ASSURANCE AND UNIT TRUST REGULATORY ORGANIZATION and USEFUL ADDRESSES.

Law Society Organization that controls the activities and behaviour of solicitors in England and Wales and administers the Legal Aid scheme. There are separate Law Societies for Scotland and Northern Ireland. They are RECOGNIZED PROFESSIONAL BODIES (RPBs) under the Financial Services Act 1986 and form part of the self-regulatory system to provide protection for investors, including dealing with complaints from the public. See REGULATION and USEFUL ADDRESSES.

LCE See LONDON COMMODITY EXCHANGE and USEFUL ADDRESSES.

Lead bank The financial institution which organizes large borrowings, on behalf of a company or country, from a group of lenders. It sets the fees and rates to be charged as well as taking ultimate responsibility for the loan.

Lease An agreement under which the owner of an asset or property gives someone else the right to use, or hire, it for a fixed period of time, normally in return for receiving some money in advance or payments in instalments, such as rent. Often a lease can be transferred by sale to different owners with the approval of the freeholder, to whom ownership of the property finally reverts.

Leaseback Arrangement whereby the owner of a property sells it to obtain cash or capital, on condition that he can continue to use the property for a specified period in return for rent or an agreed payment.

Leasehold Right, given under a lease, to own or use land and buildings for a specified period in return for an immediate payment or payment by instalments.

Leasehold mortgage Loan of a property to a borrower, who owns only the lease, not the freehold. Can be difficult to obtain if the lease has only a relatively short time to run.

Ledger Accounts in a double-entry

book-keeping system. The debits and credits are all recorded in the ledger. Originally the term referred to a bound book in which the accounts were entered by a ledger clerk.

Ledger balance The figure listed on a bank account showing either the amount owed to the holder (credit) or owed by the holder (debit).

Ledger fees Charges made by a bank for entries in an account to cover the cost of transactions such as cheques and standing orders.

Legacy Personal property left under the terms of a Will. Includes money, stocks, furniture and leasehold (but not freehold) property.

Legal aid Government scheme under which a person with limited financial resources is provided with help towards the cost of paying the legal expenses involved in court actions. See LAW SOCIETY.

Legal assets See ASSETS.

Legal charge Another name for a MORTGAGE.

Legal day Full day, lasting until midnight. This means that the date specified, for example for payment of a debt, extends right up until midnight.

Legal estate Ownership of an interest in a freehold or leasehold property.

Legal liability Having responsibility to settle a debt or make good a possible loss or damage.

Legal mortgage Loan given for the purpose of buying a property or land, where the lender not only holds the title deeds as security but also has the power to claim possession of the property, if the loan is not repaid when due, without first having to apply to a court for an order of possession. It is thus significantly different from the standard EQUITABLE MORTGAGE, in which a court order is required first to obtain possession.

Legal tender Form of money, coins and notes which by law must be accepted in settlement of a debt. In Britain, notes issued by the Bank of England have unlimited legal tender in that they can be used for the payment of debts up to any amount. So do £1 coins. However, smaller coins need be accepted only up to certain maximum levels: 20p in the case of copper and bronze coins; £5 for 5p and 10p silver and cupro-nickel coins; and £10 for 50p coins. To qualify as legal tender, the offer of money must consist of the country's legal currency, have no conditions attached, and exactly equal the amount due. If lenders accept a greater amount than the debt due, they are then legally obliged to provide change in legal currency. If the offer of legal tender is refused, the debt is not wiped out but the lender forfeits the right (lien) to appropriate the borrower's property if the debt is not paid; nor is he entitled to charge any further interest. In England and Wales (but not in Scotland or Northern Ireland), the Bank of England has a monopoly of issuing coins and notes that are legal tender in England and Wales. Scottish and Irish coins and notes are generally acceptable throughout the United Kingdom but they are not legal tender in any part of the country.

Lender of last resort Normally the central bank of a country, which uses the position to help regulate the economy. In Britain, the Bank of England will always lend money on request to the discount houses supplying the banking system, but only on its own terms and conditions. By changing these terms and conditions, it can control the supply and cost of money entering the system.

Lessee Person to whom the lease of a property is granted by a 'lessor'.

Letter of allotment Letter from a company informing an applicant for shares or stock in a new issue as to the amount he or she has been allocated. The letter is then exchanged for a certificate; but in the meantime it can be used as proof of ownership in any dealings or as security for a loan. See PROVISIONAL ALLOTMENT LETTER.

Letter of credit Document issued by a bank or other financial institution guaranteeing that it will allow a prospective borrower credit up to a stated amount for a specified period. This allows the borrower to draw up cheques or bills of exchange up to that amount in the knowledge that they will be automatically accepted. The purpose for which the loan guarantee is required is agreed beforehand and any bills must conform with this purpose. Widely used in foreign trade, especially for dealing with unreliable payers: the buyer arranges with a bank to open a letter of credit in the country of the seller, who is then able to receive payment only when presenting the relevant documents that the transaction has been completed satisfactorily.

Letter of licence Document recording that creditors (lenders) of an insolvent debtor will agree not to press for payment for a stated time, in order to give the borrower extra time.

Letter of lien Document signed by a

borrower giving the lender authority to sell goods held by a third party on behalf of the borrower, should the debt not be repaid when due.

Letter of renunciation Issued by shareholders, not wishing to take up a rights issue of shares, renouncing them either absolutely or in favour of a third party.

Letters of administration Document issued by the Probate Court appointing someone to be administrator of the estate of a person who has died. See PROBATE.

Letters patent Granted to inventors once they have obtained a patent. They can then be used to assign the rights of the invention to other parties.

Level term assurance Policy which simply pays out an agreed fixed sum on the death of the policy-holder whose life is covered. Since no payment is made if the policy term expires, the premiums tend to be cheaper than those for policies which pay bonuses or return the original capital.

Leverage US term for GEARING, where a limited amount is used to generate higher borrowings. Leveraged investments are those which require only a margin or proportion of the total sum involved actually to be paid up, such as futures trading, greatly increasing the potential rewards and losses.

Leveraged buyout A method of taking over a company by using limited assets, including possibly those of the target company, to borrow money to finance the purchase. A popular method of financing takeovers, particularly for managements wishing to control their own company or for minority shareholders seeking to obtain full control. Financial institutions,

including banks, which believe the new owners would make the business more profitable, are often prepared to provide the necessary help to mount a takeover bid by offering existing shareholders high-interest stock. The cost of this stock can place a heavy burden on future profits if the bid succeeds; but very often parts of the company are then sold off to reduce the debt.

Levy Introduce or collect a tax, such as customs duty on imported goods or on a specific activity like gambling.

Liabilities Debts owed by a business or organization to its creditors or owners.

Liability General term used to describe a debt of some kind.

Liability insurance Policies in the accident insurance class that protect the insured against the cost of paying compensation for loss, damage, sickness or death.

LIBOR See LONDON INTERBANK OFFERED RATE.

Licensed conveyancers See REGISTERED LICENSED CONVEYANCERS.

Licensed deposit takers Institutions or companies authorized by the Bank of England under the 1987 Banking Act to take in deposits of money. See DEPOSIT PROTECTION FUND and MONEY SHOPS.

Lien The right to hold something as security, particularly against a debt, until the claim has been satisfied or the debt discharged.

Lien on shares Right most companies have under their articles of association to take possession of, and sell, stock held by any shareholders owing the company money.

Life annuity An insurance policy that provides for payment of an annuity only during the life of the recipient.

Life assurance or insurance Policy taken out on the life of a person or persons. There are many variations. Assurance policies, covering acts that must eventually occur, such as death and retirement, vary from merely paying out a fixed sum on the death of the assured to providing extra bonuses (with profits) or an annuity on retirement. Term and endowment policies are for a fixed period of time, at which point they mature. A term policy provides life cover merely for the period specified and pays nothing if the holder survives until the maturity date. Endowment policies provide life cover too, but pay a guaranteed sum on maturity (with or without profits, depending on the terms and conditions of the individual policy).

Life Assurance and Unit Trust Regulatory Organization (LAUTRO) One of the self-regulatory organizations, under the umbrella of the SECURITIES AND INVESTMENT BOARD, formed to provide improved investor protection under the 1986 Financial Services Act. It concentrates on controlling the activities of companies offering insurance and unit trust products. See SELF-REGULATORY ORGANIZATIONS and USEFUL ADDRESSES.

Life assurance premium relief (LAPR) Special tax relief given for insurance policies, but withdrawn in the March 1984 Budget because it was felt to have been over-exploited by the insurance companies to promote savings products.

However, policies taken out before March 1984 still qualify for the relief, and therefore are often worth retaining, rather than being replaced with an alternative savings product. The rate of LAPR was half the standard income tax rate, so in 1989 it was reduced from 15% to 12.5%.

Life assured Person on whom an assurance policy has been taken out and on whose death or retirement the agreed sum becomes payable.

Life cover Insurance that provides an assured payment in the event of death. Often included in other financial products, like endowment mortgages or investment bonds.

Life estate An interest in land for the owner's lifetime only.

Life fund Stock of money set aside by insurance companies to meet future claims of policy-holders. The money is normally invested in a range of fixed-interest stock, property and shares to achieve a mixture of capital growth and security of income. The progress of the life fund governs how much in extra profits (or bonuses) can be paid to policy-holders.

Life income An income that is payable to someone for the rest of their life, either from a life policy annuity or from rents from a property in which a lifelong interest only is held.

Life of contract The period during which something is quoted on a market, until it expires; for example, on a futures exchange the May delivery position of a particular year may be quoted for thirteen months or more prior to becoming the spot (delivery) month.

Life office Name given to any assurance

company that offers life assurance and investment products.

Life tables Statistics prepared from records of deaths to show the expectation of life at various ages and in different employments, and which are used to calculate insurance premiums and the cost of annuities.

LIFFE See LONDON INTERNATIONAL FINANCIAL FUTURES EXCHANGE and USEFUL ADDRESSES.

Lilo See LAST IN, LAST OUT.

Limit (up or down) The maximum fluctuation in prices that is permitted on certain markets during a specific period, often a day. The restriction on price movements moving too sharply up or down too quickly is supposed to reduce price volatility and possible losses to those unable to get out of the market in time. Widely used in US markets in particular.

Limitation See STATUTE OF LIMITATION.

Limited Prior to 1980, every company with LIMITED LIABILITY was obliged to put limited (often abbreviated to Ltd) after its name to underline its status. Since the 1980 Companies Act this still applies to privately owned limited liability companies, but publicly quoted companies with shareholders must instead put Public Limited Company (PLC).

Limited liability Important concession granted to companies which are formally registered with the Registrar of Companies, that the shareholders cannot be forced to contribute more than the nominal value of the shares registered in their name, that is, the original share capital. This limits their loss should the

company fail. In return for this concession, the limited liability company has to comply with the rules and regulations laid down by the Registrar of Companies, including the filing of annual accounts and balance sheet.

Limited partnership A form of partnership, consisting of some partners having unlimited liability for paying any debts, and other partners whose liability is restricted to the amount of capital they have provided to the business. The limited partners may not share in the management of the partnership, and the business must be registered with the Registrar of Companies.

Limit order An instruction to a broker or dealer in a market to buy or sell either below a stated higher price or above a stated lower price.

Lineage Charge made by newspapers for advertisements based on the number of lines, or equivalent space, taken up. Also used as a method of payment for freelance journalists contributing to a publication.

Linked policies Insurance products that are tied to specific investments, for example unit-linked, where the premiums are put into units of investment funds. See UNIT LINKED POLICY.

Liquid assets See ASSETS, AVAILABLE.

Liquidate Pay off a debt; sell for cash; go into LIQUIDATION.

Liquidation Winding up a company by appointing a LIQUIDATOR to sell its assets for cash, which is then used to pay off its debts. A person unable to pay debts can be made bankrupt, but a company has to go into liquidation.

Liquidator A person appointed to wind up (bring an end to the existence of) a company unable to pay its debts. Appointed by a court, the liquidator has to obtain possession of all the company's assets and sell them for the best cash price obtainable. The cash is shared among the creditors, and if any remains it is divided among the members of the company as repayment of capital.

Liquid capital See WORKING CAPITAL.

Liquidity ratio Comparison of the liquid assets (cash or something easily convertible to cash) available against current liabilities (borrowings).

Listed companies Those whose shares are quoted on a recognized stock market and included in the official list of securities dealt in by members of the market. See STOCK EXCHANGE and UNLISTED SECURITIES MARKET.

List price Usually refers to the recommended retail, or wholesale, selling price listed by its manufacturer. By lowering their profit margin, retailers often sell goods at below the list price in order to attract customers.

Lloyd's agents Representatives of LLOYD'S throughout the world who supply information about shipping and aviation, and also appoint surveyors to report on damage or loss, possibly settling claims on the spot.

Lloyd's (of London) Famous central marketplace for providing insurance services, particularly for shipping. The Corporation of Lloyd's does not undertake insurance business itself, but provides the premises for its members to operate from and lays down rules and regulations for the policies issued. The membership is made up of brokers, who generate the business, and underwriters who represent wealthy individuals known as 'names' by forming syndicates to underwrite insurance policies. It is the syndicates, represented by their agents in 'boxes' at Lloyd's, who provide insurance protection in return for premiums. To qualify as a 'name' and then be eligible to join one of the syndicates, the individual must be able to show evidence of personal wealth in easily realizable assets of a specified minimum amount. It is the 'names' who are ultimately responsible for paying claims and filling any shortfall if the claims should exceed the premium and investment income of the syndicate. The 'name' provides a deposit which helps provide the underlying capital for the syndicate and which is invested in a trust fund. But the 'name' also has to have more money available in reserve, just in case the claims exceed the profits earned by the syndicate, as has happened on several occasions in recent years. Since it is an individual investment, the 'name' is liable to commit all his/her personal fortune to meeting any shortfall if necessary. Nevertheless, in normal circumstances a 'name' can expect to make profits, and the rewards can be high, if risky. The money put aside by the 'name' should earn a double return – interest on the deposit held against a possible claim, plus the profits from the premiums collected by the syndicate. Lloyd's syndicates compete directly with the insurance companies in providing financial protection against a variety of risks, such as house contents and motor accident as well as specializing in business which the insurance companies will not handle. The Lloyd's syndicates spread the risks in any policies with potential large claims among themselves and with specialist re-insurance companies. They operate worldwide and are one of the biggest earners of 'invisible' exports for Britain. See LUTINE BELL and USEFUL ADDRESSES.

LME See LONDON METAL EXCHANGE and USEFUL ADDRESSES.

Loan back Arrangement available in some pension schemes whereby an individual, director or the company can borrow up to the accumulated value of their contributions. A commercial rate of interest must be paid to the pension fund on the loan. Some pension plans offered by life assurance companies can be used as security against a loan in a similar way.

Loan capital Part of the funds provided for a company or organization subscribed for a specified period and on which fixed interest is paid. Repayment may be guaranteed by a third party or secured on the company's assets. See DEBENTURE.

Loan club Private organization, often formed in factories or shops, which receives regular contributions from its members as a form of voluntary savings. The money received is put into an interest-bearing account and repaid, plus interest, on a specified date (often at Christmas time). Members are sometimes allowed to borrow sums for a short time at an agreed rate of interest.

Loan shark Slang name for an unscrupulous or dishonest lender of money, who normally charges excessively high rates of interest.

Loan stock Offered by companies seeking to raise extra working capital, under which investors are guaranteed to receive a fixed income for the duration of the loan and have the right to be repaid before the holders of capital stock, should the company go into liquidation. Higher interest rates are offered on unsecured

loan stock, where the lender has less security for repayment.

Local US term for individual members of stock markets and futures exchanges, who trade on their own account and are not members of a company or group. They are professional speculators who make their living by trading on the markets and providing the extra turnover required to help the market function effectively.

Local authority bonds Fixed-rate loans issued by local authorities or corporations to raise money, particularly for capital expenditure. Longer-term loans are obtained by issued stock on the stock market, which trades in a similar way to gilts (government securities). Shorter-term loans are YEARLINGS, so called because they are repayable after one year, but which can be traded at any time on the stock market so they do not have to be held for a year. Mortgage (or town hall) bonds, issued by local authorities, pay a fixed rate of interest for periods of up to three years.

Lock up Term use to describe making a long-term investment. Alternatively, an agreement between a bidder for a company and the takeover target, so as to discourage further bidders.

Loi Monory Share-buying incentive scheme, through tax relief, introduced in France to encourage investment and savings by private investors. Provided the model for the PERSONAL EQUITY PLANS (PEPs) in Britain, announced in the 1986 Budget, although the British version gives tax relief only on any profits earned, not on the money invested.

Lombard Street Popular name for the London money market, since many of the big banks have their head offices in Lombard Street, in the very heart of the City of London.

London Commodity Exchange (LCE) Organization that gathers and transmits information from some of the futures markets for certain commodities traded on the Futures and Options Exchange (FOX) which is run by the LCE.

London interbank offered rate (LIBOR) The basic cost of borrowing money on the wholesale money market in London, where banks and financial institutions deal in large amounts each day. The variations in the supply and demand of money set the interest rate at which it can be borrowed both for immediate (overnight) use and at some time in the future, say three months or a year ahead. LIBOR is used as the base, on which a profit margin is added, for the interest rate charged on large loans to companies and other organizations. The higher the considered risk, the higher the margin added.

In recent years, LIBOR (linked) mortgages have been introduced, whereby the mortgage interest rate is tied to movements in LIBOR, plus a fixed percentage as a profit margin for the arranger of the loan. Normally the three months forward LIBOR is used and the rate is reviewed every quarter; LIBOR mortgage rates tend therefore to be more variable, in line with movements in the wholesale money market instead of being fixed by banks and building societies.

London International Financial Futures Exchange (LIFFE) Centre for futures markets, dealing in interest rates, currencies, stock indices and options.

London Metal Exchange (LME) International marketplace for trading in base metals, either for delivery immediately (spot) or at some future date. The LME has a string of authorized warehouses throughout the world, but mainly in Europe, where stocks of metal are held to supply the market. The weekly variation in the warehouse stock figures can often influence market prices by indicating either a shortage or a surplus. The LME is widely used by metals traders worldwide, and also by speculators.

London Stock Exchange Now known as the International Stock Exchange, it is the centre for dealing in fixed-interest stock (gilts) and company shares. See STOCK EXCHANGE.

Long General term used to describe a holding in a market, usually in expectation of prices going up: 'hold a long position' or 'go long' (make a purchase). See BULL.

Long-dated security Government-backed and other fixed-interest stocks with a promised repayment date of over fifteen years in the future. See LONG GILT.

Long dozen Thirteen, instead of the normal twelve units contained in a dozen. Also known as 'baker's dozen'.

Long exchange Bills of exchange in the currency markets that will not mature (become payable) for 69–90 days.

Long gilt Government security with a maturity (repayment) date more than 15 years ahead. See GILTS.

Long hundred Comprises 120 articles, instead of the conventional 100.

Long lease A lease that has a minimum of 50 years left before it expires.

Long liquidation Selling or closing out positions held in a market, possibly in expectation that prices are going to fall, or simply to take profits made.

Long position See LONG.

Long-term liabilities Accounting term for borrowings that are not repayable within the company's next financial year.

Longs Holders of shares, stock or future commitments to buy on the futures and options markets in anticipation of prices going up. Also a shorthand term for LONG-DATED SECURITY.

Long ton Equal to 2,240 lb (20 cwt) under the British imperial weights and measures system.

Loss adjuster Independent expert called in by an insurance company to assess the value of a claim, especially if it is disputed.
    In contrast to a 'loss assessor', who is called in by the policy-holder to perform the same task.

Loss leader Something sold at below its normal price, possibly even at a loss to the seller, in order to attract more customers.

Lot Unit of trading used on markets, comprising a group of contracts or shares. Also describes a collection of articles offered for sale together as at an auction.

Lot money Charge made by an auctioneer, based on the number of lots sold.

Low cost endowment mortgage Cheaper policy for repaying a mortgage, since the payment guaranteed is lower than the size of the mortgage loan, but the deficit is normally more than filled by the annual (reversionary) and final (terminal)

bonuses. Nevertheless since the guaranteed sum is lower, the premiums are cheaper. Normally combined with a decreasing term assurance policy to ensure the mortgage is repaid in full if the policyholder dies.

Low cost whole life assurance Guarantees, at lower premiums, an assured sum in the event of death. Two policies are used: a whole life assurance that gradually builds up as bonuses are awarded over the years, and a term assurance policy that decreases in value in line with the rise in the whole life policy.

Lower earnings limit The level of salary at which employees become liable to start paying NATIONAL INSURANCE contributions. See BAND EARNINGS and UPPER EARNINGS LIMIT.

Low start mortgage Aimed at the first-time house-buyer with limited resources. The cost of the policy is kept lower than normal for the early years of contributions, but then increases to higher levels later on to compensate for the shortfall in the starting years. Normally more expensive overall, because the initial shortfall in payments means that extra interest is added to the total capital sum borrowed.

LSD Initials for pounds, shillings and pence, from the Latin: *librae, solidi, denarii*. Now used as a general slang term for money.

Ltd Abbreviation for limited (company).

Lump sum Money paid all at one time instead of by instalments. A lump-sum investment or policy means paying a single premium rather than phasing premiums over a period. When pension plans mature, the recipient is normally given the

choice of taking part of the money due in
the form of a single lump-sum payment
that is deducted from the amount available
for distribution as a pension and is tax
free. There are Inland Revenue
restrictions on the amount of a pension
which can be taken in a lump sum, since
the tax reliefs are basically given to
encourage people to provide a source of
income for themselves when they are no
longer earning. The lump sum can, of
course, be either invested (possibly in an
annuity) or spent by the pensioner or used
to pay off debts, such as a mortgage. In
the 1989 Budget the Chancellor reduced
the maximum lump sum payment that
could be taken tax free as a part of a

general package aimed at limiting the
amount of pension benefit qualifying for tax
relief. See PENSIONS.

Lutine bell   A bell rung at Lloyd's in
London to announce important news
concerning the fate of a ship in trouble or
possibly some other disaster: one stroke
means bad news, two are good news.
Seldom used these days because of
modern communications, it dates back to
1799 when a ship, the *Lutine*, insured with
Lloyd's, went down in the North Sea with
a large cargo of bullion gold, most of which
was not recovered. The bell of the ship
was, however, recovered and taken to
Lloyd's.

M

Macro-economics Overview of the economy of a country or the world from fundamental aspects such as unemployment, inflation, balance of trade and industrial activity. As opposed to 'micro-economics', which looks at small, individual units such as a particular company or person.

Mainstream corporation tax The tax deducted from a company's undistributed profits left after advance corporation tax has been deducted from dividend payments.

Maintenance General term to cover the cost of keeping plant, machinery or standard of living up to a specified level.
    Also refers to alimony payments made to support someone else, normally a divorced or separated spouse, or children. Often this is done via a maintenance order issued by a court of law.

Making a market/price Phrase used in financial markets to describe the obligation of MARKET-MAKERS to quote a price at which they are prepared to buy and sell.

Making up day Stock market term for first date when accounts should be settled.

Making up price Stock market term for the price at which transactions are carried over from one account period to the next.

Malthusianism Belief in the theory put forward by an English economist, Thomas Malthus, at the end of the eighteenth century that the growth of population will have to be controlled, otherwise the world will run out of resources. Sometimes used as a more general term to describe a gloomy or pessimistic view.

Managed currency Currency whose value against other currencies is artificially controlled by the government concerned, either directly by buying and selling in the foreign exchange market or indirectly by altering interest rates.

Managed funds Investments that are managed on behalf of investors. Often offered by life insurance companies via investment bonds and unit-linked policies for savings or mortgage repayment. Also by unit trusts that invest in other unit trusts and by offshore funds. Instead of the investor specifying the investment policy to be followed, the management of the fund assumes this responsibility. See DISCRETIONARY SERVICE and FUND OF FUNDS.

Management agreement Service offered by brokers and financial advisers under which their customers are provided with formal agreements which define the terms and objectives of how their investments will be managed. See CUSTOMER AGREEMENT.

Management buyout Situation where the management of a company takes it over by buying out the existing owners or shareholders. See LEVERAGED BUYOUT.

Management charge or fee Cost charged by companies, such as life assurance, investment and unit trust groups, for their services in running a fund. Sometimes it is a fixed flat rate, but more often a percentage of the value of the fund, calculated on an annual, half-yearly or monthly basis, is charged. The management charge or fee is supposed to pay for ongoing costs, such as the fund manager's salary, while the initial or front load charge covers the cost of launching and setting up the fund.

Manager's cheque A cheque drawn by a bank on itself and signed by one of the managers. Used when a bank is acting on instructions from a customer, who is temporarily absent and who wants bills to be settled in the meantime.

Managers share See DEFERRED SHARES.

Managing agent Person or business appointed to manage a property or company in return for a fee or commission.

Mandate Instruction, or written authority, giving another person or organisation power to act on someone's behalf in certain specified matters, such as signing cheques or operating a joint bank account.

Man-hour Unit of measurement of the amount of work done; for example, it might take 20 man-hours for a wall to be built.

Manipulation Popular term to describe the artificial control of market prices, normally by deceitful means. However, on occasions governments will manipulate a market deliberately and openly to achieve a particular purpose, such as defending the value of a currency or influencing the price of a commodity.

Margin Amount of profit made; the difference between the cost of production or buying compared with the selling price. Or the difference between the amount of a loan and the value of the security provided by the borrower. On the stock market refers to the money or security held by brokers to protect themselves against clients failing to pay their bills. Also refers to the deposit put down in cash or securities for dealing in certain markets, such as futures and options, where the full price does not have to be paid on the spot.

Marginal cost Economics term for the extra cost needed to increase the volume of production, as opposed to the overall production cost.

Marginal land Used to describe farming land that is only just worth cultivating, giving returns little above the cost of production.

Marginal rate Percentage of tax paid at the individual taxpayer's highest rate.

Margin call Demand for additional funds to maintain the original margin required at the same value compared with the size of the risk involved. For example, a 10% original margin in a futures position might need topping up if the market price has moved against the investor. In these circumstances the call for additional funds can be considerable when compared with the original deposit.

Margin dealing Trading in a market by paying only a margin – the difference between the full cost and the amount that has to be deposited initially. By dealing in this way, the potential profit in relation to the sum expended is increased greatly, but so are the potential losses.

Marine insurance Policies taken out to protect shipping risks.

Marked cheque When the bank on which the cheque is drawn adds a note or mark, stating that it is good and will be honoured.

Marked share Where the share certificate bears a mark, or record, that rights offered on the share have been taken up or exercised.

Marketable Something that can be bought or sold easily or quickly. Hence 'marketable securities' (shares or stocks actively traded on a market).

Market capitalization Method of measuring the financial strength of a company by calculating the total value of its issued shares, based on the current stock exchange or market price. This can vary considerably in line with the share price movement. It can also be applied to all the shares quoted on the stock market in order to calculate the capitalization of the whole market. Often large sums can be wiped off the total market capitalization by quite a modest fall in prices.

Market forces Underlying influences affecting market price movements, such as an industrial recession or fears of inflation.

Market-maker A person, or organization, who is prepared to buy or sell at a quoted price. On the stock market, all trading is transacted via companies which have been appointed market-makers for particular stocks and shares – a role performed by jobbers until the trading system was changed by the BIG BANG in October 1986. Specific

market-makers are authorized separately to deal in shares and in gilts (government securities). In the OVER THE COUNTER MARKET, certain companies will make a market in shares not quoted on the exchange; and in other markets, like futures, companies prepared to buy and sell as principals on their own account are known as market-makers.

Market order An instruction to buy or sell immediately at the prevailing market price.

Market price The level at which someone is prepared to buy or sell anything. Often refers to prices quoted on recognized markets, such as the stock exchange or commodity futures markets.

Market value The amount for which an asset could be bought or sold at current price levels.

Mark to market Term used in futures trading for the daily adjustment of an account to reflect the accrued profits and losses.

Married couple's allowance Under the present taxation system husbands, even if couples are separated, receive a tax-free allowance that can be used to reduce his tax bill. This is forfeited if the husband and wife opt for separate assessments and each claims a single person's allowance. But even then the husband is liable to pay tax on any investment income earned by his wife. But the whole system will change from the tax year starting in April 1990, under proposals for independent taxation first introduced in the 1988 Budget. Under the new system everyone, whether married or single, will have their own individual personal allowances that can be set against all types of income. In addition there will be a special married couple's allowance which will go to the husband first but if the husband's income is too low to use all or part of the extra allowance the unused part can be transferred to be offset against the wife's earnings. Under the independent tax system, wives will receive the tax-free allowances for income tax and annual capital gains tax exemption even if they are not working, so many couples will be able to save tax by transferring assets and income to the spouse not using up his or her allowances. However, it will have to be a genuine transfer. See TAX REFORM.

Martinmas See QUARTER DAY.

Matched bargains Practice adopted by brokers and dealers to offset purchases and sales by different clients in order to cancel each other out. Also used by OVER THE COUNTER traders to deal in shares only when there is a willing buyer or seller available.

Maternity allowance and grant Government payments to pregnant women who have been paying National Insurance contributions. Statutory maternity pay (SMP) is also available to any pregnant woman who has worked for the same company for at least six months.

Maturity Date on which an insurance policy, bill of exchange, bond, debenture or loan stock becomes due for payment or repayment. See REDEMPTION.

Maundy money Specially minted coins given personally by the British king or queen on the Thursday before Easter in a traditional ceremony.

Maximum investment plans (MIP) Endowment insurance savings policies,

investing in units of fund and with regular premium payments, that take advantage of the concession allowing tax-free income on policies held for ten years. Those taken out before March 1984 also had the advantage of LAPR (life assurance premium relief) that was scrapped in the 1984 Budget. See QUALIFYING POLICY.

Mean Used in statistics to identify an average level, which also takes into account the importance of the constituents.

Mean price Market price calculated by taking the average of the buying and selling prices. See MIDDLE PRICE.

Means test Examination of a person's income and wealth to assess whether or not they qualify for certain benefits, normally paid by the government.

Median Middle value, half-way between the lowest and highest positions in a league table of values.

Medical (expenses) policy Insurance against the costs of treatment that might result from an accident or illness, especially when travelling abroad. Sometimes provided free with other insurance, such as against loss of baggage, or for those using a credit card to pay for the journey. See PERMANENT HEALTH INSURANCE and PRIVATE MEDICAL INSURANCE.

Mediums Short for 'medium-dated securities', which mature for repayment within five to fifteen years. See LONGS and SHORTS.

Medium-term capital Funds raised for a specific period, normally repaid within five years.

MEGA Prefix used in metric system to mean a million times. One megawatt is 1,000,000 watts.

Memorandum cheque Forward or post-dated cheque given by the borrower to the lender of the loan for use only if the debt is not repaid when due.

Memorandum of association Blueprint for a company in which the founder owners put down details of its objectives, name, registered office, capital and share structure. Has to be sent to the Registrar of Companies with any application to become an incorporated company.

Memorandum of deposit Document signed by anyone depositing stocks, shares or other negotiable assets as security against a loan. It gives powers to the lender to sell the things deposited if the loan is not repaid when due.

Memorandum of satisfaction Document sent to the Registrar of Companies whenever any financial charge on the company, such as a mortgage or debenture, has been repaid wholly or in part.

Mercantile house Any business organization involved in some commercial or industrial activity.

Merchants Traders who buy and sell goods, usually in large quantities.

Merchant banks Originally, bankers that acted as financial agents or advisers to governments. Nowadays, they concentrate mainly on financing trade and industry, raising venture capital and loans, dealing in the foreign exchange and bullion markets. Also act as financial advisers for companies, managing investment and unit trusts, pension funds and private client funds.

Merger When two or more companies get together to form a single organization, as opposed to one company taking over another one.

Messuage Legal term for 'house', including the gardens and buildings that go with it.

Metallic currency Coins made from precious or base metals, as opposed to 'paper' money.

Metric system System of measurement in multiples of ten.

Metric ton (tonne) 1,000 kilograms (equal to 2,204.6 lb).

Michaelmas See QUARTER DAY.

Micro-economics See MACRO-ECONOMICS.

Mid(dle) price Middle point between the buying and selling price (bid/offer spread) used as an average market price for comparing movements in the value of the stock, share, commodity or unit trust.

Midsummer See QUARTER DAY.

Milch cows Popular term for enterprises or parts of a business that provide steady and lucrative profits, usually without too much effort.

Minimum lending rate (MLR) The lowest rate at which the Bank of England will lend money to the wholesale money market, therefore used as a means of controlling interest rates. See BASE RATE.

Minorities Term used to describe outside shareholders in the subsidiary of another company.

Minority interest A holding of shares in a company that is not large enough to give controlling interest.

Mint Produce coinage, or an organization that produces coins. The Royal Mint in Britain is state-owned and has a monopoly to produce the government's coins and notes which are LEGAL TENDER.

MIP See MAXIMUM INVESTMENT PLANS.

MIRAS See MORTGAGE INTEREST RELIEF AT SOURCE.

Mixed economy Term used to describe national economies which have both public and privately owned enterprises and institutions.

MLR See MINIMUM LENDING RATE.

MMC (Monopolies and Mergers Commission) See USEFUL ADDRESSES.

M0 See MONEY SUPPLY.

Mobility allowance Government benefit paid to disabled people.

Monetarists Economists who believe that a country's or the world economy can best be controlled by restrictions on the supply of money, especially on bank lending.

Monetary compensatory amount (MCA) Term used in the European Community's Common Agricultural Policy to describe subsidies and duties used to make up the difference in the value of individual currencies.

Monetary economy One based on exchanging goods for money, rather than bartering.

Monetary unit Standard currency of a country.

Monetize Fix official money value of a metal or alloy when used as a coin.

Money Term derived from 'Moneta', one of the surnames of the Roman goddess Juno in whose temple Roman coins were minted. Moneta itself derives from the Greek word 'mnemoyse', meaning 'act of memory'. Over the years money has been used to describe any article that is acceptable as a means of payment, measure of value or store of wealth.

Money at call Short-term loans for up to fourteen days, made by banks to other financial institutions or brokerage firms.

Money broker Dealer in the money market who arranges short-term bank loans to other financial institutions.

Money capital Funds held by a company in cash with a view to purchasing assets.

Money market Dealings by financial institutions, such as discount houses, banks and the government, in wholesale supplies of money and short-term loans. Used, for example, to put surplus balances on deposit overnight in order to earn interest, and to set the rates paid for bills of exchange, offered by the Treasury, to the discount houses. The money market, dealing in funds owned by financial institutions, sets the basic rates of interest for the banks and the cost of retail money.

Money market accounts Special interest-bearing deposit accounts which pay interest on surplus balances, based on the current rates available in the money market plus a percentage profit margin for the bank or financial institution. These accounts normally require a minimum balance to be held on deposit and often link the interest rate paid with the size of deposit. They also tend to discourage use of the account by imposing special charges for withdrawals or restricting the size and number of payments.

Money order Way of making small payments via the Post Office. Only available from certain post offices that are both money-order and telegraph offices. Money orders can be crossed like a cheque so that they have to be paid to the bank; or, for an extra charge, arrange for payment instructions to be sent by telegraph overseas. See INTERNATIONAL MONEY ORDER.

Money purchase scheme Name given to a pension policy, where the benefits paid out are based on the amount of the contributions put in and how successfully they have been invested. Unlike the final salary scheme favoured by most companies, money purchase schemes do not guarantee a rate of pension. The eventual pension depends on the size of the lump sum, built up by investment of the contributions, which is available to buy an annuity at the time of retirement. The size of the pension also depends on the proportion of the lump sum retained by the recipient, which is restricted up to a maximum permitted level, and the annuity rates available at the time of retirement. The advantage of money purchase schemes is that they are flexible, easy to transfer from one employment to another and tailored much more to individuals than group final salary schemes. They are,

therefore, the basis of PERSONAL PENSIONS. See CONTRACTED OUT MONEY PURCHASE SCHEME and PENSIONS.

Money shops Retail outlets, usually in main streets, set up by finance companies to provide loans and banking services. They normally charge higher rates of interest than the major banks because of the greater risk involved in lending to someone who is not a regular bank customer.

Money stock Fixed-interest stock due to be repaid at a specified date in the near future.

Money supply Total of all the money held by persons and organizations in a country at a particular time. However, in Britain various definitions are used to measure the money supply. M0 (monetary base) consists of the total coins and notes in circulation held by the commercial banks and the Bank of England. M1 consists of the notes and coins in circulation, plus private sector current and deposit sterling accounts held with clearing banks. M2 adds private accounts held with deposit banks and discount houses. M3 is the broadest measure, including all private and public sector deposit accounts held, including those held by UK residents in other currencies. £M3 excludes the foreign currency accounts.

Moonlighting Having, in addition to regular full-time employment, a part-time job or jobs, usually in the evening or at night – hence the name. Often these extra earnings are not declared to the taxman, although they ought to be.

Moral hazard Insurance term to justify extra charges for insuring someone, or a class of employees, who are considered to be unreliable, careless or more likely to be dishonest.

Moratorium Agreement to allow more time for a debt to be paid.

Mortality tables See LIFE TABLES.

Mortgage A legal charge on land or property acting as security for a loan. Often known as home loan. Under a mortgage contract or deed, the owner of land or property (the 'mortgagor') borrows money and in return gives the lender ('mortgagee') an interest in the land or property. This means that it is homebuyers who give mortgages to building societies, banks or other lenders, not the other way round, as is generally supposed.

There are two main types of mortgage: an EQUITABLE MORTGAGE, where the lender holds the title deeds of the property, but has to take legal action to gain possession or sell it; and a LEGAL MORTGAGE, where the lender has complete control of the property. Mortgages can also be given on ships or yachts and on goods and chattels. Interest-only mortgages, where the borrower only repays capital at the end of the agreed period for the loan, are usually linked with savings schemes, such as endowment policies, pensions or Personal Equity Plans. See REPAYMENT MORTGAGE.

Mortage bond Document acknowledging a debt and specifying land or property owned by the borrower.

Mortgage debenture See DEBENTURE.

Mortgage deed Sets out the terms and conditions of the mortgage contract between the borrower and the lender.

Mortgage interest relief at source (MIRAS) The system under which the lender automatically deducts on behalf of the government basic-rate tax relief available by lowering the level of payments sought. However, higher-rate taxpayers have to apply direct to the Inland Revenue for any additional relief due to them.

Mortgage protection policy Assurance taken out with repayment mortgages on the life of the borrower to provide for repayment of the mortgage should he or she die prematurely. A term assurance policy is used with the sum assured declining in line with the amount of the loan paid off, although a normal life policy is usually also acceptable to the lender.

Mortgage (home-loan) rate The interest charged on the money borrowed. This can be a fixed rate, for a period of years at least, but most lenders prefer to make it variable in accordance with the rise and fall in the cost of money. Mortgage rates tend to move in line with the bank base rate, but some are linked to LIBOR (London Interbank Offered Rate). The rates also vary in accordance with the size of the loan in relation to the income of the borrower or the value of the property. Also the type of mortgage – straight repayment, endowment or pension – and the security provided by the borrower.

Mortgage relief The special annual tax-free allowance given on the interest payments (up to a maximum limit) on loans taken out by private individuals to buy a home. See MORTGAGE INTEREST RELIEF AT SOURCE and TAX REFORM.

Mother's allowance See WIDOW'S ALLOWANCE.

Motor insurers' bureau Organization set up by insurance companies to provide protection for motorists involved in accidents, either with a hit-and-run driver or where there is no proper third party coverage.

Moving average Statistical term used to track market price movements over a period and thus even out the fluctuations.

Multiple Figure used by stock market analysts to calculate the PRICE-EARNINGS RATIO of a share after dividing the net profit by the number of shares, to calculate the earnings per share.

Municipal bond See BOND.

Mutual An organization that is owned by its members, not by outside shareholders; any profits made are therefore shared by the members. Building and friendly societies have traditionally been mutuals; so have many of the insurance companies (known as 'mutual offices') whose capital is made up of the premiums paid by policy-holders, who are entitled to any profits or surpluses made.

Mutual funds US term for unit trusts, or collective investments where money is pooled together and managed by a professional fund manager.

Mutual insurance Policies issued by a mutual (non-profit-making) insurance company. The policy-holders share the profits in the form of additional benefits, but they are also liable for extra contributions if losses are incurred.

Mutual redemption reference library Elaborate name given to the central list of clients kept by members of the stock exchange, which they check before taking on new business to see whether the client is in dispute with, or owes money to, another member of the exchange.

N

Naked debenture See DEBENTURE, MORTGAGE.

Naked option A highly dangerous position in the options market, where the grantor of the option does not have the underlying asset or shares in case the option is exercised; or alternatively has not covered (hedged) the risk of the option being taken up. See OPTIONS.

Name day Stock exchange term for the date when stockbrokers show the names of buyers to sellers as a prelude to the settlement of accounts.

Narrower-range investments See TRUSTEE INVESTMENTS.

Narrow market When there is a limited supply available for trading.

Narrow money The country's money supply when measured under the M1 definition. See MONEY SUPPLY.

National association of securities dealers automated quotations system (NASDAQ) Computerized dealing system, via screens, operated in the United States in competition with the traditional stock markets. Shares dealt in are mainly smaller size, over-the-counter stocks not traded on the big stock exchanges, but some of the larger company shares are dealt in too. Model for the new trading system (SEAQ) adopted by the London stock exchange after the BIG BANG in October 1986.

National debt The total amount of money borrowed by a government on which it has to pay interest. In Britain it is managed by the Bank of England on behalf of the Treasury. A large part of the debt will never be repaid, but the lenders constantly change in accordance with dealings in government securities (gilts). In recent years the National Debt has been reduced by the government using surplus funds to buy, instead of sell, gilts.

National development bonds Old issues of government stock introduced in 1964 but withdrawn in 1968. Interest is no longer payable, so any holders should surrender them immediately.

National Girobank Previous name of Girobank, the banking subsidiary company of the Post Office, which provides an alternative service to the clearing banks and building societies. Its main advantage is that cash deposits and withdrawals can be made over the counters of post offices, which are far greater in number than the branches of individual banks. It also provides an easy way of making payments without having to go through the formalities required to open a clearing bank account. Since becoming a public limited company in October 1985, Girobank has extended its services to compete directly with the banks, including personal loans and mortgages. Business and private account holders are able to use the Transcash system for transferring money both at home and abroad at no additional cost. Girobank was put up for sale to the private sector in 1988.

National insurance State scheme to provide protection against sickness and unemployment, as well as providing other benefits such as allowances for the disabled or mothers-to-be, and pensions. It also helps fund the National Health Service, with the aid of contributions from the Treasury. NI contributions are compulsory for everyone earning more than a specified minimum amount, which is adjusted in line with inflation. They are based on a percentage of earnings in a band between the minimum, or lower, earnings level and a maximum, or upper, earnings level. The higher the earnings between these two levels, the higher the percentage of contributions paid both by employers and employees, although they pay different rates. There are separate rates for the self-employed and for voluntary contributions. The amounts paid by employers and employees vary in accordance with whether the employee has decided to contract out of (leave) the State Earnings Related Pensions Scheme (SERPS) which provides pension benefits over and above the basic state pension. Those contracted out of SERPS pay lower National Insurance contributions, since they receive reduced pension benefits. It is only possible for employees to contract out of SERPS if they are members of an alternative pension scheme, either through the company scheme or via a personal pension, that provides benefits at least equivalent to SERPS.

National Savings Offshoot of the Treasury used to raise revenue for the government from private investors, in particular by selling a range of savings products, sweetened with tax-free concessions. Was part of the Post Office until 1969, when it was made an independent operation, but still retains its link by selling its savings products and a range of government securities (gilts) over post office counters. The range of products available from National Savings includes deposit accounts, PREMIUM BONDS and a variety of bonds and certificates offering various returns, depending primarily on how long they are retained. The interest paid is either tax free or is paid gross (without tax being deducted), so is particularly suitable either for non-taxpayers or for high-rate taxpayers; there are therefore often restrictions on the maximum investment that can be made, in order to prevent high-rate taxpayers obtaining too great concessions. The interest paid, especially on short-term National Savings products, is highly sensitive to government policy and is therefore adjusted frequently. Ultimately, by using its exclusive powers to provide tax-free concessions, the government can make National Savings products very competitive if it wishes to raise additional revenue, especially as they have the security of being government-backed. In 1989 National Savings introduced a new product offering a guaranteed rate of interest over five years. See CAPITAL BONDS.

National Savings stock register (NSSR) One of the services operated by National Savings is to maintain a range of government securities (GILTS) that can be bought at post offices on favourable terms, including low commission charges. Interest is paid gross (without tax being deducted at source), making them particularly suitable for non-taxpayers. A list of the gilts on the register, available for sale, is obtainable at post offices, which will handle the purchase, normally at much cheaper cost than buying gilts on the stock exchange through a broker. The disadvantage is that no advice is available as to the best to choose, and the selection of gilts offered is limited to those on the register.

NAV See NET ASSET VALUE.

Near money Investments which can be turned quickly into cash.

Negative covenant Agreement by formal deed, undertaking not to do something.

Negative easement Right to prevent owner of land from doing something, for example blocking access.

Negotiable instrument or security Right to ownership or payment that can be transferred from one person to another, for example a bank note, bearer bonds and share certificates, bills of exchange.

Net(t) Amount actually due, after deduction of tax, costs and other charges, discounts or rebates.

Net annual value Figure used as the basis for calculating the amount of rates payable on a house or property. It is estimated by deducting allowable expenses – repairs, insurance, etc. – from the gross value (the annual rent that would have been received if the property was let). See RACK RENT.

Net assets See ASSETS.

Net asset value (NAV) An important indicator of a company's financial standing, it is obtained by dividing the net assets total by the number of shares. If the share price is below the net asset value, the company is vulnerable to takeover because it could simply be sold off at a profit, providing the net assets are assessed on their true market value. The success or otherwise of funds, like investment or unit trusts, is also judged by the rise or fall in the fund's net asset value.

Net income What remains after the deduction of taxes, National Insurance and other compulsory payments.

Net interest The sum actually received by a lender (or investor) after deduction of tax.

Net margin The profit made by a seller of goods or services, after deducting expenses.

Net profit Surplus left for a company after deducting all expenses, including taxation and payments to minority shareholders, from the gross profit.

Net worth Difference between total assets and total liabilities in a business. For private individuals, it is often used to define the amount of wealth available in quick assets (cash or something that can easily be turned into cash) and assets that might prove difficult to turn into cash quickly if at all: a private residence, share in an estate or goodwill in a business that might be difficult to pass on.

Net yield Return on capital invested on capital investment or deposit after allowing for deductions, such as charges or taxes. See GROSS YIELD.

New for old Insurance policy, normally for house contents, that pays sufficient money to cover the replacement cost of the insured item(s) damaged or lost.

New issues Shares or stock offered for sale for the first time. See FLOTATION.

New time Term to describe share transactions during the last two days of an account period on the stock exchange for settlement in the next account period.

New York Stock Exchange (NYSE) Largest stock market in the United States. Known as the 'big board', because of the number and size of companies' shares traded there.

Nickel US coin worth five cents, often used to describe any coin of little value. Also a leading base metal used in the manufacture of coins and stainless steel.

Nikkei Dow An index used to track share price movements on the Tokyo Stock Exchange. Similar to the FT Industrial Ordinary Index and the Dow Jones Industrial Average indices, it is based on the share price performance of a basket of large, top-quality, Japanese industrial companies which are considered to be market leaders. See INDEX.

Nil paid shares Special type of share that does not have to be paid for until a specified date, normally used when a company is raising extra cash by a RIGHTS ISSUE. Even though not paid for, they can be traded on the market against their future value.

Noble Generic name for the platinum group of metals. Also name of a platinum coin that is legal tender in the Isle of Man, but which is basically sold to investors, like gold coins, as a 'store of wealth'.

No-claims bonus (discount) Device used by motor insurance companies in particular to discourage claims, especially for small amounts, and to retain business. The policy-holder is offered a discount (bonus) on the premium paid if the policy has been held for a number of years without any claim being made. After a period of years the discount can be a large percentage of the premium payment. The discounts (bonuses) offered vary from policy to policy.

No-load funds Unit trusts which do not make an initial (front-end load) charge. Instead they have higher annual management fees and, usually, special penalties for selling out in the first five years.

Nominal Face value of something, such as coin, stock, or share, which may bear no relation to its actual market price. 'Nominal price' may also be a rough guide to a market price, although no actual trading has taken place at that level.

Nominal accounts Section of a company's ledger account referring to estimated expenditure and revenue.

Nominal assets See ASSETS, FICTITIOUS.

Nominal capital The amount of capital that a company is authorized to issue with a stated face value, although it may issue only part of the permitted total. See AUTHORIZED (SHARE) CAPITAL.

Nominal coupon or interest The rate of interest stated to be payable on a stock at its par (face) value. With government securities (gilts), the actual interest rate is governed by the capital price paid for the stock, together with the nominal interest; for example, £100 worth of Treasury 2·5% bought for £50 would give an interest rate of 5%.

Nominal damages Small sum ordered to be paid to the winner of a court action to indicate that only a minor loss has been suffered and no great harm has been done. In some cases the award of nominal damages is viewed as a loss, since the winner of the case receives little reward and may suffer serious financial loss in having to meet legal costs while receiving little compensation.

Nominal value See PAR VALUE.

Nominal yield See NOMINAL COUPON OR INTEREST.

Nominee Person or organization appointed to act on behalf of a third party or parties. Often used to disguise the identity of someone dealing in shares. Also insurance term for the person on whose life an annuity policy is based.

Nominee company A company specially formed to hold stocks and shares on behalf of a third party, which may be given as a guarantee against a loan.

Non-assented stock Where the holders do not agree to sell their interest in return for other stock but want to receive payment in cash instead.

Non-contributory pensions Schemes where employees do not have to make any payments, with the cost instead being borne by the employer; widely used in the Civil Service, where the government is the employer, and by some companies. The disadvantage is that early leavers may find themselves with no pension or a very much reduced pension which cannot be transferred to a new employer.

Non-cumulative preference share Type of preference share where the dividend does not accumulate if not paid every year.

Non-domiciled Someone who takes up residence in a foreign country. To achieve non-domicile status for tax purposes, a Briton must show the intention to live abroad permanently.

Non-forfeiture period Time given by an insurance company following non-payment of a policy premium to allow the insured to

choose whether to surrender the policy or convert it into a paid-up policy. If the insured dies during this period, the insurance company is liable to pay the assured sum, but can deduct any unpaid premiums.

Non-marketable securities Government stock that cannot be traded on the stock exchange and which forms part of the NATIONAL DEBT, such as savings bonds and certificates.

Non-negotiable instrument Where the right to receive payment cannot be transferred from one party to another, for example cheques that are made out to a named recipient.

Non-participating share A preference share that carries no right to a share in the profits but instead receives a fixed rate of dividend.

Non-qualifying policy Opposite of QUALIFYING POLICY.

Non-profits (endowment) policy An insurance policy where the sum assured is fixed from the start and no extra bonuses (profits) are added. In the case of endowment mortgages, a non-profits policy will merely guarantee to repay the capital sum borrowed to buy the property. This means that there will be no additional lump sum representing profits made from investing the premiums. Has to a large extent been supplemented by the low-cost, with-profits, policy.

Non-resident Persons and organizations regarded by the Inland Revenue as living permanently outside the United Kingdom.

Non-standard Term used by insurance companies to describe products that require specialist cover, like timber-framed houses or cars altered from the original manufacture.

Non-voting shares Type of share whose holder has no right to vote at the company's meeting. These often include owners of preference or A-class ordinary shares.

Nostro account Banking term, based on the Italian for 'our account', used to describe an account held in another country in the local currency.

Notary Public official, usually a solicitor, authorized to witness signatures on legal documents and the swearing of affidavits.

Not in order Words written on a cheque when it is returned unpaid because of a mistake, such as words and figures not agreeing.

Notice accounts Deposit, interest-bearing, bank or building society accounts where withdrawals of money can be made without losing interest only by giving (a specified period of) notice first.

Notice in lieu of distringas Legal device used to stop the wrongful transfer in ownership of shares.

Notional income Unrealized gain, such as a house owner living in his or her property rent-free.

NSSR See NATIONAL SAVINGS STOCK REGISTER.

Numbered account A bank account identified by a number only. Particularly associated with Swiss banks, which use numbered accounts to disguise the identity of the account holder, since the laws of that country give high priority to secrecy and the bank usually cannot be forced to reveal the name of the numbered account holder.

Numismatics Collecting and study of coins.

NYSE See NEW YORK STOCK EXCHANGE.

O

Obligation In financial terms, a commitment to pay a debt or fulfil a contract.

Occupational lease Agreement that allows a tenant to live in, or take possession of, a property for a specified number of years.

Occupational pension Official name for a company, or business organization, pension scheme. To qualify for exemption from tax it has to be approved by the Inland Revenue and the Occupational Pensions Board to ensure it complies with the rules and regulations laid down by the government. To contract out of the State Earnings Related Pension Scheme (SERPS) it must provide at least equal benefits. Most occupational pensions are FINAL SALARY schemes. Under the changes proposed in the 1989 Budget the benefits that can be provided by an approved scheme qualifying for tax exemption relief are limited to a maximum final salary, which in turn restricts the size of pension (two-thirds of final salary) and tax-free lump sums (one and a half times final salary) that can be paid. The 1989 Budget imposed a top final salary for pension scheme purposes of £60,000, meaning a maximum pension of £40,000 and lump sum of £90,000. However, these figures will be adjusted regularly each year in line with inflation. Members joining the schemes after March 1989 will be able to retire with the maximum pension of two-thirds salary any time between the age of 50 and 70, provided that 20 years' service has been completed. Meanwhile another innovation introduced was that employers are now at liberty to provide additional 'top up' benefits without any restrictions through unapproved schemes, which do not qualify for tax relief. The object of the changes was to 'cap' the size of the tax concessions given by pension schemes and limit their use as a 'tax shelter' by the wealthier employees. See PENSIONS.

Octroi Historical term for a local tax on food and household articles brought into an area governed by a local authority.

Offer by tender Method of selling new issues of stocks and shares by inviting bids from interested buyers and basing the allocations on the highest prices bid. See TENDER.

Offer for sale Invitation to buy a new issue of shares or stock. The offer may be at a fixed price or by TENDER, and sometimes a mixture of both with a proportion being often at a flat rate. Often handled by an ISSUING HOUSE, which then becomes the sponsor or UNDERWRITER.

Offer of amends Legal term for an offer to pay compensation for a wrong said to have been done.

Offer price Level at which a share, stock, unit trust or unit-linked assurance policies are available for sale. For new issues this can be either a flat, fixed rate or the highest bids received under a tender offer. In a BID/OFFER SPREAD, the offer is the selling price.

Offer to bid The difference between the price at which something, say a unit trust, was bought and the price at which it can be sold. This is a true reflection of the profit made by investors since it compares the original amount spent with the actual proceeds of sale.

Offer to offer Comparison between the selling price of unit trust over a period of time, measuring how the fund has performed but without taking into account charges. It provides a true comparison of performance, but also overstates the real return achieved since investors pay the offer price when buying, but receive only the lower bid price, after deductions for charges, when selling. See BID/OFFER SPREAD.

Office of Fair Trading (OFT) Government organization set up to administer the Fair Trading Act, protecting the rights of consumers. In particular it investigates any agreements, or company mergers and takeovers, that might restrict competition, and advises the government as to whether they should be referred to the Monopolies Commission for further investigation.

Official list Prepared daily by the Stock Exchange in London to provide a record of all sales and purchases of stocks and shares listed on the exchange and the current prices. It also gives details of dividend dates, rights issues, convertible stock and other information.

Official quotation Price of a stock or share contained in the Stock Exchange daily official list.

Official receiver Government employee in the bankruptcy court who is appointed to conduct, or supervise, the financial affairs of someone unable to pay their debts (a bankrupt) or a company that is being wound up for the same reason. On occasions, particularly when criminal actions or fraud are suspected, the official receiver may submit a report to the Department of Trade and Industry in the case of a company, or to a court when dealing with personal bankruptcies.

Official referee A law court official who reports, and sometimes makes a ruling, on matters requiring a special knowledge that a judge or jury are unlikely to have.

Official rate (of exchange) See EXCHANGE RATE.

Official reserves Stocks of gold and foreign currencies held by governments to help pay international debts as a last resort. The size of these reserves is one indication of a country's financial strength.

Official support Term used to describe action taken by the Bank of England on behalf of the government to buy sterling on the foreign exchange markets, to try and put up its value against other currencies. Alternatively, when the Bank intervenes in the gilts and money markets to keep interest rates up by support buying.

Offshore companies Set up by banks, insurance groups and other financial institutions in countries outside the UK tax system, to provide services specifically for expatriate investors not liable to UK tax. Can also be legally used by UK residents, providing they comply with the relevant tax regulations.

Offshore funds Unit trusts and funds

that are operated in countries not subject to UK tax laws or rules and regulations. They cannot be promoted for sale in the UK unless the host country has rules and regulations for protecting investors approved as being in line with those in the UK and therefore qualifying as one of the DESIGNATED TERRITORIES. Alternatively they can be directly authorized by the Securities and Investment Board, or qualify as a UCITS (Undertaking for Collective Investments in Transferable Securities) scheme that can be sold throughout the European Community. Offshore funds themselves often pay no tax or only the local tax of the host country, but once profits are remitted into the UK they become subject to UK tax legislation and have to be declared to the Inland Revenue. See UMBRELLA FUNDS.

OFT See OFFICE OF FAIR TRADING.

Old age pension Normally refers to the basic government pension, based on the National Insurance contributions paid over the years.

Old Lady of Threadneedle Street
Nickname for the Bank of England dating back to the Napoleonic Wars when a famous cartoon was published portraying the Bank of England, which is housed in Threadneedle Street in the City of London, as an old lady being attacked by politicians who wanted further supplies of gold to fund the war against Napoleon.

Old money Existing capital invested in a company.

Oligopoly When a market is controlled by a small number of interested parties, who are then in a position to manipulate prices.

Ombudsman Shorthand term for the

Parliamentary Commissioner for Administration, who was appointed by the 1967 Act to provide independent arbitration in complaints by the public against unfair treatment by government organizations. Complaints to the Parliamentary Commissioner have to be passed on by Members of Parliament (MPs) only, and his powers are limited by restrictions on what can be investigated. Local authorities have a number of commissioners who handle complaints. In recent years separate ombudsmen have been appointed to provide independent arbitration into complaints against banks, building societies, insurance companies and unit trust groups; they are, however, arrangements set up by the industries themselves and in some cases they cover only organizations that are part of the scheme. Like the Parliamentary Commissioner, the industry ombudsmen can deal only with specific complaints in certain ways and they have limited powers of enforcement. See COMPLAINTS and INVESTMENT REFEREE.

On account Part payment of a sum owing.

On cost Expense that has to be paid, whether or not anything is produced or sold.

On risk The time from which an insurance company will pay claims against the policy even if the paperwork has not been finalized.

Ono (or near offer) Term used by seller when seeking a bid from a prospective buyer close to the sale price quoted.

OPB See OCCUPATIONAL PENSIONS and USEFUL ADDRESSES.

Open cheque A cheque which has not

been crossed and can therefore be cashed over the counter. A crossed cheque can be 'opened' by the payer writing 'pay cash' over the crossing and signing the alteration.

Open credit Arrangement with a bank to make payments up to a specified amount to someone without an account there.

Open-ended Contract or arrangement without fixed limits. An open-ended mortgage, for example, has no fixed date for repayment.

Open-ended fund Where there is no limit, such as a unit trust, on the amount of units that can be issued by the fund. As opposed to an INVESTMENT TRUST which as a company is a 'closed-end fund'.

Opening price The value of a stock, share or futures at the start of the trading day.

Open interest Outstanding purchases or sales in a market, particularly futures, which are due for settlement at some time in the future. The size of the open interest often indicates how active trading conditions are in the market and whether it is oversold or OVERBOUGHT.

Open market option Right introduced in the Finance Act 1978 to transfer an accumulated pension fund from one assurance company to another in order to obtain a higher annuity payment rate when retiring. It is important to check that this option is included with a personal pension plan, so that the best annuity rate can be obtained on retirement. The option has to be exercised before any benefits can be taken out from the fund built up by the original assurance company.

Open outcry System of market trading,

particularly used for futures transactions, where dealers communicate by word of mouth on the 'floor' of an exchange. Verbal contracts to buy or sell at the price shouted out are concluded on the spot; they are later confirmed in writing and displayed on the market screens.

Operating assets Those being used in the active management of a business.

Operating expenses The cost of running a business, excluding the costs of materials and production.

Opportunity cost Measure of the theoretical loss incurred when an asset is put to one use rather than another.

Option An agreement under which the payment of a premium entitles the buyer to buy or sell something at an agreed ('strike' or 'exercise') price by a specified date. If the strike price is reached before the option expires, then the buyer is entitled to demand that the grantor either supplies stock (CALL OPTION) or takes delivery of stock (PUT OPTION). The premium paid to the grantor represents a cash deposit to purchase the right to exercise the option even though it may or may not be taken up later. The premium charged is based on the likelihood of the options being exercised. The longer the time period, the greater the risk for the grantor and the higher the premium. Higher premiums are also charged on options where the level at which they can be exercised is close to the current market value or already IN THE MONEY (when it can be exercised profitably). A 'put' option gives the right to sell and a 'call' the right to buy, whereas a DOUBLE option gives the right either to buy or to sell. Options are used in the futures and stock markets as a means of speculating on a future price movement with only the premium at risk.

Alternatively they can be used to guard against a loss in the market resulting from an unexpected move in the price, thus protecting a profit already made. This is known as 'hedging'. Grantors of options, who sell the right to buy or sell, benefit from receiving the premium in advance, which is pure profit if the option is not taken up. 'Call' options, giving the right to buy, provide protection for the grantors against the loss in value of stock held, since the premium compensates for the fall in price needed before the option is exercised. Protection against a 'put' option being exercised can be obtained by purchasing the stock on the market if the price starts rising to the level where the option might be worth exercising. An extremely dangerous practice is to grant a NAKED OPTION, where there is no stock held to deliver if the 'call' (right to buy) is exercised and no protection is taken against the 'put' (right to sell) being exercised. The losses involved can be considerable if there is a large price movement in the market. See IN-THE-MONEY, OUT-OF-THE-MONEY and TRADED OPTIONS.

Option(al) bond See BOND.

Option mortgage Government scheme to help first-time buyers whereby borrowers have the choice of either receiving tax relief in the normal way on mortgage interest payments, or paying a subsidized, lower interest rate and receiving no tax relief.

Option to purchase Right given to shareholders, or employees, to buy shares in a company at a favourable price. Alternatively, a right given to buy a property at any time before a specific date.

Order and disposition Provision in a case of bankruptcy giving the creditors

(lenders) the right to take and sell goods not owned by the bankrupt.

Order cheque Way of making a cheque more flexible by adding the words 'or order' after the payee's name. For example, a cheque made out to 'John Smith or order' means the bank can either pay the money direct to John Smith or to someone else on his instructions.

Ordinary account Special deposit account offered by National Savings for small investors who want immediate access to their savings. Interest is paid on balances held in the account for a complete calendar month.

Ordinary capital Part of a company's financial backing held by shareholders who have the right to receive a share of the profits (dividends) after the holders of fixed-interest stock and preference shares have been paid. Owners of 'ordinary shares' therefore run the greatest risk, in that they receive nothing for their investment if the company does badly. On the other hand they are likely to receive the greatest reward if the company does well.

Originator Term used by banks to describe the initiator of DIRECT DEBIT payments. They are vetted by the banks to ensure they are reputable since they are in effect issuing instructions for drawing money from the account of the bank's customer.

OTC See OVER THE COUNTER MARKET.

Out-of-the-money option An option whose exercise or strike price is well above or below the current market value, the underlying security. The option is therefore unlikely to be taken up unless the market either rises or falls substantially. See IN-THE-MONEY OPTION and OPTIONS.

Outcry market See OPEN OUTCRY.

Output tax Part of Value Added Tax (VAT) that is added to the invoice price at each stage of production and distribution by the supplier of goods and services. It is passed on by the recipient to the Customs and Excise after the relevant INPUT TAX (payments charged) has been deducted.

Overbought Term used to describe the view that a market has risen too high, as a result of too much buying, and is due for a correction downwards. Opposite of 'oversold', when it is considered that a market has been driven down too far.

Overcapitalized When a company has more issued capital, in the form of loans and shares, than it can use profitably, thereby undermining the dividends available for payment to ordinary shareholders.

Overdraft A temporary loan provided by a bank to its customers. The rate of interest charged depends on whether the overdraft has been previously authorized or is simply the result of the customer drawing out more money than the amount deposited in the account. Banks tend to penalize unauthorized overdrafts by charging very high rates of interest and also imposing charges on any transactions. If the bank considers the overdraft to be excessive to the customer's resources, it will start to refuse to make payments or insist that a proper arrangement for a longer-term loan, with some kind of security, be negotiated. The rate of interest charged on an authorized overdraft, arranged beforehand with the bank, depends on the size of the loan and the bank's view of the risk of its not being

repaid. The higher the risk, the higher the interest rate. A permanent overdraft facility or arrangement can be made, so that the customer is entitled to borrow up to a certain amount without prior consultation but may not actually need to do so.

Overdraw Take out more money than is deposited in an account.

Overnight money A loan made by a bank to enable a deal to take place, on condition that it is repaid the following day. Also the interest earned by a bank in putting money on deposit with the MONEY MARKET, for repayment the next day.

Overriding commission Fees paid to brokers who find companies willing to underwrite (guarantee) a new issue of shares or stock.

Oversold See OVERBOUGHT.

Oversubscribed When the applications for an issue of stock or shares exceed the amount available.

Over the counter market (OTC) Shares in companies not quoted on a stock exchange that are nevertheless offered for sale to investors by brokers and dealers who 'make a market' (buy and sell) in them or arrange matched bargains (putting together buyers and sellers of the same stock). Often used by companies who may be too small or not be able to qualify for listing on a stock exchange. The risks of investing in unregulated markets, where the dealers are in control and may have a vested interest, are considerable. But the rewards of buying shares in expanding companies can also be great, and it is a highly popular form of investment in the United States. In London as a way of providing more order and regulation to dealings in this type of shares, the stock exchange started a THIRD MARKET in 1987 for companies not willing, or able, to join the main exchange or the Unlisted Securities Market (USM).

Overtrading When investors become involved in dealings beyond their resources. Alternatively, when a company tries to do more business than its working capital will allow.

P

Package insurance Policy which covers a number of different risks. See BLANKET INSURANCE.

Paid-up capital The total amount of stock and shares, issued by a company, that has actually been paid for, not including amounts owed.

Paid-up policies Endowment and some life assurance policies where the contributor has stopped paying premiums before the maturity date of the policy has been reached. Provided premiums have been paid for a certain specified period, the policy can be converted (the terms are changed) so that the beneficiary still retains an interest and receives benefits when the maturity date is reached. The eventual return is based on the premiums paid and the profits earned by the insurance company with the sum invested. If a policy is converted in this way early on, the sum left to accumulate is reduced by all the charges made by the insurance company in setting the policy up, so in some cases the paid-up value is very small.

Paper credit Promises to pay money at some future date, which can therefore be used as security for an immediate loan.

Paper money Notes with no value in themselves, except for the face value printed on them with a promise to pay the bearer a specified sum. Popular description of money with no solid backing, whose value can be undermined by inflation or currency value changes.

Paper profit Increases in the value of unrealized investments or unsold assets. A house, for example, may appreciate in value but this is only a paper profit for the owner until it is actually sold. In times of inflation, or when changes are made in the value of currencies, a company may report a rise in profits on paper in spite of earning less in real terms.

Parent company Owner of subsidiary companies in which it has at least a controlling interest.

Pari passu Term used when a new issue of stocks or shares is offered for sale with the same rights and status as the existing capital.

Part exchange Method of paying for something by providing only part of the purchase price in money, while the remainder is made up with something of sufficient value to reach the equivalent of the full cost. Particularly used when buying new goods and receiving a discount on surrendering the old goods which are being replaced.

Partial loss In insurance policies, refers to payments on claims covering only the cost of repairs, not the full replacement.

Partial tender See TENDER FOR SHARES.

Participating (or profit-sharing) bond See BOND.

Participating insurance See MUTUAL INSURANCE.

Participating preferred share or stock Type of share or stock where the owner receives not only dividends or interest, but also a proportion of any profits made, usually above a specified amount.

Partly paid Shares whose full nominal value has not been paid and for which there are further 'calls' to be paid. Method used in large issue of shares (like the privatization issues) where investors are encouraged to participate by being able to spread payment over a period of time rather than having to find the whole sum immediately. The share price on the stock exchange is based on the partly paid value, until the 'calls' for further instalments have been completed.

Partnership Association of two or more people in carrying on a business. The partners do not draw salaries or get paid interest on any capital invested. Instead they each receive an agreed share of the profits.

Par (or nominal) value Face value of a share or stock, as opposed to its market value. Bonds and fixed-interest securities are redeemed at their par value – the original figure at which they were issued. If they can be bought for a cheaper price, they are described as being below par in value. Above par is when something is valued above its issued price.

Passive bond See BOND.

Patent Exclusive right, granted by approval of the government Patent Office, to be the sole person to make and sell, or to authorize others to make and sell, a newly invented machine or process. The life of a patent is set at 16 years, but in certain cases this can be extended by a further 5–10 years.

Patrimony Wealth that has been passed by inheritance through the male line of a family: from father to son to grandson, and so on.

Pawn Deposit an article of personal property as security against a loan, for repayment within six months, and with seven days' grace. If the loan is not repaid within six months, the pawnee (a pawnbroker or moneylender) has the right to sell the goods pawned at a public auction and retain enough of the proceeds to cover the loan and any interest due. Any balance must be returned to the pawnor (the borrower). The goods pawned are redeemable up until the time they have actually been sold. However, pledges valued at £2 or less can be retained by the pawnbroker at the end of six months and seven days. For loans over £5, a special pawn ticket must be given and signed, with a duplicate signed by the borrower; and, if lost, tickets may be renewed by a magistrate. Loans under £50 are regulated by the Consumer Credit Act provisions, but for over that amount common law rules apply.

Pay as you earn (PAYE) The most common method of collecting income tax from full-time employees. The employer, using the individual tax code supplied for each employee by the Inland Revenue, automatically deducts income tax direct from the salary payment and remits it to the government. Special tables are used to calculate an average amount to be deducted from each salary payment made throughout the financial year, from 6 April to the following 5 April. When an employee leaves, the employer has to provide a form showing the gross pay to date in the current financial year and the amount of tax deducted.

Pay as you earn code The figure calculated by the Inland Revenue which governs the amount of tax deducted from an individual employee's salary under the PAYE system. The code is based on the various tax relief allowances which the individual is eligible to receive.

Pay-back period Time over which the return (yield) from an investment adds up to the original outlay. This is an important measure to decide whether an investment is worthwhile or not.

Pay cash Words written on a crossed cheque by the payer, instructing the bank not to insist on the cheque being paid into a bank account.

PAYE See PAY AS YOU EARN.

Payee The person or organization whose name appears on a cheque, or bill of exchange, as recipient of the payment to be made.

Payment for honour When a person, other than the borrower, decides to pay a debt to protect the honour of the borrower. Also known as 'payment supra protest' for bills of exchange that have been paid in this way.

Payment in kind When goods or services are supplied, instead of money, to pay a loan or bill.

Pay-roll List of the number of employees in an organization and the amounts they are paid.

Payroll giving See GIVE AS YOU EARN.

P/E See PRICE-EARNINGS RATIO.

Peculation Dishonest appropriation of money or goods, particularly from public organizations, by a person to whom they have been entrusted. See EMBEZZLEMENT.

Pecuniary Equivalent to 'money' or 'a monetary interest'; for example, pecuniary gain or reward means to receive money, while an investment is a pecuniary interest.

Penalty Punishment, normally a payment of money, for breaking the law or for failing to repay a loan or honour a contract.

Penalty bond See BOND.

Penalty clause Provision for a sum of money to be paid, or rights forfeited, if a contract is not honoured.

Penny One of the oldest British coins. It was originally made of pure silver to the weight of 24 grains, the measure used to pay dues to feudal landlords, which became the pennyweight in the TROY WEIGHT scale. £1 sterling was equal to 240 pennies, which became the same number used in the imperial monetary system. Later made of bronze instead of silver as the coinage became debased from gold and silver. At one stage the penny had a cross on the reverse and was divided into four parts, from which the farthing and halfpenny were derived.

Prior to decimalization, the penny was denoted by the symbol *d*, derived from 'denarius', the lowest-value Roman coin. To mark its change of value, from 1/240th to 1/100th of the decimalized pound, its symbol was changed to p, and it was renamed the 'new penny', although the 'new' has subsequently been dropped and it is now popularly known as a 'pee'.

Penny wise Be careful with money,

inclined to save rather than spend. But the old saying, 'Penny wise, pound foolish', meant that by paying too much attention to small details, the larger and more important implications could be missed.

Pennyworth Originally meant as much as could be bought for a penny. Nowadays means receiving value for money.

Pension Payment, usually in regular instalments like an ANNUITY, made to someone having reached retirement age (or before in certain circumstances, such as to a widow or widower), to a disabled person or to reward service with the government or armed forces. The Social Security Act 1986 brought a radical change in the provision of retirement pensions once the legislation started to be implemented in 1988. One of the Conservative Government's main objectives in the legislation was to encourage employees to leave (contract out of) the State Earnings Related Pensions Scheme (SERPS), introduced in 1978 by a Labour Government. The Conservative Government disliked the SERPS scheme in principle, but it was also calculated by the government actuary that, if the scheme was left unchanged, it would face a crisis by the year 2020 and the level of contributions required to fund the pledged pension payments would have to be raised to an unacceptably high level. This was due to a combination of reasons. For a start, older (retired) employees were tending to live longer than previously forecast, meaning more payments to be made. Additionally, the post-Second World War 'baby boom' that had boosted the population came to an end in the 1960s; this meant there would be an influx of employees reaching retirement age after 2020, while the contributions would simultaneously be falling as a result of the declining labour force and fewer younger

workers. The government's original proposal was to scrap the SERPS scheme altogether; but this drew such a storm of protest, even from the government's own supporters, that a compromise was evolved.

Under the new system the SERPS benefits have been sharply reduced. The pension payments are now based on an average of lifetime earnings, including years of low or nil salaries, and restricted to a maximum of 20% of 'band earnings' – the salary range on which National Insurance contributions are calculated between a minimum and maximum level. Furthermore the pension paid to a surviving spouse is halved instead of being maintained at the full rate as previously. Under the old system, the pension payments were based on an average of the 20 years of highest salary up to a maximum of 25% of band earnings.

In spite of the reduction in benefits, it is still worthwile for older people (45+ years for men and 40+ for women) to stay in SERPS, since the level of contributions required exceeds the benefits received when compared with other pension alternatives on the market. But for younger people it is more economical to contract out and possibly come back in at a later date.

As an additional encouragement to leave the scheme, the government provided a special incentive payment. Until April 1993 anyone contracting out of SERPs will be able to claim a rebate of 2% of National Insurance contributions, over and above the normal rebate of contributions given when leaving the scheme. These two rebates can be used by themselves to provide the funding for an APPROPRIATE PERSONAL PENSION. Alternatively, the rebates can be included as part of the larger payments required to fund a PERSONAL PENSION or a company pension scheme that has not already contracted out.

This links up with the other main objective of the 1986 Social Security Act, which was to 'liberalize' pensions, thus encouraging more companies to provide schemes, without facing huge costs, and enabling employees to change jobs more easily without losing built-up pension contributions. Under the old regime, most companies had tended to use FINAL SALARY PENSION SCHEMES, where the full benefit of receiving a guaranteed pension is gained only by employees staying in the scheme until, or close to, the specified retirement age. 'Early leavers' are heavily penalized: they cannot draw any pension payments until retirement age, so their contributions are 'frozen' until that date. From January 1985 the interest on 'frozen' contributions is supposed to keep pace with inflation, as measured by the Retail Price Index, but only up to a maximum of 5% annually. The real problem is that the 'frozen' pension is based only on the employee's salary and level of contributions, up to the time of leaving the scheme – so by the time retirement age is reached, the payments due are often pitifully small. In order to provide a guaranteed pension – the great advantage of final salary schemes – most companies made membership of the scheme compulsory for all employees, so as to provide a sufficiently large 'pool' of contributions used primarily to benefit those who stayed until retirement age. Under the new legislation, companies can no longer make pension scheme membership compulsory as a condition of employment. To avoid getting locked into a final salary scheme, and facing the prospect of severe loss of contributions by leaving early, employees can instead take out an individual personal (portable) pension, maybe even persuading the employer also to make some

contributions. Alternatively, companies can provide MONEY PURCHASE SCHEMES, where the benefits are based on the return obtained from investing the contributions and there is no liability if the scheme keeps financial reserves to ensure it is able to pay a guaranteed amount. In addition to making contributions, the company can offer other benefits, like group insurance, at cheaper rates, and pensions for spouses and dependants which usually cost extra with a private personal pension. With benefits based on contributions made, rather than the number of years spent in a 'collective' pool, it is much easier to assess the transfer value of a money purchase scheme so that employees can leave and take their pension contributions with them.

It is also easier to offer a choice of pensions. Some (older) employees may prefer the 'security' given by deposit-based schemes, run by banks and larger building societies, where the contributions are put into an interest-bearing account and, together with the tax-free income earned, are used to buy an annuity at retirement date. Alternatively, to achieve growth in the value of the capital as well, in order to stay in line with inflation, the contributions can go to a managed tax-exempt investment pension fund that can be unit-linked (invested in SUB-FUNDS) to obtain a wider spread of investments.

To be approved by the Inland Revenue and thus obtain the tax concessions, company pension schemes have to comply with certain rules and regulations, including a specified 'normal' retirement age. Further radical changes made in the 1989 Budget, however, made the situation even more confusing. To put a 'cap' on the extent to which pension funds can be used as a 'tax shelter' it was decided to lower the maximum benefits that could be paid from approved schemes that qualified for tax exemption. In the case of occupational (company) schemes this has been done by simply lowering the pensionable final salary. However, employers are entitled to provide 'top up' benefits, without restriction, through unapproved schemes that do not qualify for tax relief. The age limit at which the maximum tax-exempt pension can be provided was lowered and at the same time many of the restrictions surrounding Additional Voluntary Contributions were abolished, making it easier for employees both to retire early or to increase their company pension benefits to the maximum permitted level. If the combination of the company scheme and AVC contributions produce excess funds, above the permitted level, the excess amount will be returned to the employee, subject to a special tax charge to compensate for the tax relief already given.

The size of contributions, based on a percentage of earnings, that can be made to a personal pension was increased, but these are subject to similar restrictions on the maximum benefits that can be paid out of approved, tax-exempt, schemes. See ADDITIONAL VOLUNTARY CONTRIBUTIONS, MONEY PURCHASE SCHEMES, PENSION MORTGAGES and PERSONAL PENSIONS.

Pensionable service Number of years an employee has been in a pension scheme, which is taken into account when calculating the pension due.

Pension fund Money or assets set aside to provide pension payments. The funds, normally managed by either assurance companies or investment houses, have to make allowance for long-term objectives, with guaranteed payments to be funded many years into the future. Therefore they have to adopt a cautious investment strategy to ensure that enough income is generated for them to meet their commitments. To achieve this kind of safety, they tend to spread the risk by investing in a wide range of alternatives, from fixed-interest securities like government stocks (GILTS) to property and shares. This mixture, made in the interests of safety over the long term, often means that pension funds, in spite of benefiting from tax-free concessions, achieve lower returns than investment funds catering for relatively short-term periods, like unit trusts.

Pension mortgage Arrangement linking the repayment of a mortgage with the proceeds of a pension plan. The borrower takes out a loan to help buy a property, for repayment at the end of a specified period, say 25 years, and meanwhile agrees to pay interest on the full amount of the loan until it is repaid – an interest-only mortgage. At the same time the borrower agrees to make the capital repayment of the loan, when due, from the proceeds of a pension policy, either existing or a new plan taken out for the purpose. It is most tax efficient, since the borrower receives double tax relief: the relief available on the mortgage interest payments, and the tax relief available from investing in pension schemes. So, in effect, tax relief is received both on the interest payments and on the capital repayment of the mortgage. The disadvantage of this arrangement is that it is rather inflexible: money invested in the pension plan cannot be withdrawn until the policy-holder reaches retirement age; for a younger person, this means locking money away for a long period.

At the same time there are Inland Revenue restrictions on the size (reduced in the 1989 Budget) of the lump-sum payment (needed to repay the mortgage) that can be taken out of a pension scheme.

It is also a somewhat artificial
arrangement in that by law the proceeds
of a pension cannot be assigned, like an
endowment policy, for some specific
purpose such as repaying a loan. PEP
(Personal Equity Plan) mortgages cannot
be assigned either. However, pension
mortgages offer tax relief on the way in
and, therefore, provide a valuable tax
'shelter' while saving up to pay off the
loan. In reality, the lender is merely
trying to ensure that the borrower has
sufficient funds to repay the mortgage
when due. More practically, the lender
also often benefits from the commission
paid on selling a pension policy, which
usually also includes life assurance
cover.

Until 1988, pension mortgages were
available only to the self-employed with
personal pensions; but changes in the
pensions system from 1988 now make
them available to a much wider section.
There are several different varieties of
pension mortgages, dependent on the
pension policy taken out which can be
unit-linked by investing in the units of
sub-funds, and therefore not provide a
guaranteed sum, since the return is
dependent on the performance of the
funds and the market they are investing in.
If that performance is poor and not likely
to achieve the capital sum required to
repay the mortgage, the holder may have
to increase premiums or extend the
mortgage. To overcome the inflexible
disadvantage of pension schemes
mentioned above, very often the total
premiums paid are divided up to cover
several different policies, so that (if
required) one or more of them can be
converted into PAID-UP POLICIES by
discontinuing payments. Converting
policies in this way can, however, be
expensive, since all the charges are
deducted from the early premium
payments.

Pension plans or schemes National
Insurance contributions provide all
employees with a basic state pension. The
STATE EARNINGS RELATED PENSION
SCHEME (SERPS) is a voluntary addition
that can be contracted out of, provided
that it is replaced with a scheme giving at
least equal benefits – not a difficult task.
There are then several additional
alternatives. One is a
NON-CONTRIBUTORY PENSION scheme,
where the employer pays all the
contributions; or there are the
contributory schemes under which
contributions are made by both the
employer and the employee, with the
employer normally providing a bigger
proportion. These contributory schemes
may be divided into two main alternatives:
FINAL SALARY and MONEY PURCHASE.

With the final salary version, the
employee's pension is based on the
number of years in the scheme, providing
a guaranteed percentage of the salary
being earned by the employee on
retirement or when leaving the scheme.
The attraction is that the employee
receives a guaranteed pension. The
disadvantage is that the main benefits
accumulate during the last few years
before retirement; if an employee leaves
the scheme before retirement, the
pension is frozen until the retirement date
is reached and may be worth very little by
that time, taking into account inflation and
the steady rise in salaries in the interim.
At the same time, final salary scheme
payments are difficult to transfer
effectively, since they are tailored to meet
the needs of a particular group of
employees and often may not fit in well
with another scheme with a different
mixture of employees and different basic
objectives. The transfer value of a final
salary scheme is also likely to be low for
someone replacing it with a personal
pension, since the guaranteed pension is

based on contributions from a group over a period of years being used to provide benefits to individuals in turn.

With the money purchase version, the employee basically receives as a pension the value of the contributions made, and the money earned from investing them, less charges. There is no guaranteed sum, so the pension is dependent not only on the amount of contributions made but also on the investment return achieved; a poor investment performance directly affects the pension paid, so do the annuity rates available at the time of retirement, since the sum accumulated in the scheme is used, after deducting any lump-sum payment required, to buy an annuity and provide regular pension payments in that way. The main advantage of a money purchase scheme is that it is much easier to transfer, since it is based on individual contributions rather than depending on a group of employees – although, as with other company schemes, a proportion of the contributions is used to provide benefits such as assurance protection against early death and pensions for dependants.

The money purchase system is the basis used for all PERSONAL PENSIONS, in which the employee usually makes the sole contributions. These are obviously the most flexible, easily transferable and adaptable to changing needs by raising or lowering premiums, plus individual insurance cover. However, they do not normally have the benefit of employer contributions, so the amount of money going into the pension fund is proportionately smaller.

Employees can also boost their pension by Additional Voluntary Contributions (AVCs) schemes that are either taken with the company scheme or with another pension provider, known as Free Standing Additional Voluntary Contributions (FSAVCs).

PEP See PERSONAL EQUITY PLANS.

Peppercorn rent Traditional term for a token (normally very small) rent, paid primarily to establish that the property is leasehold and owned by someone other than the occupant or leaseholder. The term goes back to the Middle Ages when pepper was quite a valuable spice, and dried berries of the pepper plant were used to pay rents. As supplies of pepper became more plentiful and its value dropped, the peppercorn rent was retained for cases in which owners of property only want to safeguard their legal rights and are not looking for a source of income.

Per capita income The average amount received by individuals, measured by dividing the total income by the number of heads (*per capita* in Latin).

Per diem payments Daily ('by the day' in Latin) payments.

Performance bond See BOND.

Performing rights Held by the owner of the copyright in a literary work, musical or play, to control or license performances to the public.

Perk (short for perquisite) Extra incentive given to employees, such as company car or expense allowance. Alternatively, offered to shareholders as an inducement to buy stock in a company offering discounts on goods or services it provides. See BENEFIT IN KIND.

Permanent assets See ASSETS, CAPITAL.

Permanent health insurance (PHI) Policies or plans offered to provide protection against loss of income as a result of a prolonged sickness or disability. It can be taken out by individuals or by organizations on behalf of their employees, possibly linked with a company pension scheme. Payments start after a deferred period, as defined in the policy, and are based on the size of the insured's salary. They are intended to cover the shortfall between the insured's normal salary and state payments under the National Insurance scheme, so they are limited to 75% of the normal salary. However, provision is usually made for contributions to a pension scheme to be maintained as well. Benefits, which may increase the longer the illness lasts, can be tax free for the self-employed for a period, but payments from a group PHI policy are taxable in the normal way.

PHI is not the same as insuring against the cost of private medicine bills or against sickness or accidents. See UNIVERSAL (LIFE) PLANS.

Perpetual annuity A payment, in instalments, made for a period of time that has no fixed end, such as the interest on an undated (irredeemable) bond or government security.

Perpetual bond See BOND, ANNUITY.

Perpetual debenture See DEBENTURE, IRREDEEMABLE.

Perpetuity Legal term for period of time that has no limit. Payment in perpetuity means, therefore, one lasting for ever.

Personal accident policy Insurance to provide a lump sum or regular payments if the insured is accidentally killed or injured. The size of the payment depends on the premium paid, the nature of the injury sustained and the profession of the insured. Some policies include insurance against sickness of all kinds or of specific kinds. See MEDICAL EXPENSES POLICY.

Personal allowance The amount someone is allowed to earn before becoming liable to income tax. The amount varies according to the status of the individual, whether married or single, at the moment but will be the same for men and women when independent taxation is introduced from April 1990. The size of allowances are constantly adjusted by the Chancellor of the Exchequer, normally in the annual Budget, to provide higher or lower relief against paying tax. It is adjusted in line with the rate of inflation if the Chancellor wishes merely to maintain the same real rate before tax becomes payable. See AGE ALLOWANCE.

Personal assets See ASSETS.

Personal cheque One drawn by a private person, as opposed to a company or organization. A personalized cheque is one where the bank has put the name and number of the account on the cheque before issuing it to the customer.

Personal equity plans (PEPs)
Government scheme, originally announced in the 1986 Budget and introduced in 1987, aimed at encouraging wider share ownership. It allows taxpayers to invest, up to a maximum amount each fiscal year, in the UK stock market and draw the benefits out free of either income or capital gains tax. PEPs are based on the French Loi Monory scheme, but that gave tax relief on the money going in to be invested in shares, while PEPs only give exemption from tax when profits and earnings are paid out. So PEPs tend, therefore, to have more appeal to the high-rate taxpayer rather than encouraging smaller investors (who may well not be liable to pay capital gains tax in any case) to venture into the stock market. Indeed the original scheme, as envisaged in 1986, failed to achieve much support since it was considered too complicated, with too

many rules and restrictions that put up the costs and made it difficult to sell.

However, PEPs received a huge boost in the 1989 Budget. The maximum amount that could be invested was raised substantially. So was the percentage (now half) of the total that could be put into unit or investment trusts. At the same time many of the restrictions were abolished, including the previous provision that the funds had to be invested for a minimum of a calendar year and a day to qualify for the tax concessions. Under the new regime, the only restriction is on the amount that can be invested in any fiscal year, from 6 April to 5 April.

Another innovation, introduced with privatization issues in mind, was to allow new issues of shares to be transferred into a PEP at the issue price value, providing this is done within 30 days and does not breach the maximum investment limit.

It is also now possible to switch all the funds into cash, if the prospects for the stock market look bad, but to avoid this being used as a tax-free deposit account, composite rate tax (the tax automatically deducted from interest on bank and building society deposit accounts) has to be paid on the interest.

These changes have made PEPs considerably more attractive both for buyers and sellers. The increase in the amount that can be invested, and removal of most of the restrictions, has brought charges down. So it makes economic sense for investors to give first priority to a PEP when buying unit trusts, investment trusts or shares. The only remaining major restriction is that all the shares bought must be UK market stocks, and the unit trusts and investment trusts eligible for PEPs must have at least 75% of their holdings in UK stocks. Alternatively a much smaller amount can be put into investment and unit trusts investing in non-UK shares but this still

means by far the majority of holdings are confined to the UK market only. So there is an element of inflexibility, and high risk, on being confined to invest principally in only one market. Nevertheless PEP funds have a considerable advantage from the tax-free concessions that should enable them to perform better, especially over the longer term, than funds paying tax, as well as benefiting investors.

PEP funds also provide an alternative vehicle for repaying mortgages. They are much more flexible than endowment mortgages in that there is no restriction on withdrawing money at any time. So any excess profits can be taken out to reduce the mortgage loan if wanted, or a surplus tax-free fund built up that can be used at any time.

Personal identification number (PIN) Multiple-figure number given to holders of plastic cards to identify themselves when using the card in automated cash machines or paying bills via EFTPOS or with a debit card. Issuers of plastic cards advise holders to keep the PIN number separate from the card itself for security reasons.

Personal loan Term used by banks to describe lending to individual customers for the purpose of private expenditure, such as buying, say, household goods or a car for private use. The loans are negotiated for repayment over a specified period at an agreed rate of interest. If security can be provided, it is often cheaper to negotiate an OVERDRAFT at a lower rate of interest, if possible.

Personal pensions Schemes which allow individuals to make their own pension arrangements and normally be responsible for all the contributions. Prior to 1988, personal pensions were confined mainly to the self-employed, but the 1986

Social Security Act allowed – indeed encouraged – personal pensions to be taken out as a replacement or addition to the STATE EARNINGS RELATED PENSIONS SCHEME (SERPS) or company/occupational plans. Under the new legislation, personal pensions can be supplied by banks, larger building societies, and unit trust groups, as well as by insurance companies, provided that the scheme is approved as providing benefits at least equal to SERPS. The advantage of personal pensions is that they are more flexible, can be tailored to individual requirements and may easily be transferred on a change of employment with no loss of benefit, which is why they are commonly described as 'portable pensions'. They also allow pension payments to start at an earlier retirement age than state or company schemes. The disadvantages are they are all MONEY PURCHASE SCHEMES, with no guaranteed pension on retirement, and therefore vulnerable to poor investment performance or unfavourable annuity rates at the time of retirement. Normally, they do not include contributions from employers, although these might be given as an extra benefit by some companies. In addition, they may not include pensions for spouses or dependants or automatic life assurance benefits, which can be obtained much more cheaply by a group scheme, especially for individuals with a poor health record. An APPROPRIATE PERSONAL PENSION basically meets the requirements needed to leave (contract out of) SERPS and take advantage of the special incentive, available until 1993, offered by the government in the form of a 2% rebate of National Insurance contributions. The 1989 Budget included proposals to allow increased contributions to be made into personal pensions from the age of 35 upwards, and also provisions for scheme members to manage their own investments. But the same 'ceiling' on the maximum amount that can be paid, with the tax exempt concessions, applied to occupational or company schemes also applies to personal pensions. See FINAL SALARY and MONEY PURCHASE SCHEMES and PENSION.

Personal relief The amount an individual can earn free of tax. See PERSONAL ALLOWANCE.

Personal representative Someone appointed, either as executor or administrator, to take over the financial affairs of a deceased person. If the deceased has made a Will, the personal representative will be one of the executors named. If no Will has been made, the personal representative is the administrator appointed by a court to deal with the estate of the deceased.

PET See POTENTIALLY EXEMPT TRANSFERS; PROPERTY ENTERPRISE TRUSTS.

PETA See PURE ENDOWMENT TERM ASSURANCE.

Petrodollars Name given to the large sums of money, accumulated by the oil-exporting countries after the oil-price explosion in 1973, which could not be spent immediately and were therefore deposited in US-dollar-based accounts.

Petty cash Money kept in hand especially to pay small bills on the spot or to reimburse expenses incurred or likely to be incurred.

PHI See PERMANENT HEALTH INSURANCE.

Physical stocktaking Check on the amount of stock held at a specific time by counting and measuring rather than by relying on calculations from the records of sales and purchases.

Piece-work Way of relating employee's wages or salary directly to the number of units produced in a particular period. It is an alternative to wages based on the length of time worked, although the two methods are often combined to provide a productivity bonus.

PIN See PERSONAL IDENTIFICATION NUMBER.

Pink book Annual government publication on the UK balance of payments during the previous year.

Pink (preferential) form Special application form for employees to use when wishing to buy shares in a subsidiary or new company owned by their employers. Under stock market regulations, a company is allowed to set aside for employees up to 10% of shares in a new company issue.

Pin money Traditional term for small allowance given by a husband to his wife or daughter to spend on dress or dressmaking materials. Alternatively, refers to money saved by a woman from a housekeeping allowance, marriage settlement or from casual employment earnings.

Pit Name given to trading areas or boxes on a market, particularly the futures exchanges in Chicago and New York.

Placing Method of issuing shares or stocks, normally in fairly small quantities, by persuading private or institutional investors to buy them at a fixed price, rather than offering them for general sale

to the public. Used either when a private company wants to spread its shares among a wider spread of holders, thereby converting to a public company, or when a block of shares in a company is for sale and its disposal on the open market might undermine the price.

Platinum card Plastic charge card that is one step above a gold card, in that it offers greater benefits, but its holder has to be more wealthy. As a precious metal, platinum is normally more expensive than gold – although this is not always the case – and is considered by many investors, especially in Japan, as an alternative 'store of wealth' to gold or silver. It is an industrial metal but has similar uses to those of gold in jewellery, coins and special investment bars or ingots. See NOBLE.

PLC See PUBLIC LIMITED COMPANY.

Pledge Article delivered by a borrower as security against a loan. See PAWN.

Pluvius insurance Policy against loss of income or revenue caused by rain, storm or other bad weather conditions.

Poison pill Tactic used by a company to try and resist an unwanted takeover bid. The idea is to make the target company less attractive to the predator by giving rights committing the company to sell stock at a reduced price as soon as the unfriendly bidder has acquired a certain percentage of the total stock.

Polarization Term used under the Financial Services Act to describe the difference between agents selling financial products from specified, or 'tied', sources and independent agents offering a range of products from a variety of sources. Tied agents have to make it clear that they are representing the interests of one particular company.

Policy-holders' protection act
Passed in 1974, the Act guarantees that in the event of a UK life assurance company collapsing financially, the policy-holders will be assured of receiving no less than 90% of the value of their policies. They are reimbursed by a reserve fund made up from levies on all UK life companies.

Poll tax Alternative name for the Community charge, being introduced by the government to replace local authority rates. It is capitation (per head) tax based on a register, or poll, of names.

Pooled investments See INVESTMENT CLUB.

Portable pensions Pension plans which can be transferred when the beneficiary changes employment. All PERSONAL PENSIONS are portable, and so are some occupational schemes within sectors of industry or government.

Portfolio Entire collection of investments held by an individual or an organization, such as a unit trust, pension fund or insurance company. The purpose of a balanced portfolio is to have a mixture of different investments, earning income or gaining in capital value, to diversify risk and spread opportunities for profit.

Postcheques Issued by post offices and backed with a postcheque card, they can be used to withdraw cash in local currency from offices in many different countries.

Post-dated Cheques or other promises of payment, which cannot be cashed until a specified date in the future. Normally issued when the borrower does not have

sufficient funds available to meet an immediate payment.

Post obit. bond See BOND.

Post Office stock register See NATIONAL SAVINGS STOCK REGISTER.

Potentially exempt transfers (PET)
A lifetime gift which, under the Inheritance Tax regulations, becomes free of tax if the giver lives for seven years after the date of the gift; so such gifts made to individuals or to trusts are potentially exempt for tax purposes. If the giver dies within the seven-year period, a sliding scale of tax is charged, with the rate declining in accordance with the number of years since the gift was made. The reduction from the full rate starts after three years, going down to zero after seven years. See INHERITANCE TAX.

Pound Derived from the Latin 'pondo', the pound was originally a measure of weight, which was also used to denominate 240 silver pennies, equalling one Troy pound, which became known as the pound sterling. It was also equivalent to twenty shillings. Several other names, including 'broad', 'laurel' and 'unite', were used until 1816, when the 20 shilling gold sovereign became the basic currency. When a rise in the value of gold made the sovereign coin worth more than 20 shillings, the Treasury in 1914 issued one pound notes, which took over as the basic currency in Britain. In 1982 the pound note was replaced by a coin, but larger denominations of pound notes (starting with the five pound note) continue to be issued.

Poundage Unofficial name for tax or commission based on the pound weight or value, including postal and money orders.

Pound cost averaging Term used to describe the effect of saving or investing by regular instalments. It means that, over a period of time, the fixed amounts paid will buy more or less, depending on the fluctuating value of the asset being bought; and this will result in an average purchase price paid being less than the arithmetical average of the market prices over the period. Particularly applicable to investment trust or unit trust savings schemes.

Pound foolish Cliché used to describe practice of neglecting to take care of large sums of money as a result of too great attention to small transactions. See PENNY WISE.

Poverty trap Situation occurring when a rise in wages will result in a worker either losing state welfare benefits or paying more tax, thus ending worse off in real terms.

Power of attorney Legal document, signed and sealed, authorizing someone to perform specific or general acts on behalf of another person or organization. See ENDURING POWER OF ATTORNEY.

Power of sale Authority held by one person to sell property owned by another person who owes an outstanding debt.

Precept Order directing the payment of money.

Pre-emption Prior right to purchase, given to a person or organization.

Preference capital Part of a company's capital issued in the form of preference shares. Holders have a right to a fixed rate of dividend out of net profits before any dividend is paid on ordinary or deferred shares. There are several different classes

of preference capital, including CUMULATIVE, NON-CUMULATIVE, PARTICIPATING and REDEEMABLE PREFERENCE SHARES.

Preference dividend Dividend payable on preference shares or stock.

Preferential duty An import duty at a specially low rate on goods from a favoured country or source of supply.

Preferential payments Payments which receive priority in distributing the estate of a bankrupt or of a company which has gone into liquidation.

Preferred (preference) stock Part of a company's share capital, its holders rank second, after LOAN STOCK holders, in entitlement to a fixed rate of dividend before any payments to ordinary shareholders, and priority after creditors to any distribution of assets if the company goes into liquidation. The reduced risk and fixed dividend enjoyed by preferential shareholders are offset by their not benefiting as much as ordinary shareholders if the company does well.

Premium A sum paid in addition to the market or face value of an asset. Alternatively, used to describe the payments made to insurance and pension policies; or an advance payment, especially in leasing or renting property.

Premium (savings) Bonds Form of investment, with no guarantee of any return, offered by the state-owned National Savings to appeal to those wishing to take a gamble without risk of losing the original stake. After a bond has been held for three months after purchase, it is entered into the weekly and monthly draws for prize money, with the winning numbers being selected by a computer nicknamed ERNIE (Electronic Random Number Indicator Equipment). The prize money, which is paid completely tax free, is divided up among a certain number of bonds, grouped together for the draw, to provide a specified overall rate of interest which then all goes to the winning numbers at the expense of those unsuccessful in the draws, who get nothing. The overall interest rate, or prize money, is varied in accordance with the general trend in normal interest rates. The bonds can be bought in post offices or banks by anyone over 16 years old and on behalf of under-16-year-olds by parents, guardians or grandparents. They can be encashed at any time for the original sum paid. The only loss suffered is the depreciation in the value of money, due to inflation, while the bond is being held earning nothing. The holder of the bond is also losing the potential interest that could be earned from a normal investment; but this is a fairly unimportant factor with small holdings of Premium Bonds, which have the chance – albeit remote – of earning a great deal more if lucky in the prize draw. Clubs and organizations with small surpluses of cash find Premium Bonds an attractive alternative investment with the possibility of a major addition to funds being received tax free for a relatively small outlay.

Prepayments Payments in advance.

Preserved (pension) benefits If employees leave a pension scheme early before retirement, they are entitled to have the contributions they have made 'frozen' and paid out when retirement age is reached. See DEFERRED PENSION.

Pre-tax profit Net profit made by a company before tax has been deducted.

Price-earning ratio (P/E) Method used by analysts to rate companies by comparing the market value of the shares and the profit for the year. The taxed profit is divided by the number of ordinary shares to obtain the EARNINGS PER SHARE figure. This is then divided by the current market price to give the P/E ratio. A high ratio means the share price has been pushed up by the expectation of increased profitability, while a low ratio can indicate that the share is good value at its current level.

Price ring Manufacturers or dealers who get together to control the level at which something is bought or sold for their own advantage.

Price support Help given, usually by a government or governments, to prevent a market value falling below certain specified levels. Price support operations are also often organized by dealers and investors to bolster the value of a share by offering to buy at a certain level.

Prime costs Those incurred in the production and distribution of a product.

Prime (lending) rate US equivalent of the BASE RATE of interest in the UK, charged to the most credit-worthy customers by banks.

Principal Money loaned, or supplied, to help establish a venture. Also a direct participant in a contract or someone employing an agent or broker to act on his behalf.

Prior charge Security, such as debenture, loan stock or preference stock, that ranks before ordinary shares for the payment of dividend, interest or distribution of assets.

Prior lien debenture An additional debt

which, with the agreement of the debenture holders, carries the first claim to payment of interest and repayment of capital.

Private banks Describes any bank that is not state-owned; but normally applies to banks which are not members of the clearing system.

Private (limited) company One that does not offer shares or stock to the public and which does not allow members to transfer shares without the approval of other shareholders. It must have at least two members.

Private medical insurance Policy under which the insured is repaid, up to previously agreed figures, the cost of private medical services. Often taken out by companies or organizations on behalf of their employees as an additional perk or benefit in kind. From April 1990 tax relief, at the highest marginal rate, will be given on private medical insurance policies for anyone over 60 years old. The tax relief will be allowed to the person of any age paying the premiums, providing that the beneficiary of the policy is over 60.

Private sector That part of a country's economy which is owned and operated by privately owned companies and organizations, not by government departments or state-owned corporations (the public sector).

Private treaty A contract, normally to buy or sell, reached by personal bargaining or agreement, as opposed to a public offering or auction.

Private trust A trust set up for the benefit of a specified person or persons, as opposed to a charitable or public trust.

Privatization Sale of government-owned assets to the public (private hands) by offering for sale shares in a newly created public limited company to be quoted and traded on the stock exchange.

Privy Purse Government funds allocated by parliament to the monarchy to meet their personal expenses.

Probate Official approval by the Probate Registry that a Will has been proved legally. It has to be obtained before the executor named in the Will can start settling the affairs of the deceased. Probate need be obtained only if the value of the estate exceeds £5,000.

Probate price The price used to assess the value of shares in an estate for inheritance tax purposes. It is estimated on the 'quarter up' principle, that is, the lowest price quoted in the Official Stock Exchange list, plus a quarter of the difference between the lower (sell) and upper (buy) prices quoted in the list.

Proceeds The sum of money received from a business deal or sale of assets.

Procuration fee Payment made to someone for their services in arranging or negotiating a loan.

Productive assets See ASSETS, ACTIVE.

Professional indemnity Insurance against losses from negligence or fraud by employees of a business, often taken out by partnerships or private companies, for example solicitors and estate agents, to protect themselves against claims that might be made by clients against them.

Professional valuation Assessment of

the value of assets by someone who claims to have the necessary expertise, and who could therefore be considered guilty of negligence if the valuation proves to be incorrect.

Profit and loss account Important section of an organization's annual report which sets out to show the net profit during the accounting period. This is done by deducting from the gross profit all expenses incurred in production, distribution, administration and financing, taking into account any additional income that might have been received. Also shown are the tax charges, dividends paid and retained profits.

Profit margin The money made by a business, prior to taxation charges, expressed as a percentage of total turnover. The movements in this margin can give a good indication of the strength of a business, since it provides a guide to the efficiency of the company or the competition faced.

Profit related pay
Government-approved scheme, first announced in the 1986 Budget, giving tax relief, up to maximum ceiling, on extra payments made to employees based on the increased profitability of the company.

Profit sharing Arrangement under which the owners of a business agree to distribute some part of the profits made to the employees, normally over and above their normal salaries but sometimes instead of paying salaries. See EMPLOYEE SHARE OWNERSHIP PLANS (ESOPs) and EMPLOYEE SHARE SCHEMES.

Profit-sharing bond See BOND, PARTICIPATING.

Pro forma invoice Used when a seller requires payment before delivery of goods or a service.

Program trading Term coined in the United States to describe computer-based dealing systems, used mainly by professional investors.

Progressive tax Tax, for example income tax, that increases or decreases in line with the amount of taxable income.

Promissory note Document containing an unconditional promise to pay a certain sum of money, to a specified person or to the bearer of the note.

Prompt date Day when payment is due for goods bought, especially in the commodity markets and at auction sales.

Proof of debt Document signed by a creditor (lender) when making a claim against the estate of a bankrupt person.

Property bond See BOND.

Property enterprise trust (PET) Investment fund which buys commercial property in those enterprise zones that offer special tax concessions.

Property funds Specialized investment funds which buy property on behalf of investors, insurance companies and pension scheme managers.

Proportional tax Tax imposed at a fixed, flat rate.

Proprietary office Insurance company which belongs to shareholders, as opposed to a 'mutual', which is owned by the policy-holders.

Proprietary product One that is produced and sold solely by the owner of a

proprietary right, such as a patent which
forbids others from selling or making the
same product.

Prospective multiple The likely
earnings per share used to calculate the
PRICE-EARNINGS RATIO.

Prospective yield The return (dividend
or interest) expected on an investment.
See INITIAL YIELD.

Prospectus A document giving details of
an offer to the public of shares, stock or
debentures, especially in new issues or
ventures. It is a legal document which
must contain specified facts and figures to
ensure that the prospective investor is
properly informed.
   Also part of a proposal form issued by
insurance companies to outline various
policies available.

Protected bear or bull Someone with
an outstanding sale or purchase in a
market, who has taken defensive
measures against incurring a potential
loss, possibly via the futures or options
market.

Protected (no claims) discount
Arrangement in an insurance policy to
retain the no-claims discount, even if a
claim is made. This usually involves paying
an additional premium, but is sometimes
offered free as a sales inducement to
certain classes of policy-holders who are
considered less likely to make a claim in
any event.

Protective duty Tax imposed, normally
on imported goods, to safeguard an
existing domestic industry from cut-price
competition.

Provident fund Savings scheme set up
for employees of an organization, run by

trustees who are responsible for investing
the money. Often used to describe the
activities of FRIENDLY SOCIETIES.

Proving a will See PROBATE.

Provision In accounts, setting aside
money for the replacement of assets, lost
or reduced in value, and allowing for
doubtful debts and other liabilities which
cannot be quantified accurately.

Provisional allotment letter Form
sent by companies making a RIGHTS
ISSUE, notifying shareholders how many
shares they have been allocated.

Proxy Written authority from
shareholders transferring the power to
vote on their behalf. Also used to describe
the persons holding the right to vote on
behalf of others.

PRP See PROFIT RELATED PAY.

PSBR See PUBLIC SECTOR BORROWING
REQUIREMENT.

PSLR See PUBLIC SECTOR LENDING
REQUIREMENT.

Public account Bank account for money
collected by government and local
authority departments.

Public accountant See CERTIFIED
ACCOUNTANT.

Public company See PUBLIC LIMITED
COMPANY.

Public corporation Government-owned
organization which manages a nationalized
industry or service, like the Post Office or
British Broadcasting Corporation.

Public deposits Balances of the funds

held by government departments at the Bank of England.

Public expenditure Money spent by the government in providing public services, such as roads. 'Public investment' is government money spent on fixed assets, such as hospitals.

Public issue Offer of shares or loan stock in a company, made by inviting the public to apply. See FLOTATION and PRIVATIZATION.

Public lending right System under which authors receive payments from government funds, based on the number of times their books are borrowed from public libraries.

Public liability insurance Policy, compulsory for some businesses, to cover any losses that might be suffered by members of the public as a result of mistakes or negligence. See PROFESSIONAL INDEMNITY.

Public limited company (PLC) A limited liability company whose shares, or loan stock, are available to the public, although not necessarily listed on a stock exchange. The total number of shareholders must exceed seven, but there is no restriction on the right to transfer shares to other shareholders.

Public sector borrowing requirement (PSBR) Shortfall between the amount spent by a government and the amount raised by taxation. The balance needed to bridge the gap is borrowed from the public by selling government securities (GILTS) and National Savings products to investors.

Public sector lending requirement (PSLR) Surplus of money held by the

government as a result of the amount raised by taxation exceeding expenditure. The government reduces the surplus by buying back securities (GILTS) it had previously sold to raise money.

Public trustee Government department within the law courts whom any member of the public can appoint as an executor or administrator of their Will, as legal guardian of children, or as trustee.

Public utilities Organizations which provide the public with essential services like electricity, gas, water and transport, often owned by the government. Many of them, however, have been privatized in recent years by the government, turning them into limited companies and offering the shares for sale to investors.

Puisne mortgage A legal mortgage not backed up with deposit of the title deeds of the property, although it may be listed by the Land Charges Registry. It therefore has a lower priority for repayment than other mortgages on the same property.

Purchase tax Tax levied on certain goods at the point of sale, it has since been superseded by VALUE ADDED TAX.

Pure endowment Type of life assurance which is really a savings plan. It provides no protection against death but pays out the value of the premiums paid, plus profits made from investing the premiums, when the policy matures after a specified period. In some policies the premiums are repaid if the policy-holder dies before the repayment date.

Pure endowment term assurance (PETA) Schemes that were devised to help reduce liability to pay CAPITAL TRANSFER TAX (CTT), before it was replaced by inheritance tax in the 1986

Budget to block the loophole exploited by the PETA plans.

Put The right to sell something at an agreed price by a specific date.

Put option An option giving the buyer the right to sell the underlying share or financial instrument at a fixed price on or before a specified date. Opposite of CALL OPTION, which gives the right to buy.

Pyramiding Building up a holding in a market by using the first deals to finance further transactions. Hence 'pyramid selling' under which the original promoter of a product sells the rights of sale to other promoters, who may in turn sell them on to further groups of sellers.

Q

Qualification shares Some companies require directors to hold a block of shares in order to qualify as a director.

Qualified accounts Term used when auditors are unable to say that the accounts represent a 'true and fair' view of the company's financial position. Sometimes this is genuinely true because not sufficient information is available, but it is often used as a warning that something is going wrong.

Qualifying policy Assurance policy whose benefits are paid free of tax, provided specified rules and conditions are followed. The policy must be held for 10 years, or three quarters of the original term agreed, and the premiums must be paid regularly, at least once a year, and must be spread evenly over the life of the policy. The policy must also include an element of life assurance cover. The amount payable on death must be a minimum of 75% of the sum assured, unless the policy-holder is 55 years of age or older, when the percentage of the death benefit is reduced by 2% a year. (So life cover for a 60-year-old has to be only 65% of the sum assured.) The policy is not really tax free, since tax is paid by the insurance company on the fund during the life of the policy.

Quantum An amount of money specified in value, instead of as a percentage of proportion; thus: 'the quantum paid is £1,000, representing 1% of the total earnings of £100,000'.

Quantum meruit Legal term referring to a payment for goods or services ordered by a third party when no price was agreed, or for work done by someone under a contract before it was broken by a third party. Literal translation from the Latin is 'as much as he deserved'.

Quarter day Legal term to define one of the four days in the year on which quarterly payments, especially of rent, should be made or tenancies be reviewed. In England and Wales, the four quarter days are: Lady Day (25 March); Midsummer (24 June); Michaelmas (29 September) and Christmas (25 December). In Scotland they are Candlemas (2 February); Whitsun (15 May); Lammas (1 August); and Martinmas (11 November).

Quartiles Comparative values that are arranged in accordance with the value in the middle of the order (median) into four sections; thus values above the median are the two upper quartiles, while those below are the two lower quartiles. Much used by unit trust groups to describe the comparative rankings of their funds against competitive unit trusts. The objective, of course, is to have unit trusts in the upper quartiles – signifying above-average investment performance.

Quasi-loan Legal term to describe loans made by companies to directors who are liable for repaying them to the company.

Quasi-money Assets that can be used

as a substitute for cash. See NEAR MONEY.

Queen's shilling Historical payment that used to be given to those joining the British army. See KING'S SHILLING.

Queer Street Traditional slang term to describe someone who is in financial trouble and is likely to go bankrupt.

Quick assets See ASSETS.

Quid Traditional slang term for £1 (originally 20 shillings). Hence 'quids in' means making a good profit on a deal.

Quietus Release from a debt or other liability. Provide a receipt.

Quotation Market price, or estimate of the cost of a service or policy. To seek a quotation refers to companies applying for approval to have their shares traded on a stock exchange.

Quoted company or investment Shares or stocks that are traded on a recognized market. See LISTED COMPANIES.

R

Rack rent A rent payment that is considered to represent the full value that can be got for a property, and could therefore be seen as being rather high.

Raider Stock market term for an individual or company that mounts takeover bids for companies, usually with a view to making a short-term profit.

Rake-off Slang term for share of the profit in a deal, often as the result of a hidden or illegal commission.

Ramp Organized effort to push up artificially the market price of something, usually the shares of a company quoted on the stock exchange. This can be done in several ways: by organizing concerted buying by different parties, spreading rumours or giving a falsely optimistic view of the company. Used when a company wants to inflate its share price for some reason, possibly to help finance a takeover or dispose of a large holding.

Random walk theory Theory that market prices do not fluctuate in prescribed patterns, as believed by those using charts or graphs to predict future price movements.

Rate of exchange The value of a currency of one country as compared with currency of other countries. See EXCHANGE RATE.

Rate of return The amount of money –

dividends, interest or capital growth – received on an investment. See YIELD.

Ready cash or money Notes or coins available for immediate payment. Hence the slang term 'readies', meaning cash in hand.

Real assets See ASSETS.

Real chattel A leasehold interest in land.

Real cost See OPPORTUNITY COST.

Real estate Alternative name originating in the United States for property, or an interest in land and buildings.

Real investment Investment made not for financial gain but on behalf of the community, such as in hospitals and schools.

Realizable assets See ASSETS, QUICK.

Realization The sale of assets for cash. A realization account is often used when winding up a business; it takes in all the assets and sale of proceeds, pays out the debts, and any balance left over is paid to the creditors.

Realized profit Amount made on the disposal of an investment or asset.

Real property Traditional term for ownership of a freehold or specified rights over freehold land.

Real security Mortgages for REAL PROPERTY.

Real terms Value of money or other asset, after taking into account the impact of inflation or currency changes that may reduce its purchasing power in the future; for example, an insurance policy may promise to pay a large sum of money at some date in the future, but when the payment time is reached the money may be worth considerably less in real terms, especially if there has been high inflation in the intervening period.

Rebate Allowance made to reduce a payment due, or return an overpayment. Similar to a discount, except that a rebate can be returned at a later date after the payment has been made.

Receipt Formal acknowledgement of a payment.

Receiver Person appointed, usually by a court, in cases of bankruptcy or insolvency; or when there is a disagreement about ownership; or when a partnership is dissolved; or to manage the affairs of someone mentally incapable. Holders of DEBENTURE stock can also appoint a receiver if a company has been acting in a manner which harms their interests. Normally a receiver is responsible for the collection of income and assets for distribution to the creditors until debts outstanding are paid in full. Sometimes, however, the receiver is also appointed manager, to carry on a business. See OFFICIAL RECEIVER.

Receiving order Instruction made by a court to put the OFFICIAL RECEIVER in charge of a person or company which is insolvent and unable to pay outstanding debts.

Reciprocal insurance See MUTUAL INSURANCE.

Recognizance Pledge made to a court of law to forfeit a sum of money if a named person does not attend the court on a specified date or stop activities which might cause a breach of the peace.

Recognized investment exchange (RIE) Stock market in UK authorized to handle dealings for the public, since its rules and regulations comply with the terms of the Financial Services Act 1986 giving protection to investors.

Recognized Professional Bodies (RPBs) Organizations, like those for accountants, actuaries, insurance brokers and solicitors, which are authorized by the SECURITIES AND INVESTMENTS BOARD (SIB) to regulate the activities of their members in offering investment products and services, provided these represent only a small part of the firm's total business. The RPBs ensure that their members are complying with the terms of the Financial Services Act 1986 in providing proper protection for investors. See SELF-REGULATORY ORGANIZATIONS and USEFUL ADDRESSES.

Recompense Payment as a reward for some service or to compensate for a loss.

Reconstruction of capital When a limited company decides to change its share ownership, often because it is in financial difficulties. It may amalgamate or merge with another company, form a new company or enter into a SCHEME OF ARRANGEMENT.

Recovery stock Stock market term for a share which has fallen in price but is considered to have the potential to climb back up in value again. Some groups offer funds investing primarily in recovery stocks.

Recurring endowment policy Type of policy aimed at lower-paid industrial workers, which pays out after a specified period (five, seven or ten years) but which gives the policy-holder the choice to transfer the cash sum received into a further policy for a larger assured sum.

Redeemable bond See BOND, CALLABLE.

Redeemable debenture See DEBENTURE, IRREDEEMABLE.

Redeemable preference shares Shares in a company which it can buy back at any time it chooses from the holder.

Redeemable stock Security paying a fixed interest, which can be repaid at a stated redemption date, or earlier, at the wish of the issuer of the stock.

Redemption Paying off a loan or recovering ownership of a property by paying off the mortgage.

Redemption date Time when certain types of security, especially government stocks, are due for repayment by the borrower.

Redemption yield On a fixed-interest security, with a redemption date, the yield (or earnings) is calculated by combining the interest together with the capital profit (or loss) that would be made on the repayment date. Thus, if the security is bought at £98 and its redemption value is £100, the £2 capital profit is taken into account when calculating the total or redemption yield. Particularly used to calculate the value of GILTS (government securities).

Reducing balance insurance Policy where the sum assured decreases in value by a fixed percentage each year. See LOW COST ENDOWMENT MORTGAGE.

Redundancy payment Compensation money paid to employees whose jobs cease to exist, and they therefore become unemployed through no fault of their own. The amount of compensation paid is normally calculated on the length of service with the company and the wage being received at the time, although the government lays down the minimum amount payable. Several companies offer insurance against being made redundant, with policies that are often linked with the repayment of loans, such as mortgages.

Refer to drawer Phrase written or stamped on a cheque which a bank will not cash. Usually this is because the issuer of the cheque does not have sufficient funds in an account to cover the payment, but sometimes it is because the words and figures written on the cheque do not agree. The phrase is a polite way of the bank suggesting that the recipient should get in touch with the writer of the cheque. Some banks use instead the phrase 'return to drawer'.

Refinance Paying off an existing loan by borrowing new money, often at a lower rate of interest. Usually used with bonds and debentures, but also for increasing or decreasing the size of a home loan. See REMORTGAGE.

Refunding bond See BOND.

Refuge capital See HOT MONEY.

Registered bond See BOND.

Registered capital See AUTHORIZED (SHARE) CAPITAL.

Registered debenture See
DEBENTURE, BEARER.

Registered licensed conveyancers
Individuals who have qualified as members
of the Council for Licensed Conveyancers,
and are therefore authorized to handle
conveyancing work, involving them in
buying and selling land or property, in
spite of not being solicitors. The Council
was formed by the Administration of
Justice Act 1985 which ended the previous
monopoly of conveyancing work held by
solicitors, with the objective of creating
competition and bringing down costs. To
qualify, a licensed conveyancer has to pass
an examination, undergo training and be
approved as being a 'fit and proper'
person. Certain exemptions, however, are
made for those with experience in
conveyancing, such as former solicitors
who decide to set up independently. It is
not possible to be a licensed conveyancer
and a solicitor at the same time. See
USEFUL ADDRESSES.

Registered share/stock Where the
name of the owner is listed on the
company's register.

Registrar Person or company
responsible for keeping a record of
shareholders. Often this task is
undertaken by a large bank; but some unit
trust groups use outside registrars to
handle all the paperwork involved,
although this can also be done in-house.

Registrar in Bankruptcy Official of the
bankruptcy court who holds a public
examination of cases and decides whether
to declare the debtor bankrupt.

Registrar of Companies Government
official whose department is responsible
for the listing, and keeping records, of all

limited companies. See USEFUL
ADDRESSES.

Registrar of Friendly Societies
Keeper of the list of approved friendly
societies, who by registering qualify for
various rights and powers. See FRIENDLY
SOCIETIES and USEFUL ADDRESSES.

Registration fee A small charge levied
by companies when transferring
ownership of shares or stock.

Regressive tax A tax that is charged at
a reducing rate as the amount to be taxed
increases. Opposite of PROGRESSIVE
TAX.

Regular premium policy Endowment
or life assurance where the premiums are
paid over a period of time at specified
intervals – weekly, monthly, quarterly or
annually. The same method is used for
'regular savings schemes', for example in
investment and unit trusts, or for
PERSONAL EQUITY PLANS, where the
investor decides to make contributions at
intervals over a period of time, rather than
just making a single down-payment. See
POUND COST AVERAGING.

Regulation The Financial Services Act
1986, aimed at providing increased
protection for investors, transformed the
whole regulatory structure for investment
in the UK. It followed a series of scandals,
mainly centred in the City of London, in
which investors were defrauded by
dishonesty or mismanagement; but there
were too many loopholes in the law to
press successful prosecutions under the
old Prevention of Frauds Act. The
government decided therefore to bring in a
completely new set-up to regulate
investment businesses. As from 1988,
when the new legislation became
operational, it became a criminal offence

for an investment business to operate without having received authorization that it was 'fit and proper' to do so.

Furthermore, to retain that authorization, investment businesses have to comply with the general rules and regulations laid down by the Financial Services Act and with the specific regulations of the organization with which they are registered. The system created by the Financial Services Act 1986 is known as self-regulation, since it allows each sector of the financial services industry to have its own organization. However, these SELF-REGULATORY ORGANIZATIONS (SROs) and RECOGNIZED PROFESSIONAL BODIES (RPBs) come under the umbrella of, and are answerable to, the main 'watchdog' organization, the SECURITIES AND INVESTMENTS BOARD (SIB). The SIB in turn is answerable to the government, primarily via the Department of Trade and Industry, and to the Bank of England. The SIB authorizes some business direct, notably the banks, and has a model rulebook that sets the minimum standards for the self-regulatory organizations, who then have additional rules tailored for their particular sector. In 1988, when the system started operating, there were five separate SROs – the Association of Futures Brokers and Dealers (AFBD); the Financial Intermediaries, Managers and Brokers Regulatory Association (FIMBRA); the Investment Management Regulatory Organization (IMRO); the Life Assurance and Unit Trust Regulatory Organization (LAUTRO); and The Securities Association (TSA), including members of the London stock market and overseas dealers operating in the UK.

Each SRO has its own separate officials and secretariat for monitoring the behaviour of its members, ensuring its regulations are complied with and arrangements are made for dealing with complaints. However, there is a common compensation fund to meet losses, run by the SIB. The Recognized Professional Bodies (RPBs), which are approved by the SIB, cover firms like those of accountants and solicitors, where some investment services may be provided, but this is not the main bulk of their business; they are therefore answerable to their own professional organization and do not need to comply with all the SIB rules and regulations. However, if their investment business is sufficiently large, then the firms either obtain authority to operate from the appropriate SRO or form a separate subsidiary to do so.

The definition of 'investment business' is very wide, and the rules and regulations under the Financial Services Act cover every aspect, from advertising and marketing to charges and commissions, the behaviour of salesmen, individual authorization of employees, appointed representatives or tied agents, and the giving of 'best advice', as well as the application of the 'know the customer' principle. From the general public's point of view, the SROs of most direct importance are FIMBRA, which has the largest membership of independent intermediaries and brokers dealing directly with the public; TSA, covering the stock markets; and the AFBD, regulating futures and commodity exchanges. However, complaints and disputes are also handled by RPBs, such as the Law Society and accountancy organizations, and by the special Ombudsmen appointed to provide independent arbitration for disputes with banks, building societies, insurance and unit trusts.

Financial companies operating in overseas, or offshore, countries have to gain approval from the SIB to offer investment products or services in the UK. However, products that comply with the European Community's standard regulation for collective investment funds (known as UCITS) can be sold freely in the UK. So can those offered by companies in DESIGNATED TERRITORIES or countries whose rules and regulations have been approved by the SIB as being compatible with those operating in the UK. See COMPLAINTS, OMBUDSMAN and USEFUL ADDRESSES.

Regulatory tax Government duty whose prime objective is to control or discourage some activity, like smoking, rather than to raise money.

Reimburse Repay money spent on behalf of someone else.

Reinstatement insurance Fire or accident policy where the insurer promises to pay claims based on replacing or rebuilding the insured goods, without taking into account any wear or tear that might have taken place.

Also used to refer to reviving a life policy, after it has lapsed because of non-payment of premiums. If the policy-holder decides to resume paying premiums, the insurance company will consider reinstating the policy.

Reinsurance Used by insurers to share or spread the risk of insuring, particularly where large payments could be involved. The original insurer contacts one or more other insurance companies, sometimes specialist reinsurance groups, who agree to cover a proportion of the risk involved, in return for a percentage of the premium money. Lloyd's of London, in particular, spread the risks by operating through syndicates who each take on a proportion of the potential loss. Although the risk is spread, the original insurer remains liable to meet any claim. Bookmakers practise a form of

reinsurance when they lay off bets with other bookies, so as to limit the amount they might lose.

Remittance Sum of money sent from one place to another. Hence 'remittance man' is someone living abroad, receiving money from his home country or being paid to stay away from his home country.

Remittance slip Form sent out with invoices for payment so that the recipient can more easily identify details of the payment made.

Remortgage Take out a new loan to replace the existing mortgage. Can be used as an alternative to taking out additional mortgages (second, etc.) on a property; but there may be a danger of losing the tax concessions allowed on the first mortgage. May also involve paying extra legal and valuation fees. See SECOND MORTGAGE.

Removal bond Promise to pay any duty that may be chargeable on imported goods removed from a customs warehouse for manufacturing or processing.

Remuneration Money paid for a service, including employment, as opposed to paying for goods.

Remunerative Something that is profitable or brings a satisfactory return.

Renewable term assurance Life policy that gives holders the option to renew at the end of the specified term covered, without having to provide new evidence of good health. However, this option is usually limited to holders below a certain age level.

Renewal notice Form sent out to insurance policy-holders as a reminder that the renewal premium for continuing the policy is due for payment.

Renounceable certificate Form sent to shareholders notifying them of their new holdings following a CAPITALIZATION ISSUE.

Rent Money charged for the use of land, property, goods or services.

Rental The amount of rent received, or the charge for hiring goods and services.

Rentier Someone who lives on the income received from rents and investment in fixed-interest securities.

Renunciation See LETTER OF RENUNCIATION.

Repairing lease Where the leaseholder, or tenant, is liable to pay for any repairs to the land or property.

Reparations Money paid for injury, loss or damage, or to right a wrong.

Repayment mortgage Home loan in which the borrower pays back the original capital, and the interest due, during the period of the mortgage. Normally the repayments are covered by a fixed sum each month, which is adjusted to take into account any change in the interest rate – although often the sum can remain the same and the time period for repayment be changed instead. In the early years the repayments cover primarily the interest due and very little of the capital; but over the years the position is gradually reversed – an important point to bear in mind for tax purposes, since tax relief is given only on the interest paid, not on the capital repayment. Usually the lender insists on the borrower taking out separate insurance cover on a repayment

mortgage to cover death or even unemployment. This pushes up the cost, when compared with interest-only endowment or pension mortgages, which normally have built-up insurance included with the policy taken out to repay the capital sum of the mortgage.

In recent years there has been a switch away from repayment mortgages because interest-only mortgages are claimed to provide better value. More to the point they also provide extra commission for the lender, such as a bank or building society, or for the broker selling the mortgage. In fact the choice between a repayment and an interest-only mortgage should depend on the rate of interest, the tax position of the borrower, and the cost of the additional insurance cover required for a repayment loan compared with the endowment or pension policy being used to repay the capital. It is also important to bear in mind that an endowment or pension scheme is likely to be less flexible for the borrower in changing circumstances, since there is an additional commitment to a form of savings plan in addition to the mortgage. See ENDOWMENT MORTGAGE, PENSION MORTGAGE and PERSONAL EQUITY PLANS.

Replacement cost Accounting term used to indicate the sum needed to replace an asset, rather than its original historical cost, which is likely to be lower: an important point to bear in mind when insuring goods or property. In the case of property, however, the cost of replacement (in the event of fire or other damage destroying the building) may be less than the valuation, which includes the cost of the land.

Replevin Legal term for the right for a person to reclaim goods that have been taken away, possibly because of a disputed debt. While the court is considering the matter, the owner of the goods is entitled to regain possession of them on signing a replevin bond that guarantees they will be returned if the court decides against him or her.

Report and accounts See ANNUAL REPORT.

Report and valuation Surveyor's report on a property, it does not cover a full structural survey but gives more information than a valuation report only. Often used by home-loan borrowers, who in any event have to pay for a valuation report for the mortgage lender.

Re-present When a cheque or other form of promissory note is not honoured by a bank, the owner is often asked to re-present it again at a later date when sufficient funds to cover it may have been provided.

Repurchases The purchase of a security by the issuer of the share or stock. Most widely used in unit trusts to describe the sale by investors of units, which are repurchased by the managers of the fund.

Requisitioning Taking possession of goods or property without the permission of the owner, normally by governments in times of crisis.

Resale price maintenance (RPM) An agreement between manufacturers, wholesalers and retailers not to sell goods below a certain price. Such agreements are forbidden in Britain under the Restrictive Trade Practices Act, unless it can be proved that the agreement operates in the public interest, as with the Net Book Agreement.

Reschedule debts Device to help

borrowers who are unable to pay back the capital or interest on the agreed date; the lender agrees to new dates for repayment, although he sometimes insists on a higher rate of interest or a guarantee from a third party that the new payments will be made. Mainly used in international lending, where poor or underdeveloped countries have proved incapable of paying loans received either from banks or from other countries' governments. The rescheduling in these cases is often organized by the INTERNATIONAL MONETARY FUND.

Reserve capital That part of a company's authorized issued capital that will be called up only in the event of the company being wound up. See UNCALLED CAPITAL.

Reserve currency Leading currencies that are considered to be important enough always to be in demand, and therefore suitable for governments to hold as part of their official reserves, in the knowledge that they can always be traded. The US dollar has been the main reserve currency since the end of the Second World War, replacing sterling to a large extent. But in recent years the Deutschmark, Swiss franc and yen have also been in strong demand as reserve currencies.

Reserve fund Accumulated profits of a business which, instead of being paid out in dividends to the shareholders, have been used to help finance its expansion by acquiring assets.

Reserve price The lowest price (at an auction) which the seller is prepared to accept. If the reserve is not reached, the article for sale is withdrawn.

Also used to describe the minimum price for some fruit and vegetables, fixed under the European Community's Common Agricultural Policy.

Reserve ratio See CASH RATIO.

Residuary legacy The amount of a deceased person's estate left after specific bequests in the Will have been settled and all debts and expenses paid. The residue is then divided up according to the terms of the Will.

Retail Price Index (RPI) Government measure of the cost of living and rate of inflation, compiled from the price movements of a 'basket' of consumer goods and services, rated by their importance in everyday life. Food, for example, carries a high rating in the index, which is issued monthly by the Department of Employment.

Retained profits See RETENTIONS.

Retention money Amount held back from payment to a contractor in case the contract is not completed on time or the work is not satisfactory.

Retentions Amount of a company's profit left after all deductions, including the payment of dividends to shareholders. These retained profits are used to increase the company's assets or reserves.

Retirement annuity An assurance policy that provides for payment of a pension from the date of the annuitant's retirement. Often used to describe personal pension taken out by self-employed.

Retirement pension One that starts from the date when employees give up work and continues until death. It may be either a government pension under the National Insurance scheme or a company pension.

Return on capital The amount of income received from an investment of capital. The return is usually expressed as an annual percentage; for example, earnings of £1,000 on an investment of £10,000 would equal a return of 10%.

Return premium Sum paid back by an insurance company when a policy is changed or stopped.

Return to drawer See REFER TO DRAWER.

Revalorization of currency When a government decides to replace its existing currency with a new unit, usually because the old currency has suffered from a sharp drop in value.

Revaluation Increase the value of assets (or a currency) to bring them more into line with their up-to-date market value. Companies frequently revalue their assets, particularly property and long-term investments, to a more realistic level so as to increase the net asset value backing the share price.

Countries revalue their currencies when they have a consistent surplus of exports over imports and their currency is considered to be undervalued against other currencies.

Revaluation reserve Surplus funds put aside as the result of a revaluation and sale of assets.

Revenue Money received, or taxation income paid to the government. Also shorthand term for the INLAND REVENUE.

Revenue accounts Book-keeping term for that section of accounts in which the money received or coming into the business is recorded.

Revenue reserves Surplus funds, kept back voluntarily by directors of a company, which may no longer be required at a later date and can be distributed to shareholders in the form of a dividend instead.

Reverse takeover When one company purchases another company, but in reality the company bought assumes control. Often used by small private companies which acquire larger, publicly quoted companies listed on a stock exchange.

Reverse yield gap Theoretical amount lost in income terms when an investment in shares or property falls short of the amount that could be earned from a cash deposit in a bank, building society or fixed-interest government security (gilt or National Savings product).

Reversion Legal term for the right to possess land, property or money at some future date; for example, when a lease expires, assets in a trust fund become payable, or an assurance policy matures.

Reversionary annuity Life assurance policy that provides for regular payments to start on the death of the insured to a third (named) party for the rest of their life. If the named person dies before the insured, the policy comes to an end and no payments are made.

Reversionary bonus The additional amount that life assurance companies add to with-profits policies at regular intervals, representing the extra profits made on investments. The size, and frequency, of reversionary bonuses depends on the profitability of the assurance company and its investment performance. But once a reversionary bonus has been declared, it cannot be withdrawn and is added to the value of the policy as a proportion of the sum assured. If the policy is encashed early, before it has matured, a reduction in the bonuses is calculated in line with the time the policy has been in force. Reversionary bonuses are normally allocated on a regular basis, either annually or once every three years, unlike the TERMINAL BONUS which is decided only when the policy reaches maturity.

Reversionary interest Term used to describe the right held by someone under a REVERSION. Reversionary interests can often be sold to raise cash for immediate use by the existing owner and transferred to someone else; for example, the sale of an endowment policy, due to mature some years ahead, usually fetches a higher price than if it is simply surrendered to the insurance company. The sale of a future inheritance or the freehold of a property can also be used to provide immediate funds for the original owner and future assets or income for the buyer.

Reverter to settlor A form of trust devised to reduce liability to capital transfer tax, before it was replaced in 1986 by inheritance tax. Trusts established before March 1986 are still effective, but are no use as a tax-avoidance device after that date.

Revocable letter of credit One that can be cancelled or changed.

Revolving credit Arrangement under which a bank makes a loan for a fixed period; it can be used at any time by the customer and be renewed when amounts have been repaid, thus providing a constant borrowing facility.

Revolving fund Reserve of money from

which loans are made, it also receives repayments, plus interest, of the loans, so that the size of the fund is preserved to enable continuous lending and re-lending of money.

RIE See RECOGNIZED INVESTMENT EXCHANGE.

Rights issue Device used when a company wishes to raise additional money. It offers existing shareholders the right to buy more shares at a price normally below the current market value. The number of shares offered is based on the existing holding – for example one new share for every ten shares already held. In this way each shareholder retains the same percentage of shares in the company as previously, provided the full rights issue is taken up. However, shareholders who do not want to buy any extra shares can sell their right to do so on to a third party at a price which recognizes that the shares are being acquired at below market value. The 'rights letter' from the company outlining the offer is used for sale to the third party, either privately or via a stockbroker or dealer.

Rights letter See RIGHTS ISSUE.

Ring trading Term used to describe dealing sessions on the commodity markets, specifically the London Metal Exchange. Originally when metal traders gathered together, one of them drew a circle in chalk which they all stood round, and this became known as ring trading – the periods when dealing is carried out by OPEN OUTCRY instead of via the telephone or screens.

A more disreputable use of ring trading is when manufacturers or dealers get together to control market prices to their own advantage – an illegal practice if it works against the public interest.

Riot risk Insurance term for a risk that is not covered by a household policy unless special clause is included (at extra cost) to give protection against malicious damage caused by rioters.

Risk capital Money that is considered to be at risk because it is being used in an investment or venture that could well fail. From an investor's point of view, risk capital is money that could be lost without too much hardship being created and which can therefore be used for speculative investments offering potentially higher rewards. See VENTURE CAPITAL.

Roll-over relief Taxation term used to describe occasions when the payment of capital gains tax can be deferred or delayed. For example, investors who effectively sell their shares when accepting new shares in a company making a takeover are not liable for tax on the profits made until selling the new shares; and companies can defer the tax liability on selling a fixed asset if the proceeds are used to buy a replacement.

Roll-up funds Funds where the profits are not distributed in the form of income but instead are used (rolled up) to increase the value of the units. This device was widely used when income tax was payable at higher rates than capital gains tax, to reduce the liability of investors paying high rate income tax. It is still favoured by investors who want to make deferred capital gains tax profits instead of taking immediate income. See DISTRIBUTOR FUNDS.

Rounding Increasing a value to the next highest whole number.

Rounding-up charge An upwards adjustment in unit trust prices that is used to avoid inconvenient fractions when calculating charges. However, from 1988 the use of rounding up by unit trust management groups was severely restricted, since it had been widely used to make 'hidden' profits for the groups. It is still permitted, however, with insurance products.

Royalties Money paid to authors and composers for their work, based on the volume of sales and a percentage of the price; also to owners of copyright material or patents; also to owners of land from which minerals are being extracted.

RPB See RECOGNIZED PROFESSIONAL BODIES and USEFUL ADDRESSES.

RPI See RETAIL PRICE INDEX.

Rubber cheque US slang term for a cheque that the bank refuses to honour or which 'bounces'.

Run on a bank Sudden rush by depositors to withdraw their money from a bank, normally because they feel it is unsafe and may soon not be able to pay out. The most feared happening for a bank, since it involves paying out short-term funds (cash) when a lot of the bank's assets may be held in longer-term assets that cannot be sold immediately. The bank can therefore be made insolvent, even if it has adequate overall reserves.

S

See STOCK EXCHANGE AUTOMATED QUOTATIONS SYSTEM.

Salary Derived from 'salt money', the amount that used to be paid to workers so that they could buy salt. Now widely used to mean the regular wage paid to an employee.

Saleage The proportion of the production of a commodity that is of saleable quality.

Sale and leaseback An arrangement under which the owner of an asset (such as a property or machine) agrees to sell it to someone else, but only on condition that it is leased back to the original owner for use for an agreed period of time and at an agreed rent. This device is normally used by companies to raise extra money for the business at the expense of reducing the value of its assets.

Sale as seen When something is sold without any guarantee of its quality being given by the seller.

Sale or return An agreement that allows the buyer to return goods to the seller within a specified period of time. Widely used as an incentive to persuade shopkeepers to buy items, like newspapers and magazines, which often have to be sold quickly before they become out of date and hence worthless.

Sale ring An auction, or sale, where the buyers form a ring round the auctioneer or the goods, such as cattle, being sold.

Sales agent Person employed by a manufacturer, or distributor, to sell goods on their behalf either on a salary or on commission.

Sales tax Tax imposed at the point of sale, based on a percentage of the selling price, like VALUE ADDED TAX.

Salt away Popular term for storing, or saving, money for future use. See SALARY.

Salvage money Reward given, usually by shipowners, to a third party responsible for saving the whole or part of a cargo.

Salvor's lien The right of someone who has saved a cargo to retain it until the claim for salvage money has been agreed.

Samurai bonds Loan stock issued by non-Japanese concerns on the Tokyo market, denominated in yen but not subject to local tax paid by the Japanese.

Sans frais French for 'without expense', sometimes written on a bill of exchange to signify that the issuer of the bill will not be responsible for any expense which might be incurred in obtaining payment.

Save and borrow account A bank account which acts as a monthly savings plan while also providing an automatic source of borrowing up to an agreed amount. The account holder agrees to save a fixed sum each month and earns interest while there is a surplus balance, but pays interest when the account is overdrawn. May also be called a revolving credit account.

Save as you earn (SAYE) Scheme under which employees agree to have a regular sum deducted from their wages or salaries to be put into a savings plan. In some instances a bonus is paid if the savings are retained for an agreed period of time.

Savings accounts An account offered by banks, building societies or the National Savings organization which gives a higher rate of interest on money deposited in return for restrictions on withdrawal of the money.

Savings and loans North American equivalent of building societies in Britain.

Savings bank See NATIONAL SAVINGS BANK.

Savings bonds and certificates Government-guaranteed savings products offered by NATIONAL SAVINGS.

SAYE See SAVE AS YOU EARN.

Scale fee Charge for work, based on a standard scale of fees rather than on the amount of work actually done. Widely used by professions like solicitors and accountants, as well as government departments.

Scalpers Market dealers who buy and sell small quantities, usually with a low profit margin, so as to make small but quick returns.

Scheduled territories Countries that

use sterling as their main or reserve currency.

Schedules A, C, D, E, F See TAX SCHEDULES.

Scheme of arrangement or composition Method used by a debtor to avoid being made bankrupt, under which a plan, formally recorded in a deed, is drawn up for only part of the debt to be paid. The scheme must be approved by creditors representing at least three-quarters of the outstanding debts and by the Bankruptcy Court.

Scrip Certificate or receipt given to holders of bonds and debentures, See BEARER SCRIP.

Scrip-holder A person or organization owning scrip.

Scrip issue Shares that are given to existing shareholders in a company free of charge. They are created by using some of the company's reserves of capital, and are allocated in proportion to the shares already held – for example one new share for every ten held. Apart from benefiting shareholders, a scrip issue is also used by companies whose shares have become difficult to buy and sell because of a shortage of supplies, to make more available to the market without reducing their value.

SDRs See SPECIAL DRAWING RIGHTS.

SEC See SECURITIES AND EXCHANGE COMMISSION.

SEAQ See STOCK EXCHANGE AUTOMATED QUOTATIONS SYSTEM.

Secondary bank See FINANCE COMPANY.

Secondary market Term used to describe buying and selling of something that originated elsewhere.

Second-class paper Promissory notes, bills of exchange or cheques guaranteed by someone whose commercial reputation is not of the highest class; in other words, there is a greater risk involved.

Second mortgage An additional mortgage taken out on a property on which there is already an existing, or principal, mortgage. A second mortgage, which is often used to provide security for a loan, is registered as a legal charge but bears a higher risk, since the holder of the principal or first mortgage has priority in being repaid, if necessary from the sale of the property, and usually holds the title deeds. As a result of this greater risk, interest charges on second mortgages are usually higher, sometimes considerably higher. See REMORTGAGE.

Secret reserves Accounting term for reserves deliberately not shown in a company's balance sheet. See HIDDEN RESERVES.

Secured creditor Someone holding a mortgage or some other form of collateral or security provided by the borrower of a loan. So the lender is 'secure' even if the loan is not repaid.

Secured debenture See DEBENTURE, MORTGAGE.

Secured loan Where the borrower of money provides some form of collateral or security that can be cashed in by the lender if the loan is not repaid. Because of the reduced risk, the rate of interest charged on secured loans is usually much less than the cost of unsecured loans.

Securities General term mainly used to describe stocks and shares, although it can also apply to all form of 'paper' investments. Formerly referred solely to debts or claims that were secured in one way or another and were therefore considered to be safe.

Securities and Exchange Commission (SEC) The state-backed organization in New York which controls the activities of all the US stock exchanges and other markets where securities are traded, primarily to ensure that investors are protected against fraud.

Securities and Investment Board (SIB) Main regulatory organization set up in 1985 to provide improved protection for investors by implementing the Financial Services Act 1986. The SIB is the umbrella organization that supervises, and controls, the other self-regulatory organizations (SROs) created to deal with different sectors of investment protection – stock market dealings, life insurance and unit trusts, futures and options, and all sellers of financial investment products. All companies involved in providing or selling collective investment services have to be authorized by one of the self-regulatory organizations or by the SIB itself. The SIB rulebook lays down the minimum standards required for the individual organizations and approves general policy. The SIB is indirectly controlled by the government, through the Department of Trade and Industry and the Bank of England; but it operates as an independent unit whose task is to ensure that investors receive the benefit of the protective powers introduced in the Financial Services Act, which superseded the Fraud Preventions Act. It also approves RECOGNIZED PROFESSIONAL BODIES (RPBs) and

DESIGNATED TERRITORIES. See
COMPLAINTS, REGULATION and USEFUL
ADDRESSES.

Securities Association (TSA) One of
the self-regulatory organizations, under
the umbrella of the Securities and
Investments Board, set up under the
Financial Services Act 1986 to protect the
interests of investors by controlling and
regulating the stock markets and
stockbrokers. It is closely associated with
the London (International) Stock
Exchange, sharing the same offices and
secretariat. See COMPLAINTS,
SELF-REGULATORY ORGANIZATIONS and
USEFUL ADDRESSES.

Securities market Place where
securities are bought and sold, such as the
Stock Exchange in London.

Security Something of value provided
by a borrower that can be cashed in by
the lender if a loan is not repaid as
promised. Very often some form of
security or collateral is insisted on before
a loan will be granted. Or alternatively,
the lender will charge a higher interest
rate, if security is not provided, because
of the greater risk involved in making the
loan.

Securitization Arrangement under
which mortgages (home loans) are
assigned by the original lender to a third
party who becomes responsible for the
loan; however, the terms and conditions
for the borrower should remain the same.
Useful way for mortgage lenders to
provide more home loans while restricting
the amount of capital committed.

Seed capital Money provided to help
start a venture or project, often by
financing the research and development
needed to judge its potential.

See-safe An agreement to sell goods to a
retailer on a SALE OR RETURN basis. In
some cases the customer pays for the
goods on delivery but is entitled to claim
the money back if they remain unsold at
the end of an agreed period.

Segregated account Bank account that
is deliberately kept separate by someone
holding money on an individual client's
behalf. The idea is to provide greater
protection for the client by operating a
separate account which can be easily
identified and checked, so that if anything
goes wrong there is a much better chance
of the money being kept safe. Putting
client's money into a segregated account is
a compulsory requirement for financial and
investment advisers under the Financial
Services Act. It does not provide
guaranteed safety against fraud and
negligence, since segregated accounts are
normally operated by the adviser or the
company holding them on a client's behalf.
So the funds in a segregated account can
be misappropriated without the client's
knowledge. At the same time a liquidator
can take control of the funds in segregated
accounts to meet the demands of creditors
generally.

Seigniorage Profit made by a
government from issuing coins. It is the
difference between the cost of
manufacture and distribution compared
with the face value.

Self administered pension
Arrangement under which contributors to
a pension scheme retain control of the
management and distribution of the fund.

Self-assessment System existing in
some countries, notably the United
States, where taxpayers prepare their
own annual returns, which are then
subject to checking by the tax authorities.

Self certification Facility offered by some mortgage lenders for borrowers to certify their own income or financial resources without having to provide additional independent evidence. Because of the obvious extra risk involved, the lender normally confines the mortgage to a lower percentage of the value of the house or alternatively charges a higher interest rate.

Self finance Fund the start, or expansion, of a business without borrowing money from outside sources.

Self-liquidating Loan that is repayable out of the product for which it was necessary to borrow money; for example, money borrowed by a builder to complete a house for sale, or by a farmer to finish harvesting a crop.

Self-regulatory organizations (SROs) Organizations set up under the 1986 Financial Services Act to regulate the various sectors of the financial and investment community. They have to be recognized (authorized) by the umbrella watchdog organization, the Securities and Investments Board (SIB), which sets the standard minimum rules. The SROs, which became operational in 1988, included the ASSOCIATION OF FUTURES BROKERS AND DEALERS (AFBD), FINANCIAL INTERMEDIARIES, MANAGERS AND BROKERS REGULATORY ASSOCIATION (FIMBRA), INVESTMENT MANAGEMENT REGULATORY ORGANIZATION (IMRO), LIFE ASSURANCE AND UNIT TRUST REGULATORY ORGANIZATION (LAUTRO) and THE SECURITIES ASSOCIATION (TSA), Although subject to overall control by the SIB, each SRO operates independently in its own sector and has wide-ranging powers to investigate complaints and maintain constant supervision to ensure that members comply with the rules and regulations. If any company fails to comply with the rules, it can be closed down and banned from operating. The older-established self-regulatory organizations (like the Law Society and Institute of Chartered Accountants) were reclassified as RECOGNIZED PROFESSIONAL BODIES (RPBs) which are permitted to authorize their members to offer investment services, provided they do not constitute a major part of the total business. See COMPLAINTS, REGULATION and USEFUL ADDRESSES.

Self tender When a company buys back its own shares. This usually happens either when the company wants to increase its earnings per share by reducing the capital required or to fight a hostile takeover bid.

Seller's market When prices are over-valued, or there is a surplus supply or lack of demand, pushing prices downwards. See BEAR MARKET.

Selling out Situation on the stock exchange when a buyer fails to take up shares, and they are therefore sold by the broker for the best price obtainable. The buyer is then liable to make up the difference, if any, between the original price offered and the actual price received.

Selling short Making a sale of something that the seller does not possess but which he hopes to acquire back at a lower price, thereby making a profit. However, the short seller can suffer unlimited losses if the price goes up instead of falling, so it is a dangerous practice for non-professional traders. Term also used in a more general sense to indicate the belief that something is not worth its current value or rating.

Separate assessment Tax option given by the Inland Revenue when a husband and wife want to be treated as separate individuals for tax purposes, normally because their joint earnings make it beneficial for each to have a personal allowance and forgo the joint allowance given for married couples. However, from April 1990 a completely new system of independent taxation is being introduced and the separate assessment will disappear. See MARRIED COUPLE'S ALLOWANCE and TAX REFORM.

Sequestration The appropriation of a property by a third party appointed by a court of law, when the ownership is in dispute or while the estate of a bankrupt is being divided up.

SERPS See STATE EARNINGS RELATED PENSION SCHEME.

Service charge Payment for providing a particular service. This may be for arranging a loan or supplying management or supervision. It most commonly applies, however, to the additional cost added on to hotel and restaurant bills as an extra payment, tip or gratuity, to waiters and other staff, in return for their services.

Servicing a debt Paying the interest due on an outstanding loan.

Settlement Paying a bill or outstanding debt. Also legal term for creating a trust, either by deed or by Will, to hold and administer property and/or other financial assets, on behalf of the beneficiaries.

Settlement day The date on the stock exchange when contracts to buy or sell shares have to be settled or paid. It is normally on a Monday, ten days after the end of the stock exchange account period. Also known as 'account day'.

Settlement discount Allowance, or reduction in price, given by a seller for prompt payment by a buyer.

Settlement terms Discounts allowed by a seller for payments made by specified dates.

Severance pay Money paid to employees of a company who lose their jobs through no fault of their own or when their contract of employment comes to an end. See REDUNDANCY PAYMENT.

Severe disablement allowance Government benefit paid to those who are unable to work because of being disabled, and are not able to claim sickness or normal invalidity benefit because they have not paid sufficient National Insurance contributions to qualify.

SFO See SUPERANNUATION FUNDS OFFICE.

Shadow director Someone who is not a named director of a company, but is still able to give directions or instructions to the Board.

Shady deal Slang term for a transaction that is considered to be dishonest.

Share accounts Term used for building society deposit accounts with no fixed investment period. It signifies that the depositor is viewed as a shareholder, or part owner, of the society, and there are restrictions on the maximum investments that can be held by individuals. At one time, share accounts were treated by the Inland Revenue like shares in a company, and were therefore eligible for indexation relief against capital gains tax; but that concession was withdrawn in the 1988 Finance Act.

Share allotment See ALLOTMENT LETTER.

Share broker See STOCKBROKER.

Share capital The total number of shares and loan stock issued, or authorized to be issued, by a company to raise the funds needed to start up and carry on the business. The amount of share capital is shown on the company's annual balance sheet listing the various different types of shares and loan. This represents the net worth of the business, after deduction of the amount owed to creditors.

Share certificate Legal document issued by a company to holders of shares to provide evidence of ownership. It outlines, in accordance with details listed on the company's share register, the type of share held, the quantity and serial numbers for identification. Thus when shares are bought and sold, say through the stock exchange, the certificates are given to the buyer as proof of the change of ownership and the new shareholder's name is listed on the SHARE REGISTER.

Share exchange Simple method used by companies wishing to merge together by swapping their share holdings. Alternatively, share exchange schemes are offered in investment products such as unit trusts, where the investor's existing holding of shares are taken instead of cash, and changed into units, after deduction of any capital gains tax that might be payable.

Shareholding The amount of shares, or stock, held in a company.

Share index or indices A device used to measure the change in the value of shares traded on a market by putting their prices together and tracking them on a collective basis. The index can be made up of the bulk of the shares traded (like the Financial Times All-Share index in London) or of a smaller number of actively traded shares in leading companies selected to represent the market as a whole (like the FT-SE 100 index). In addition, special indices are compiled, made up of shares from particular sectors of the market, such as gold-mining companies.

Share option or stock option Right given to buy or sell shares or stock at an agreed price. In the options market, this right is bought by payment of a premium; but in many company schemes it is used as a reward or incentive for employees or key staff. Employee share option schemes receive special tax relief as part of a government drive to encourage wider share ownership and provide an incentive for employees to take a greater interest in the profitability of the company employing them.

Share premium The amount at which a share is valued, over and above its nominal or face value. Thus a £1 share trading at £5 would have a premium of £4.

Share register List of shareholders which must be kept by every public limited company to identify who holds the shares, the amount paid and the date of purchase. The register must be kept open for at least two hours a day to be available for examination free by any shareholder, or by anybody else on payment of a nominal inspection fee.

Share shop Popular name for a retail outlet, like a department store, that sells shares and other financial products to the general public.

Share split When the price of a share is

considered to be too high for trading purposes, a company may decide to split the shares up, for example by allocating to existing shareholders four new shares at £5 each for one old share valued £20. This makes the shares easier to buy and sell, since they can be traded with smaller outlay of money per share.

Share transfer Form that is used to notify formally any change of ownership of shares. It is sent, together with the SHARE CERTIFICATE, to the registered office of the company so that the details of the new owner can be entered in the SHARE REGISTER.

Share warrant Form of share certificate issued to shareholders stating that they own a specified number of fully paid shares, but not mentioning the name of the shareholder. Indeed the shareholder's name is struck off the share register when the warrant is issued. As a result, ownership of the shares can be achieved by simply transferring the warrant. See WARRANTS.

Sharks Slang term for greedy people who make money by ruthless, often dishonest means. See LOAN SHARK.

Shell company A company that exists in name only, and is not actively engaged in business. They are often used as a cheap way of launching a business without having to go through the process of setting up a company, or alternatively to make use of their listing on a stock exchange. Sometimes shell companies are left dormant for future use, or to act as a vehicle for building up a group of different companies.

Shilling Former unit of currency used in the UK and some of the countries in the British Empire. There were 20 shillings in the £, and each shilling was worth 12

pennies. Believed to originate from Germanic term, 'skilling'.

Short Market term used to describe the trading technique of selling stock, not owned by the seller, in anticipation of being able to buy it back before the delivery date falls due at a lower price and so make a profit. Thus 'going short' means selling in anticipation of prices falling and is the opposite of taking a LONG position in anticipation of prices going up. 'Shorting' the market is a highly dangerous practice, since if prices rise instead of falling, the seller has to acquire stock and can be held to ransom by holders of the available stock. However, many professional traders reckon they make more money by 'going short', against the natural trend to buy; and on occasions 'short' selling is used to depress the price of a share or stock before making a takeover bid or purchase. A safer way of 'going short' is to buy a PUT OPTION. See BEAR.

Short bill A bill of exchange payable on demand or within a period of ten days.

Short-change Deliberately give a bad deal, such as a shopkeeper giving the wrong change in hopes that the customer will not notice.

Short covering When sellers have sold stock they do not possess, in hope of profiting from a fall in prices, the sale eventually has to be 'covered' by a matching purchase whatever happens. If the market shows signs of going up instead of down, sellers will often 'cover' their 'short' positions quickly in order to avoid suffering losses. See SELLING SHORT.

Short-dated securities or stock
Fixed-interest bonds, bills and securities, including gilts, that are repayable in less than five years' time.

Short form report Accountant's report included in a company prospectus, which details the trading record, the source of funds and the latest balance sheets.

Shorthold tenancy Tenancy that is limited to a period of between one and five years.

Short lease Lease that has less than 50 years to run before the property reverts to the owner of the FREEHOLD.

Short notice accounts Savings accounts with banks or building societies where the depositor has to give advance notice of withdrawal in order to take out the money without loss of interest. In return, the depositor is given a higher rate of interest than for accounts where money can be drawn out immediately without notice.

Shorts Sellers in a market; alternatively, abbreviated version for short-term government securities (gilts) which are due for repayment within a maximum period of five years.

Short-term capital Money borrowed for a limited period, such as a bank overdraft.

Short-term deposits Money deposited with banks, building societies and other financial institutions which can be withdrawn at short notice. Normally the longer the term of the deposit, the higher the interest rate paid, although on occasions when there is a shortage of instantly available money this does not apply.

Short-terminism Colloquial phrase to describe the attitude of investors, fund managers or companies, being preoccupied with making quick profits

rather than a steady return over a period of years.

Short ton Measurement of weight used in the United States equal to 2,000 lb, as compared with the metric tonne (2,204.6 lb) and the long ton (2,240 lb).

Shunter Broker in a provincial stock exchange who matches up transactions with those on the London Stock Exchange.

SIB See SECURITIES AND INVESTMENT BOARD and USEFUL ADDRESSES.

Sight draft Bill of exchange payable when it is presented, irrespective of when it was issued.

Silent partner See SLEEPING PARTNER.

Silver Precious metal that is historically an alternative to gold as a store of wealth, Mined, either by itself or in association with other metals (notably copper, lead and zinc), silver was used as the basis for the currency and coinage in many countries. According to the Bible, Judas betrayed Jesus for thirty pieces of silver. Unlike gold, it also has important industrial uses, notably in the manufacture of photographic film and in the electrical and silver-plating industries.

Silver bullion Ingots or bars, the form in which silver is traded primarily either physically or via the futures markets. However, the main sales to the public of silver are in the form of coins or jewellery.

Silver standard Monetary system under which the value of the currency unit was based on a specific weight of silver and normally includes coins made out of silver.

Simple interest Interest calculated on the original capital sum or loan only, and not including any accrued interest. See COMPOUND INTEREST.

Sinecure Employment that requires little work done, even though a good salary may be paid.

Single bond One that contains no payment conditions.

Single liability US term for LIMITED LIABILITY.

Single option Option that carries either the right to buy (call) or sell (put), but not both.

Single person's allowance Amount of money that can be earned before tax starts to be deducted. The allowance is usually increased in the annual Budget to compensate for the effects of inflation, but this does not always apply. In the 1988 Budget it was announced that from April 1990 everyone, whether they are married or not, would be eligible for a single person's allowance, under the new independent taxation regime aimed at eliminating the previous discrimination between married and non-married couples. See TAX REFORM.

Single premium Insurance policy where only one (initial) premium is paid instead of a series of regular payments. Hence with single premium INVESTMENT BONDS, an initial lump-sum payment is made at the start, although this can often be supplemented by additional amounts later.

Sinking fund Money put aside, usually in regular instalments, for a specific purpose: either to repay a debt, redeem outstanding shares or stock, replace an asset, or frequently to cover the cost of repairs to a property. Leaseholders in a house, for example, may well have to contribute to a sinking fund held by the freeholder to ensure that money is available for emergency repairs or restoration.

Sinking fund policy A life insurance policy under which a fixed sum of money is payable on a specified date, whether or not the insured person is alive on that date. Also known as CAPITAL REDEMPTION POLICY.

Situation rent The extra amount that is charged for land or property deemed to be better situated than a similar property.

Skint Having no money, being penniless, possibly as a result of having been skinned or fleeced.

Slate club Alternative name for LOAN CLUB, derived from description of loans being 'put on the slate' (originally written down on a slate) for payment at a later date.

Sleeping partner Someone who invests money in a partnership and has a right to a share of the profits, although taking no active part in the management. Also known as 'silent partner'.

Sliding peg or crawling peg Monetary arrangement in some countries to adjust automatically the value of its currency in line with the rate of inflation.

Sliding scale Method of varying charges for work done according to the amount involved, the time spent or profits made.

Slow assets See ASSETS, ILLIQUID.

Sluice-gate price Minimum import price level fixed by the European Community

under its Common Agricultural Policy for
pig-meat, eggs and poultry, aimed at
protecting domestic producers from
competition.

Slush Slang term for forged bank notes.

Slush fund Slang term for money or
assets put aside specifically for making
secret payments or bribes.

Snake Shortened version of 'snake in the
tunnel', a phrase used to describe an
arrangement made between some
member countries of the European
Community to co-operate in trying to
restrict to a minimum fluctuations in the
value of their currencies. See EUROPEAN
MONETARY SYSTEM.

Soft currency Currency of dubious
value, usually from a developing or
Communist bloc country which has
balance-of-payments problems and high
inflation. There are, therefore, few buyers
of the currency, which is likely to
depreciate in value and be difficult to sell.
Opposite of HARD CURRENCY.

Soft money Paper money, as opposed to
coins.

Softs (soft commodities) General term
used to describe agricultural commodities
and futures markets, to distinguish them
from metals and minerals.

Sola From the Latin 'one and only.' Used
to describe a bill of exchange only one
document of which has been issued, with
no copies.

Sole agency An agent who has exclusive
rights to sell specific goods or property.
Estate agents with sole rights often charge
sellers lower commisssion than if several
agents have been appointed.

Sole proprietor The one and only owner
of a business.

Sole trader Someone who trades on
their own account rather than in a
partnership or as an employee of a
company.

Solicitor's lien The right of solicitors to
keep possession of documents until their
fees have been paid.

Solvency The ability to pay all debts in
full when due. A solvent company has a
surplus of assets over liabilities. See
INSOLVENCY.

South Sea Bubble Famous swindle
during the early eighteenth century when
the formation of the South Sea Company
was the climax of a period of frenzied
speculation on the stock market, which led
to share prices being pushed to artificially
high levels. When the South Sea Company
collapsed financially, the whole bubble
burst and huge losses were sustained.
This incident is often cited as what can go
wrong if the markets are allowed to trade
freely with no restrictions.

Sovereigns UK gold coin, first minted in
the reign of Henry VII. Initially it had a
value of twenty-two shillings and sixpence,
but was subsequently fixed at a value of
20s(£1) in 1817. It ceased to be circulated
as legal currency in 1914, although
sovereigns and half-sovereigns continued
to be minted until 1975. The name
'sovereign' is still used colloquially to
describe the possession of money
generally. Since the value of the gold
content far exceeds the face value of the
coins, they are nowadays bought and sold
via bullion brokers, coin dealers and banks
as a substitute for gold or for their rarity
value. Their prices fluctuate constantly, in

accordance with the changes in the cost of gold.

Spec Abbreviated version of 'speculation'. Hence, trying or buying something 'on spec' means taking a gamble.

Special clearing Method by which payment of a cheque through a bank can be speeded up, to be cleared on the same day. However, the bank imposes an additional charge for this service.

Special commissioners (of income tax) Officials appointed by the Treasury to decide on disputed tax appeals.

Special deposits Amounts of money which must be deposited by commercial banks with the Bank of England, which varies the sums required to be deposited as a means of controlling the money supply.

Special drawing rights (SDRs) See INTERNATIONAL MONETARY FUND.

Speciality debt A debt that remains in force until twelve years have elapsed. See STATUTE OF LIMITATIONS.

Special manager Someone appointed by the official receiver when the liquidation of a company that has gone bankrupt requires specialist knowledge.

Special presentation When a cheque is presented for SPECIAL CLEARING.

Special resolution Normally required for changes in the constitution of a company. Similar to an extraordinary resolution.

Special situations Market term used to describe a particular type of investment

fund, normally a unit trust, which puts money into companies that are expected to benefit from some new development, say a takeover bid, new discovery or appointment of a new management. They are, therefore, essentially high-risk funds that tend to perform either very well or very badly.

Specie Money in the form of coins, not notes. Opposite of SOFT MONEY.

Specific capital Asset that can be used only for one particular purpose, such as a machine.

Specific legacy Legacy that must be paid for a specified part of the deceased's estate.

Specific tax Tax charge based on a specified quantity, as opposed to value.

Split capital Arrangement, favoured by investment trusts in particular, under which a fund is divided up into two parts – capital growth and income shares. Holders of the income shares receive all the income received by the whole fund, while holders of capital growth shares are assigned any increase in the value of the capital invested. Thus investors with different aims – income or capital growth – are both catered for by one fund according to their preference.

Split share A share that is divided into a number of smaller units to make them easier to buy. A £10 share, for example, might be divided into four shares worth £2.50 each.

Spot cash Another term for cash on delivery. On some futures markets the spot cash price is quoted to indicate what has to be paid for immediate delivery and payment on the spot.

Spot delivery Immediate delivery.

Spot exchange Market price for immediate purchase or sale of a currency.

Spot market Dealings that take place on the commodity or currency markets for immediate delivery and payment.

Spot price The cost of something delivered immediately.

Spot rate The cost of a currency for immediate delivery, as compared with sometime in the future.

Spot transactions Buying or selling for cash, and immediate delivery, as opposed to dealing for delivery at a date in the future.

Spout A pawnbroker's shop. Hence 'up the spout' can mean being in financial difficulties, or ruined, on the assumption of being forced to pawn goods.

Spread The profit margin between the cost of manufacturing or buying something, and selling it. With shares, unit trusts and options, the spread is the difference between the buying or asking (offer) price and the selling (bid) price. On the futures markets the spread is the difference between the price for immediate delivery (cash or spot price) and the price for delivery at some forward or future date.

Spreading the risk Basic strategy of investing in different shares and investments on the grounds that they are unlikely all to fall in value at the same time. Investment in one share, for example, carries a high risk if the particular company fails. Alternatively, for further safety fund managers and private investors seek to put their money into different sectors, like

property, cash, fixed-interest securities and foreign currencies, as well as into shares, so they should be protected whatever happens. Insurers also protect themselves against potentially heavy losses by passing on some of the business to other companies. See REINSURANCE.

Square mile Popular name for the City of London financial centre, based originally on the fact that most of the big institutions – like the Bank of England, Lloyd's insurance and the Stock Exchange – are grouped close to each other within one square mile on the north side of the River Thames in London. Over the years, the term has become a general description for the whole London financial centre, even for offices and dealings outside the original square mile.

Squeeze Financial term for the situation when pressure is put on a market, a company or an individual to do something they might not want to do. The most common example is where a dealer creates an artificial shortage of supplies by buying up all the available stock and forcing prices up. This puts a 'squeeze' on sellers who had hoped to profit from prices going down. It is common practice for central banks, like the Bank of England, to force the value of a currency higher by buying heavily, thereby 'squeezing' sellers.

Stabilized bond See BOND, INDEXED.

Stag Popular stock exchange term for someone who seeks to make a quick profit by buying shares in a new issue, including privatization issues, and selling them shortly afterwards at a higher price. If the issue is oversubscribed, the market price will normally open at a higher level than the issue price, reflecting the demand for the shares, and stags can sell their allocations at a higher price than paid. But if the issue is undersubscribed, or the market price falls below the issue level for some reason, then the stag has the choice of either suffering a loss or holding on to the shares in the hope that the market price will move up. Stags are essentially short-term speculators in new issues, who buy shares only with the intention of selling quickly, rather than becoming long-term investors. Hence 'stagging' is used to describe speculative buying of new shares in a company or stock.

Stagflation Combination of slow economic growth together with rising prices, causing inflation. Worst possible scenario for a government.

Staggered directorships A defensive tactic used by companies threatened with being taken over. The appointment of existing directors is staggered over different periods of years, so they can retain control even if the company is bought out, unless the buyer pays suitable terms of compensation.

Stakeholder Person, often an estate agent or solicitor, who agrees to hold a sum of money deposited by the buyer until such time as the conditions of the sale have been met, when the buyer gives approval for the money to be paid over.

Stale cheque Cheque that has not been presented within the time period specified by the bank for payment and is, therefore, not cashable. It will normally be returned marked 'out of date'.

Stallage Rent paid, usually to a local government authority, for the right to put up a stall or booth in a market-place.

Stamp duty UK government tax on the sale of property and shares. It is imposed by the Inland Revenue, which charges a payment for stamping the documents needed to complete the purchase of a property or shares, and is normally paid by the purchaser.

Standard coinage Where the face value of coins issued equals the intrinsic value of the metals used.

Standard indemnity Normal rate of charges imposed by an insurance company to cover a specified risk, for example when a building society wants protection against lending a high percentage of the value of the property.

Standing order Instruction to a bank to make regular payments of a set amount on a set date. Also known as BANKER'S ORDER, it is more often compared with a DIRECT DEBIT. The main difference is that with a standing order the payer retains control and the bank can vary the payments only with the account holder's permission. With a direct debit, the onus for collecting payment falls on the recipient; but it can also be used in a more flexible way to collect payments of variable amounts.

State earnings related pension scheme (SERPS) Introduced by the Labour Government in 1978 to provide an additional, extra pension over and above the basic state pension rights provided by payment of National Insurance contributions. Additional National Insurance contributions are made in order to qualify for SERPS, and there is the right either to contract in (join) or contract out (not join) the scheme. Employees are automatically contracted in, unless they deliberately contract out through an alternative scheme that must provide at least the same pension benefits. Those contracted out pay a lower rate of National Insurance contributions to reflect the reduced pensions benefits. Many company pension schemes automatically contracted out of SERPS. But under new legislation that became effective in 1988, the Conservative Government gave special incentives, in the form of rebates of National Insurance payments, for individual employees to contract out of SERPS and instead take out a personal pension plan. See PENSIONS.

State enterprise Company or organization owned, or controlled, by the government.

Status inquiry Examination of financial standing of someone borrowing money or seeking credit. See CREDIT AGENCY.

Statute-barred debt A debt that cannot be recovered by legal means because its time limit has expired. Under the Limitation Act 1939, the time limit for a normal debt is six years from the end of the credit period or twelve years for SPECIALITY DEBT made under seal. However, the limitation does not apply to certain creditors, notably the Inland Revenue for unpaid tax. The time limit is also restarted if the borrower acknowledges the debt, either by making part payment or in writing.

Statute of limitations The time period set for the legal collection of unpaid debts, provided the lender has not made any application for payment. See STATUTE-BARRED DEBT.

Statutory companies Companies set up by special Act of Parliament for some specific purpose, normally for public utilities – such as the provision of electricity, gas or water – which require certain powers to be able to act for the common good.

Statutory instruments Legal orders and regulations having the force of law, which are made by government ministers, instead of being approved directly by Parliament.

Statutory sick pay (SSP) Under the government's National Insurance scheme, contributors are entitled to sickness benefit if they are unable to work because of ill-health for a period of over three days. The employer has to pay the statutory rate for the first eight weeks of absence, but can then reclaim it, together with the normal National Insurance contribution. After that period the Department of Social Security is liable to pay the statutory rates laid down, unless the employer continues to pay the employee a wage in excess of the statutory sick pay rate.

Sterling Most commonly used these days as a shorthand description for the British currency or (London) pound. However, it was originally used to describe money of a specified standard weight or fineness. It was derived from 'easterling', the name given to merchants from north Germany who settled in London in the reign of Edward I. They used as a currency silver pennies of particularly good quality, and 240 of these pennies, or 'sterlings', became equal to one pound sterling, as they weighed the equivalent of one pound troy weight of 92.5% pure silver. Later on, in 1816, the silver pound sterling was replaced as a currency in Britain by 22 carat, or 91.66%, pure gold. The term 'pound sterling' was first of all used in the foreign exchange markets to distinguish the British unit of currency from other currencies, particularly those also using units of one pound in weight. Eventually sterling became synonymous with the British currency and was used as a RESERVE CURRENCY, since it was acceptable throughout the world and linked to the currencies of many countries which are current or past members of the British Empire. Since the end of the Second World War in 1945 the economic problems suffered by Britain, leading to the reduction in value of sterling against other currencies, has meant that its role as a reserve currency has greatly diminished, being replaced primarily by the US dollar. Nevertheless sterling remains one of the major currencies, and it still retains direct links with currencies in several Commonwealth countries.

Sterling area or sterling bloc
Countries, also known as the Scheduled Territories, which use sterling as a trading or reserve currency.

Sterling bond A bond payable in sterling, despite being issued in a foreign country. Often known as a BULLDOG.

Sterling security Stock or share in which both the capital and interest or dividend are payable in sterling or in the currency of a country in the Scheduled Territories.

Sterling silver Silver goods with a standard mark inscribed by the government assay office which denotes that the fineness of the silver used is at least 935 parts pure silver out of every 1,000 parts. It thus enables the owner to estimate the value of the silver content of the goods.

Stipend Salary, or fixed regular payment for services, normally used to describe monies paid to a clergyman, magistrate or sometimes to a tutor.

Stipendiary magistrate Qualified lawyer employed full-time and receiving

payment, as contrasted to the unpaid Justices of the Peace.

Stock General financial term used to describe assets held, fixed-interest securities and share capital. Strictly speaking, stock in a company does not include shares, since shares have to be fully paid up before they become converted into stock; but in practice the term is widely used to describe holding shares or a stake in a company. Fixed-interest securities, such as gilts, are definitely stocks, specifically denominated in units of £100. There are also many different types of stock, for example bonds, which provide the owners with various rights.

Stockbroker Generic term used to describe members of the stock market, who buy and sell stock and shares on a client's behalf and are paid brokerage, or commission, for this service. The role of the stockbroker has changed greatly since a new trading system was introduced on the Stock Exchange in October 1986 (known as the Big Bang) which scrapped the old position of jobber and allowed stockbrokers to act both as a market-maker and as an agent in share dealings. At the same time, the minimum commission system was scrapped, so stockbrokers are now free to negotiate rates with individual clients, depending on the size of the deal, the status of the client and the work involved. Traditionally, stockbrokers have been specialists in advising customers on their investment strategies in the stock market and providing background research into individual shares. But stockbroking services are now offered by many organizations, including banks and building societies. However, anyone offering stockbroking services has to be authorized by the SECURITIES ASSOCIATION (TSA), the self-regulatory organization attached to the London Stock Exchange, or by the umbrella organization, the SECURITIES AND INVESTMENT BOARD (SIB).

Stock certificate A document, similar to a share certificate, issued by a company whose shares have been converted into stock, confirming that the holder is the registered owner of a specified amount of stock in the company. In some cases the name of the holder is not specified; so the bearer of the certificate is the owner of the stock, which can be easily transferred by simply passing on the certificate.

Stock cheque Special kind of draft or bill of exchange used by stockbrokers in one country to pay for stock brought from a broker in another country.

Stock exchange An organized market where securities (both stocks and shares) are bought and sold under fixed rules and regulations. The basic purpose of a stock exchange or stock market is to provide a meeting point for companies and government to raise money by selling their stocks and shares to investors, either to private individuals or to institutions like pension funds and insurance companies. Traditionally this has been achieved by creating a trading place, or 'floor', where the representatives of buyers and sellers could get together and deal. Nowadays, with modern technology and computer systems handling all the information via screens, a physical trading floor is no longer necessary and has, in fact, been abandoned in the case of the Stock Exchange in London. In other countries, trading floors have been retained, but the principle is the same: the role of stock exchanges is really to try and ensure that stocks and shares can be traded under organized and regulated conditions so that both buyers and sellers can rely on deals

being honoured by members who have been vetted to comply with specified standards of honesty and financial stability. When a company is 'listed' to allow dealings of its shares on the London stock market, it also has to meet certain criteria, and is classified accordingly, either on to a 'full' listing, the UNLISTED SECURITIES MARKET (USM) or on to the THIRD (OVER THE COUNTER) MARKET. See USEFUL ADDRESSES.

Stock Exchange Automated Quotations System (SEAQ)
Computer-based system on the London Stock Exchange used to provide a record of share dealing transactions and prices. When deals have been completed, the price information is passed to brokers via the Teletext Output Price Information Computer (TOPIC) which can then give clients up-to-date information on price movements.

SEAQ Automatic Exchange Facility (SAEF) is another computer-based system introduced on the London stock market to handle dealings (especially small-size bargains) automatically, and thus reduce expense and paperwork. Broker members of the market feed orders direct from their clients into the system, which automatically selects the best price being quoted by market-makers and completes the order with the market-making firm offering the best deal.

Stock exchange mutual reference library Central list of all clients of the Stock Exchange member-companies which is used by brokers to check, before taking new business on, whether the client has a record of defaulting or otherwise not paying money owed.

Stock indices Mathematical measures of trends in prices of stocks and shares,

compiled by plotting the average
movements to show the upward or
downward changes in markets or
individual sectors. See INDEX.

Stock option Special arrangment made
by companies, usually for key and/or
senior employees, offering them the right
to buy stock or shares in the company at a
favourable price. Often used as an
inducement to win or retain the services of
an employee, subject to certain conditions
being met, such as agreeing to remain for
a specified minimum of time. See GOLDEN
HANDCUFFS.

Stockpile See BUFFER STOCK.

Stock transfer A legal form that
simplifies the change of ownership of
stocks and shares. The form gives just the
name and address of the new owner and is
signed by the previous owner.

Stock warrant Same as a STOCK
CERTIFICATE.

Stony broke Slang term for having no
money left after using up all resources
(including precious stones).

Stop loss An order, normally given to a
broker, to close a position in a market in
order to limit the loss suffered.
Particularly used in volatile markets with
sharp price movements, like futures and
options, as a means of protection against
excessive losses.

Stopped cheque Where the bank has
been instructed by the payer not to honour
a cheque. It is then often returned unpaid
with a note saying that payment has been
countermanded (cancelled) by the drawer
or it simply orders not to pay. If the bank
pays the cheque in spite of the stop order,

it is liable to bear any loss incurred instead
of the customer.

Store card Charge or credit card issued
by retail shops for use when paying for
goods bought there as a sales inducement
or alternative to a cheque. With the
'charge card' variety, the amount owing
has to be paid in full at the end of a
specified accounting period, normally
monthly. A credit (store) card operates
like Access or Visa in that shoppers have
the option to pay off a minimum sum each
month and settle the rest later if so
desired. Because of the administrative
costs involved, store cards tend to charge
a high rate of interest on money owed.

Straddle Market term for buying and
selling for forward delivery at the same
time over the same period, to establish a
transfer of assets while limiting potential
losses from changes in the market price.
Similar to a double option See OPTION.

Strap A transaction in the options
market, comprising buying one put (sell)
and two call (buy) options at the same
time. Conversely, a 'strip' is buying two
puts and one call option.

Straights Bonds with a fixed-interest
and fixed-maturity date. See
EUROBONDS.

Street dealings Market slang term for
transactions concluded after normal
trading hours. Hence also 'street price'.
See KERB TRADING.

Strict liability Legal obligation to pay
damages, even though the cause of the
loss was purely accidental, such as cattle
escaping from a field and causing a car to
crash.

Strip See STRAP.

Structural survey An investigation of a property, usually carried out by a qualified surveyor, commissioned to examine the structure rather than to give a valuation. A precautionary measure often taken by prospective buyers of old or converted houses to find out whether costly repairs are likely to be necessary.

Sub-fund or sub-trust Investment funds or unit trusts that are part of an 'umbrella' group of funds, run by an investment manager or insurance company.

Sub-lease A lease that is given by someone who is himself leasing the property from the freeholder. Also known as 'under-lease'. Hence a 'sub-lessor' is a tenant who sub-lets a property to a sub-tenant.

Sub-mortgage When a mortgage lender borrows money under another mortgage on the same property, timed to expire a few days before the first mortgage.

Subordinated unsecured loan stock Loans made by banks where the interests of depositors take precedence over those of the stockholders.

Subrogation The legal right of an insurer to take any money received by the insured as a result of a successful claim against a third party.

Subscribe Agree to make a payment for goods (say a magazine), services (such as membership of a club) or to charity. Used in the stock market to describe an application for shares in a limited company, or an insurance agreement to take part of a risk in an insurance contract.

Subscribed capital Part of the capital of a company that is issued in return for cash, as opposed to some other form of asset, like property.

Subscription See SUBSCRIBE.

Subscription day Specified time when dealings are permitted in some unit trusts, particularly offshore funds, which do not allow daily dealings.

Subscription shares Building society shares that are normally bought by regular instalments, and are therefore a form of savings plan. They often pay a higher rate of interest than the society's ordinary account as an inducement to maintain regular payments in.

Subshare Portion of a share bought in a foreign company (since in Britain a share cannot be divided up).

Subsidiary earnings Extra income received from a subsidiary occupation, in addition to but below normal earnings from someone's main job.

Subsidy Money given to somebody, or some organization, to help pay costs. Also given by governments to allow producers of goods, such as farmers, to sell them at a specified (low) market price without suffering crippling losses that might put them out of business or force them to sack employees. Also used to subsidize exports in order to gain a market share or dispose of surplus stocks.

Subsistence allowance Extra money, often a fixed sum per day, paid to employees to cover the cost of food or other expenses when travelling or working overtime.

Substitute money Documents like bank deposits or credits that can be transferred as an alternative to cash payments.

Substituted annuity When some pension plans mature, the holders are given a choice of annuities in which to put the proceeds for payment of the pension. They are thus able to substitute one annuity for another which may provide more favourable terms.

Sub-underwriting The sponsor, or underwriter, of a big new issue of stocks or shares will often spread the risk by asking other financial institutions to support the issue.

Subvention Money given to a person or organization that is providing a service for the general good of society.

Sufferance See TENANT AT SUFFERANCE.

Sum assured/insured The amount guaranteed for payment by the insurance company under an assurance (life) or insurance (accident) policy.

Sumptuary law Regulations that can put a limit on personal spending in times of financial trouble.

Sundries account Record of dealings with occasional customers or suppliers.

Sundry debtor Borrower who owes money to a business, but not for the company's normal trading activity. It might, for example, be an employee who has taken a personal loan from the business.

Superannuate Pension off an employee.

Superannuation Pension or other payment received by someone who has retired from being employed. Used by Civil Service and other public sector employees to describe their occupational pension schemes.

Superannuation funds office (SFO) Section of the Inland Revenue that deals exclusively with pension schemes. It supervises the way both company and personal pension schemes operate and the tax concessions made.

Supplementary benefit See INCOME SUPPORT.

Supplements (National Savings) Extra interest paid out to holders of index-linked savings certificates to make them more attractive during a period of low inflation.

Surcharge An additional charge, made over and above the original payment. For example, a travel company may impose a surcharge if the cost of providing the holiday has been forced up by unexpected changes in the value of currencies. Surcharges are also often used to cover the provision of additional services.

Surety bond See BOND.

Surrender value Amount paid when an insurance policy is cancelled before it reaches the agreed maturity date. The sum is calculated by taking into account the total premiums paid and the return on investment earned. However, since the insurance companies tend to deduct their charges, and setting-up costs during the early years of the policy, the surrender value is often disappointingly low, especially if the policy has been running for only a relatively short period. Indeed if surrendered very early, the policy may have no value at all. Policy-holders can judge the extent of the charges and costs deducted by looking at the projected surrender values and comparing them with the premiums paid over the same period.

Swaps Purchase and sale of currencies

for immediate delivery, made at the same time as a purchase or sale of a currency for delivery at some time in the future. Used by financial institutions, particularly banks, to speculate in the currency markets or make a known profit from providing money for a specific period.

Swift International system for transferring money electronically between different banks.

Switching Moving investments by selling one and replacing it with another. Sometimes this involves selling shares and going into fixed-interest securities, or vice versa. Alternatively, unit-linked life insurance policies, mortgages, pension funds and unit trust groups give the opportunity to switch, either free of charge or subject to certain restrictions and costs. With a pension or mortgage fund, for example, it often makes good sense to switch into a secure, fixed-interest or cash fund when the plan is near maturity, to preserve the value already built up against a sudden drop in the share market. Some companies will automatically advise this, but others will leave it to the policy-holder. A liability to capital gains tax may be incurred by switching, since this often means taking a profit on the existing holding. But switching can also be used to establish a capital gains tax loss.

Switching discount Unit trust groups often offer special terms to their existing clients to switch from one trust to another at a special cheap rate as an inducement to retaining their business.

Syndic Person appointed by an organization (like a university) to manage its financial affairs.

Syndicate Group of people, or companies, who get together for investment or speculative purposes, particularly venture capital projects where the risks are high. Insurance underwriters in the Lloyd's exchange form syndicates to deal in specific classes of insurance.

T

Take-home pay The amount of money actually received by an employee after deductions made for income tax, National Insurance, pension funds and other contributions.

Takeover bid Offer made to shareholders of a company by another company or individual seeking to acquire their shares in sufficient quantities to gain control. If the company being taken over is a member of the Stock Exchange strict rules and regulations laid down by the TAKEOVER PANEL to protect the interest of the shareholders have to be followed or the bid will be disallowed. There is normally a time limit set for acceptance or otherwise of the offer. If the bidder gains control of 90% or more of the shares, he has the legal right to acquire the remaining 10% at the offer price. A bid can be friendly, that is recommended by the Board, or contested, in which case the bidder appeals directly to shareholders in defiance of the Board, and battle for control ensues. See DAWN RAID.

Takeover panel The organization, attached to the London Stock Exchange, which ensures that takeover bids for listed companies comply with the City Code of Takeovers and Mergers, which seeks to protect the interest of investors and shareholders.

Takings The cash received in a retail outlet for sale of goods.

TALISMAN See TRANSFER

ACCOUNTING, LODGING FOR INVESTORS AND STOCK MANAGEMENT.

Tally Originally a split of wood, divided into halves that matched each other and provided evidence of a contract when matched together. They were used as proof of loans made to the sovereign or exchequer; but nowadays the term describes the list of a ship's cargo, loaded or unloaded.

Tallyman Shopkeeper or trader, usually selling cheap goods, who accepts payment by instalments.

Talon A slip, issued with bearer bonds, that the holder can exchange for a new set of interest coupons when the earlier coupons have been used up.

Tangible assets See ASSETS.

Tangibles Investments involving actual physical possession, like diamonds, coins, wine or works of art.

Tap issue Treasury fixed-interest securities issued direct to government departments or other chosen recipients, instead of being placed on the market for general sale or put up for tender like other GILTS.

Tap-stock Readily available fixed-interest securities, usually the unsold balance of government-backed GILTS not taken when offered to the market, and therefore obtainable at a given price on demand – like water from a tap. They are divided into short taps (repayable within five years); medium taps (repayable within five to fifteen years); and long taps (over fifteen years).

Tare Allowance given for the weight of the container when assessing the value of goods.

Target price Term used by the European Community Common Agricultural Policy to describe the theoretical fair and economic return efficient farmers should receive for the sale of their products. It is fixed annually, and different methods are used to try and ensure that the target price is reached.

Tariff Scale of prices, charges or taxes. Often used by itself to refer to the tax imposed on imports.

Task pay System of basing employee's payment on the jobs completed within a specified standard time-period.

TAURUS See TRANSFER AND AUTOMATED REGISTRATION OF UNCERTIFIED STOCK.

Tax Payment of money demanded by a government to meet general public expenditure or specific purposes.

Taxable income The amount of income on which someone is liable to pay tax after all deductions for reliefs and personal allowances.

Tax and Price Index (TPI) Government index introduced in 1979 to measure the rise in wages needed to keep pace with changes in taxation and prices.

Tax avoidance Legal way of reducing

payments of tax by exploiting the allowances available.

Tax codes See PAY AS YOU EARN.

Tax commissioners See COMMISSIONERS OF INLAND REVENUE.

Tax credit A voucher indicating that a stated sum of tax has already been paid and which it may be possible to reclaim from the Inland Revenue. For example, when a share dividend is paid, the basic rate of tax is automatically deducted by the company. Shareholders who are non-taxpayers are then entitled to claim the tax back. Those liable to tax can produce the tax credit to show that they have already paid basic rate tax and have this deducted from their tax liability.

Tax disc Receipt for payment of a road fund licence, that has legally to be displayed on the vehicle to provide evidence that the tax has been paid.

Tax evasion Illegal methods of avoiding taxation payments.

Tax exempt funds Funds not liable to tax. Non-profit organizations working for the public good (like charities, religious associations, clubs and societies) can invest without having to pay taxes. Pension funds, personal equity plans (PEPS) and certain friendly societies are also not liable to pay tax, provided they comply with the rules and regulations specified.

Tax haven Independent countries (like the Bahamas, Cayman Islands or the Channel Islands) which specialize in providing a tax base for wealthy individuals and international companies seeking to reduce their tax liabilities. They either charge no tax at all or have much lower rates, and do not have taxation agreements with other countries, so their residents do not have to pay UK tax rates, for example. However, countries like the UK have strict rules about establishing tax residence overseas and thereby avoiding liability to UK taxes, and the cost of living in a tax haven country can be high.

Tax holiday Stated period of years during which a company setting up in a particular area or country is not liable to pay taxes. Used as an inducement to attract investment and new industries to boost employment or exports.

Tax point Stage at which VALUE ADDED TAX becomes payable.

Tax rebate When too much tax has been paid, the Inland Revenue will repay the excess, either by cheque or by deducting the amount from future payments.

Tax reform Changes are constantly being made in the taxation system, with new measures being announced in almost every annual Budget. Some of the changes made are merely to block loopholes being exploited legally to reduce tax payments, to correct past mistakes or to simplify the system. But tax reform is also used to reflect, and implement, the political priorities of the ruling government, since taxation is a major weapon in controlling the distribution of wealth, investment and savings. It follows that a change in government usually brings changes in taxation too. Recent years have seen some important general policy changes with the switching of emphasis from direct to indirect taxes (that is, less income tax and more value added tax) and the removal of 'shelters' (like investment in woodlands) in return for lowering overall rates. There have also been many specific changes. In the 1966 Budget, for example,

the system for collecting death duties (the tax imposed on the estates of deceased people) was changed. Capital transfer tax, which had replaced Estate Duty but had been proved vulnerable to avoidance schemes, was itself replaced by a new inheritance tax, adopting a different approach; and this was simplified still further in the 1988 Budget. The 1986 Budget also included proposals for the start in 1987 of PERSONAL EQUITY PLANS (PEPs), providing a direct government incentive in the form of tax relief to encourage wider share ownership. Big changes to make PEPs more appealing were included in the 1989 Budget, which otherwise was mainly concerned with technical adjustments and new rules for pension schemes.

By far the most radical changes were announced in the 1988 Budget proposals. The most important immediate change was the equalization of the capital gains and income taxes with the same two basic rates for both. This involves scrapping three of the higher-rate bands for income tax and the introduction of a second (higher) rate for capital gains. This meant a radical rethink in the whole strategy of private investment. Until then, the basic objective of private investors liable to higher-rate income tax was to try, where possible, to concentrate on achieving gains in the value of capital, rather than on generating income, since this involved paying the lower capital gains tax rate and avoided the higher income tax rates. The equalization of the two taxes, and the reduction in the annual exemption from paying capital gains tax, made this policy far less important.

The 1988 Budget also saw the scrapping of tax reliefs on covenants (except for charities) and maintenance or alimony payments, as well as the disappearance of several other special allowances. It also changed the basis for giving mortgage tax

relief from the person to the property, so
that from August 1988 it was no longer
possible to have more than one person
claiming mortgage relief on any one home.
This was part of the Chancellor's general
policy to stop unmarried couples receiving
tax concessions and benefits unavailable to
married couples. But the 1988 Budget also
included proposals for far more
wide-ranging changes in the taxation of
married couples, to become effective from
April 1990. From that date everyone,
whether married or not, will be taxed as
an independent individual, receiving a
'single' person's annual tax-free allowance.
However, husbands will receive a special
married couple's additional tax-free
allowance to set against their income first;
but it can also be transferred and set
against the wife's income, if the husband is
not earning sufficient to use all or part of
the extra allowance. The same transfer
system will be applied to capital gains, so
that wives will also receive an annual
exemption and husbands will no longer be
liable to pay tax on their wife's investment
income. Instead they can transfer assets
to their wives, if necessary, to use up the
wife's allowances. See CAPITAL GAINS
TAX, INHERITANCE TAX, MARRIED
COUPLE'S ALLOWANCE.

Tax return An Inland Revenue form
which taxpayers have to fill in, providing
details of the various sources of their
personal income and assets, together with
claims for any tax-free allowances, like
mortgage relief. This form provides the
basis for calculating the amount of tax an
individual has to pay each fiscal year (from
6 April to 5 April in the following year) and
to set the tax codes, used for deducting
tax direct from employee's salary under
the PAYE system.

Tax schedules System used by the
Inland Revenue to tax different types of

earnings. The five schedules A, C, D, E
and F have their own sets of tax-free
allowances and expenses. In some cases
the schedules are further divided into
numbered Cases. The five schedules are:

Schedule A: covering profits, rents and
receipts, from land or property in the UK,
although not including rents from furnished
or holiday accommodation that usually
comes under Schedule D. There are a
series of allowable tax-free expenses that
can be claimed under Schedule A.

Schedule C: covering profits, dividends
and interest earned from investments in
British government securities (GILTS) and
some stocks issued by foreign
governments.

Schedule D: income and profits earned
from a trade, profession or vocation by
self-employed or freelance workers (Case
I); earnings from investments and
payments received (Case III); income
from overseas (Cases IV and V); other
miscellaneous income (Case VI), including
rents from furnished or holiday
accommodation, although this could also
come under Case I.

Schedule E: earnings received from
employment and pension and annuity
payments.

Schedule F: earnings from dividends and
distributions paid by UK companies and
unit trusts.

(Schedule B, covering earnings from
commercially managed woodlands, was
scrapped in the 1988 Budget after it was
decided to withdraw concessions allowing
investment in forestry being used as a tax
'shelter'.)

As can be seen, Schedule E tax, usually
deducted direct by employers on behalf of
the Inland Revenue, accounts for by far
the biggest slice of tax collected. See PAY
AS YOU EARN.

Tax shelter A form of investment, like a Business Expansion Scheme or Personal Equity Plan, used to avoid paying tax quite legally. Special trusts can also be set up as tax shelters.

Tax year The twelve months, from 6 April to 5 April of the following year, is used for assessing tax liabilities, thus taking into account any changes in rates or allowances that may be included in the annual Budget announcement by the Chancellor of the Exchequer in March.

T. bills See TREASURY BILLS.

T. bond (Treasury bond) See BOND.

Telegraphic transfer A quick way of transferring money abroad, offered by banks. The bank cables the relevant instructions to its agent, or branch, overseas to allow the required sum to be withdrawn by the person named. The cost of the cable can be charged to either the sender or the recipient. A special spot (or telegraphic transfer) rate is used to convert the value of the original currency sent into the local currency.

Teletext output price information computer (TOPIC) System that provides dealers and other subscribers with stock market prices as soon as deals are struck. The information is supplied by the Stock Exchange Automated Quotations System (SEAQ).

Tel quel rate Used by a bank when buying a foreign currency bill of exchange that has some time to run before becoming due for repayment. It is based on the spot (or telegraphic transfer) rate, combined with the period of time to wait for payment and collection charges.

Temporary annuity Payments under a life insurance policy which continue for a fixed number of years, unless the recipient (annuitant) dies first. See ANNUITY.

Temporary policy See TERM ASSURANCE.

Tenancy Right of a person or organization to hold buildings or land under a lease or a settlement.

Tenant at sufferance A tenant who continues to retain possession of buildings or land after the lease giving the right to possession has expired and without the permission of the landlord.

Tenant at will A tenant who holds land under a lease which can be ended at any time by either the tenant or the landlord giving a specified period of notice.

Tenant for life Person who owns a tenancy only during their lifetime.

Tenant for years Person who holds buildings or land for only a specified number of years.

Tender Offer by a borrower to pay off a debt with the exact number of coins and notes required. See LEGAL TENDER.
  Also offer to buy or sell goods and services at a stated price, usually in competition with other tenderers.

Tender for bills An offer of Treasury Bills made each week by the Bank of England to financial institutions, mainly DISCOUNT HOUSES, who supply the clearing banks with money. The amount of money offered can be varied by the government to regulate the amount of credit available to the bank and, therefore, to their customers.

Tender for shares Method of setting the price for new issues and shares by inviting offers from potential buyers above a stated minimum level. Those offering the highest bids are allocated the stock, but if the highest price bid does not cover all the stock available for sale then the price is adjusted down to the highest point at which all the stock is sold, and this then becomes the market price. Sometimes a partial tender is used to dispose of some of the stock, while the rest is sold at a fixed price like an ordinary new issue.

Tenure The conditions under which buildings or land are held by a tenant.

Term assurance Basic (and generally cheapest) form of life policy under which a person, or persons, receives a specified payment on death within a fixed period. Nothing is paid if the person is still living when the fixed period expires. Term policies are used as a means of financial protection, for example by someone taking out a mortgage who wants it to be paid should he or she die, or against repayment of another kind of loan or to cover inheritance tax liability if death takes place within seven years of a gift being made. Also known as 'temporary policy'.

Terminable annuity Payment under an insurance policy made for only a specified number of years.

Terminal bonus An additional sum paid at the end of a with-profits life assurance policy or on the death of the insured. The bonus is not guaranteed since it depends on the returns achieved by the insurance company from investing the premiums over the years. It differs from a REVERSIONARY BONUS, which is guaranteed once it has been declared and added to the value of the policy. Nevertheless it is rare for a terminal bonus

not to be paid, since the guaranteed with-profits element is usually set at a conservative level which the insurance company should have no difficulty in achieving.

Terminal market Normally used to refer to commodity futures exchanges, although in fact it originally meant the end of the distribution chain for commodities before being sold to consumers.

Term loan A bank loan repayable by an agreed number of payments.

Term shares Building society account where the depositor agrees to leave the money untouched for a fixed period of time or suffer loss of interest for early withdrawal. These accounts normally offer a higher rate of interest; but the rate is variable and is often only guaranteed to remain at a certain premium above the society's ordinary rate. In those circumstances there is no guarantee that the society will not then lower its ordinary rate to an artificially low level.

Testament See WILL.

Testamentary trust A trust that has been created under the provisions of the will of a deceased person.

Third market Separate sector of the London Stock Exchange, formed in 1986, to provide organized and regulated share dealings for companies that were previously dealt with in unofficial dealings OVER THE COUNTER. Third market companies are primarily fairly new small ventures, offering only a proportion of their shares for dealing, who do not qualify for membership of the full market or the second tier, the UNLISTED SECURITIES MARKET (USM), and are therefore that much riskier investments. They have to produce accounts going back for no more than one year; certain new companies, with no track record at all, are allowed to be members if it is considered their future revenue is secure. Each company listed on the third market must have a sponsor, prepared to make a market in the shares so that they can be bought or sold.

Third party insurance Policy taken out that covers the insured only against possible claims for death, damages or other losses suffered by a third party (not the insured or the insurance company) as a result of actions by the insured, such as causing a car crash. It is compulsory by law for motorists, owning or driving a car, to take out third party insurance, and also for employers, against possible injury to employees at work. Owners or tenants of property also have to take out public liability insurance to protect persons invited on to their premises. In the case of compulsory third party insurance, the insurance company can be sued directly for damages if the insured fails to make a claim. Optional types of third party policies are professional indemnity insurance contracts.

Threshold allowances The amount of income or capital that is free of tax. The threshold for personal allowances and inheritance tax, for example, are normally increased each year in line with the rate of inflation otherwise they would effectively be reduced in real terms.

Threshold insurance A policy taken on the life of a parent or guardian with a lump sum payable either on death or when a child reaches a specified age, such as 18 or 21 years. Also known as a child's deferred policy.

Threshold price Minimum price for imports set under the European

Community's Common Agricultural Policy, aimed at protecting farmers within the Community from competition.

Ticket day Day when stockbrokers issue forms showing the names of buyers to sellers of stock for settlement of outstanding accounts. Also known as NAME DAY.

Tied agents Popular term for persons, or organizations, restricted to selling the products or services of a particular company or group. Many insurance companies sell their products through tied salesmen or outlets.

Tight money Term used when interest rates are high and money is in short supply for lending, usually following action by the government to cut the rate of inflation by restraints on spending.

Time bargain An agreement to sell and deliver shares on a specified date in the future.

Time-barred Legal term for the period after which civil courts will no longer hear actions seeking to enforce contracts. The periods are twelve years for regaining possession of land and property, obtaining repayments of mortgages on land, and claims against personal estates of deceased persons; three years for damages for personal injuries; one year for obtaining payments of moneylender's loans and interest. See LIMITATION.

Time charter Hiring of a ship, or space in it, for a specified time-period.

Time loan A bank loan due for repayment after a specified date.

Times covered Stock market calculation to assess the financial resources of a company by dividing the amount of money available for distribution as dividends by the sum actually paid out in dividends.

Timeshare System under which the use of a property is sold to different people for a fixed time-period each year. Especially popular with holidaymakers or those who want to live or visit another country under their 'own roof'. Some property complexes are built solely to be sold on a timeshare basis, while others are private homes whose owners live elsewhere for most of the year. Although the concept is sound, over the years timesharing has acquired a dubious reputation, because of fraudsters painting a false picture of the property, and problems over payments for maintenance. Caution is therefore recommended before signing a timeshare agreement.

Tithe Originally described the tenth part of one's income that people were expected to give to the Church for the upkeep of the priest. A living for the clergy was often valued according to the tithes attached. Nowadays tithes have become fixed payments, unrelated to the income of the donor.

Title Legal term to define ownership of an object or property. Title deeds, for example, prove ownership of a freehold or leasehold property.

To Abbreviation of 'debtor to', used on invoices claiming payment.

Token money When the face value of coins is greater than the value of the metal in them.

Token payment Repayment of a small part of a loan by the borrower to acknowledge the debt and his commitment to repay at a future date.

Toll Charge demanded for use of road or bridge, aimed at recovering the costs of building and maintenance.

Tonnage dues The charges made when a ship enters or leaves a port, based on its tonnage or cubic capacity.

Tonne See METRIC TON.

Top down Investment strategy based on broad economic and political trends rather than prospects for individual companies.

Top hat pension An extra pension usually given to key employees, such as directors of a company, as a special inducement.

Top hat policy An endowment assurance policy usually taken out by a company on the life of key employees, to provide them with additional benefits.

TOPIC See TELETEXT OUTPUT PRICE INFORMATION COMPUTER.

Top slicing Method of assessing the tax that may be payable when a life assurance policy or investment bond matures. The profit or gain on the policy, including withdrawals of income, is calculated by deducting the premiums paid. Then it is divided by the number of years for which the policy has been in force. This amount is then added on to the taxpayer's other income during the tax year when the gain on the policy is taken. If this addition puts the total income into a higher-rate tax band, then the taxpayer is liable to pay tax on the whole gain at the higher rate of tax, less the basic rate. Since the policy has already paid tax at the basic rate, no further tax is payable if the taxpayer's total income, including the gain, does not exceed the basic rate tax band.

Top-up loans An additional borrowing on top of an existing loan. May well be money for improvements to a property, on which there is already a mortgage.

Touch Slang term for borrowing money, often from a reluctant lender. Also stock market term for the best bid and offer (buying and selling) prices of a share offered by a market-maker at any one time.

Town clearing Special arrangement between clearing banks, confined to branches and offices within the City of London (a half-mile radius with Lombard Street as its centre, on the north side of the River Thames), under which cheques and bank drafts for amounts of over £10,000 are settled on the same day – that is, credited to the receiver and debited to the payer's account. The gain (and loss) in interest resulting from this speedier settlement can be very significant when large sums are involved, bearing in mind that a normal clearing takes three working days.

TPI See TAX AND PRICE INDEX.

Tracker funds Popular name for funds and unit trusts that seek to track the performance of a market index by buying a majority, or all, of the shares that make up the index. See INDEX-LINKED FUNDS.

Traded option Type of option that has a value of its own, since it can be transferred by being bought and sold on the special traded option markets. The purchaser buys the right to exercise the option, which can be a put (sale) or call (buy), and is valued according to likely profit that may be made from it being exercised on the expiry date. Thus profits from traded options are normally made by selling them at a higher level than the purchase price, rather than holding them until the expiry date. See OPTIONS.

Trading account Summary by accountants, prepared in order to compare the value of sales with the cost of the goods sold, to see if the business is making a profit or loss on sales.

Trading capital The combined value of the current and fixed assets of a business.

Trading currency A currency that can be used by importers and exporters to settle their debts, since it can be valued at a known market rate.

Tranche (French for 'slice') used to describe payment by instalments, or part of a loan due for repayment.

Transaction A business deal or entry in a bank account. Bank charges are often based on the number of transactions – both receipts and payments.

Transferable bond See BOND.

Transfer accounting, lodging for investors and stock management (TALISMAN) The London stock market's computerized system for settlement of dealings.

Transfer and automated registration of uncertified stock (TAURUS) The London stock market's computer system designed to save paperwork by allowing transfer of stocks and shares to different owners without the use of contract notes and share certificates.

Transfer certificate Document issued by a company confirming that the change in ownership of shares has been registered in its books, instead of supplying fresh share or stock certificates.

Transfer deed Fom that is signed by the purchaser of registered shares or stock so that the change of ownership may be entered on the register.

Transfer duty Government tax payable on transfers of securities, within 30 days. See STAMP DUTY.

Transfer fee Small charge that a company may make for registering a change in ownership of its stocks or shares. Very often the sum involved is so small that the company doesn't bother to collect it.

Transfer income Payments received by persons who give no goods or services in return, such as pensioners and the unemployed.

Transfer value The cash value of a pension when it is transferred from one scheme to another. Based on contributions already made, it is calculated by an actuary, following guidelines laid down by the Institute of Actuaries, assessing the likely value when the pension is due to start being paid. The transfer value must be transferred to the managers of the new scheme or into a personal pension/section 32 bond; it cannot be paid direct to the individual who will be the eventual recipient.

Transitory income Payments of an irregular nature, such as royalties on the sales of books.

Traveller's cheques Special cheques, issued by banks and many other financial institutions, which can be cashed in countries all over the world. They thus enable the traveller to avoid carrying possibly large sums of money in several different currencies. The sum received is based on the rate of exchange used for the local currency compared with the currency in which the traveller's cheque is denominated. This rate can be manipulated by the organization cashing the cheque, and extra charges may also be imposed. Traveller's cheques are paid for in advance and a commission is charged at the time of purchase and also sometimes when they are cashed; so they are an expensive way of carrying money, making large profits for the issuers. But as a special inducement the issuers guarantee to refund the value of the cheques if they are lost or stolen, provided they have been signed at the time of purchase.

Treasure trove Under British law, any money and objects made of precious metals (gold and silver) found in a hiding place have to be reported to the police, the British Museum or the nearest coroner. If the owner cannot be traced, it is deemed to belong to the government. A jury may be called to decide whether the objects found are really treasure trove, and the finder may be awarded some or all of the saleable value of the fund, but not the treasure itself.

Treasury bills (T. bills) Bills issued weekly by the Bank of England, on behalf of the Treasury, which promise to pay a fixed sum of money on a certain date, usually three months ahead. The bills pay no interest on the sums borrowed by the government, so they are offered for sale at a discount to the DISCOUNT HOUSES. The discount that the Treasury is prepared to accept can be used to regulate the cost of money for the clearing banks.

Treasury bond See BOND.

Treasury notes Currency, in the form of 10 shilling (50p) and £1 notes, issued by the UK Treasury during the 1914–18 War, subsequently amalgamated with the Bank of England notes.

Treasury stock Fixed-interest securities guaranteed by the Treasury. See GILTS.

Treasury warrant An order issued by the UK Treasury, authorizing the payment of money owed by the Exchequer.

Trial balance Method of checking accounts by putting all the debits in one column and credits in another, and seeing if they match.

Troy weight System of weights used for precious metals and gems. A troy ounce is equal to 31.1035 metric grams, and one ton of gold and silver to 746.48 kilograms.

True investment Use of money to earn a regular income, in the form of either interest or dividend.

True yield Annual income from an investment in a security, calculated as a percentage of the security's current market price after taking into account any dividend or interest payment.

Trust company An INVESTMENT TRUST.

Trust deed A legal document, made under seal, to create a trust. It appoints the trustees, states the purposes and conditions, defines the money, land or other property to be managed for the benefit of the named beneficiaries or charities.

Trustee Person appointed to handle monies or property on behalf of the beneficiaries in accordance with the terms of the trust. The trustee has widespread legal powers, but is bound to act in the best interests of the trust and its beneficiaries. See PUBLIC TRUSTEE.

Trustee in bankruptcy Officer of the bankruptcy court, who is given power to take possession of the bankrupt's property and hold it in trust for the creditors.

Trustee investments Unless the TRUST DEED specifically states the investments to be made, trusts are restricted to certain investments. Half has to be put into narrow-range investments, such as government-backed fixed-interest securities. The other half can be invested in wider-range investments, such as shares in registered companies with TRUSTEE STATUS, certain building societies, and unit trusts.

Trustee savings banks Originally formed as non-profit-making organizations in the early eighteenth century to encourage thrift among the working classes. Managed by trustees, they were allowed by the government to offer tax-free interest. In 1976 the number of individual trustee banks was reduced from 70 to four, and the tax-free interest privilege was cancelled and replaced with full banking status being granted, enabling the trustee savings banks to compete with the big clearing banks. In 1986 the TSB was 'privatized' by applying for a listing on the Stock Exchange and offering 1.5 million shares for sale to its customers and the general public. It now operates like the other main clearing bank companies.

Trustee securities See TRUSTEE INVESTMENTS.

Trustee status Special conditions that shares or debentures must meet if they are to qualify as TRUSTEE INVESTMENTS. The company has to be incorporated in Britain with a paid-up capital of at least £1 million and to have paid a dividend on all classes of its shares for at least five years.

Trust for sale Trust that forces the trustees to sell its assets as soon as possible and to distribute the proceeds to the beneficiaries. These trusts are formed to distribute the estate of a deceased person, or to deal with a bankruptcy, or with the liquidation of a company.

Trust fund Assets, including property of any kind, held in trust for the benefit of the beneficiaries.

Trust instrument A legal document, such as a Will or TRUST DEED, placing land in trust for named persons.

Trusts Legal entities set up under a TRUST DEED to take charge of and manage land, money or other property for the benefit of one or more beneficiaries. Often created under the terms of a Will to distribute the estate or to protect the interests of dependants and charities. Also

used as tax-saving devices; to wind up bankrupt companies and to administer pension schemes. See also ACCUMULATION AND MAINTENANCE TRUSTS and UNIT TRUSTS.

TSA See the SECURITIES ASSOCIATION and USEFUL ADDRESSES.

Tuppence Slang for two pennies. Hence 'tuppeny-ha'penny' means something of little or no value.

Turn The profit margin made on a deal or transaction.

Turnkey contract Arrangement whereby the contractor is left to deal with and settle all problems that may occur during the period of the contract. Payment is made when the hirer can 'turn the key' and start operations.

U

UCITS See undertakings for collective investments in transferable securities.

Umbrella funds Investment funds, often based offshore, which have a main fund or 'umbrella' that is able to invest in a wide range of sub-funds. This provides investors with a selection to choose from, ranging from money (cash) funds to currency, bond and fixed-interest securities, as well as shares in different sectors or countries. The 1989 Budget scrapped a major tax advantage previously enjoyed by offshore umbrella funds by ruling that from March 1989 any switches between sub-funds would be liable to UK capital gains tax on any gains made.

Unappropriated profits Part of the profits of a business not paid out in dividends or allocated to any particular use.

Uncalled capital Part of the issued capital of company not yet used.

Uncertificated units When dividends from a unit trust are reinvested, the amount of units bought is often so small that it is not worth issuing extra certificates. Instead they are held on the unit-holders' account and credited to them when the units are surrendered for payment.

Unconditional A takeover bid for a company is declared unconditional when the bidder has gained control of over 50% of the voting stock. Once a bid has become unconditional, the bidder is required to take up any shares offered on the same terms, even if not seeking to gain full control of the company.

Unconvertible currency One which cannot be freely exchanged for other currencies.

Undated stock A fixed-interest security which has no specified date for redemption, and therefore interest is payable for ever. Consols and War Loan are two well-known examples of undated gilts.

Underinsurance If a property is insured for less than its full value, payment on any claim may be reduced to reflect the degree of underinsurance.

Under-lease A lease given by someone who is himself also a leaseholder. See sub-lease.

Underlying holdings The shares held by a fund or unit trust on behalf of investors. The price of the units is calculated according to the market value of the underlying assets, plus any charges.

Under offer Indication that the sale of a property is being discussed with a potential buyer, although no legal agreement has yet been finalized.

Undertakings for collective investments in transferable

securities (UCITS) The standard regulation laid down by the European Community specifying the basic rules for any collective fund such as unit trust, sold within the Community. Once a fund has achieved UCITS status, it can be sold in all countries in the Community.

Underwrite Agree to guarantee someone against a commercial loss, as when making a new issue of shares. Alternatively, agree to accept liability for loss under an insurance contract; both actions in return for a fee or commission.

Underwriter A merchant bank, broker or trust which agrees, for a fee, to take up any shares in a new issue which are not sold to the public. Thus if the flotation is not a success and the market price falls below the issue price, the underwriter faces making a loss. Alternatively, underwriters in the insurance industry fix the premium rates and conditions of policies, to take into account the likely risks involved in providing insurance cover.

Underwriting agent Insurance salesman.

Undischarged bankrupt Bankrupt who has not been released from the restraints imposed by the bankruptcy court, such as not being able to be a director, own any property, or hold any public office.

Undue debt Loan which is not yet due for repayment.

Unearned income Income not arising from employment, but instead from dividends, interest or rents. There is no longer any distinction for tax purposes, as there was in the past, between earned and unearned income. The allowances apply to both sorts.

Unearned increment Increase in the value of land or buildings as a result of rising demand, rather than because of any improvements or repairs.

Unfranked income Investment income in an investment or unit trust that is liable for corporation tax. Normally represents earnings from overseas holdings, since dividends from UK stocks and shares are paid with basic-rate tax already deducted and are therefore not liable to any additional tax.

Unified bond or stock See CONSOLIDATED BOND.

Unitization The dividing up of an investment fund into units of equal value. The most common example of this being done is with INVESTMENT TRUSTS, whose price on the stock market is influenced by supply and demand, and may on occasion be well below the value of the underlying assets and securities owned by the trust. To take advantage of this discount, a bidder may take over the trust and unitize it by turning it into a unit trust fund. The value of the new units for sale is then based on the underlying assets owned, not on the previous share price.

Unit linked mortgage or pension See UNIT LINKED POLICY.

Unit linked policy Way of spreading investment from a single managed fund into a selection of funds. Instead of the policy-holders' premiums going into an individual fund, they are used instead to buy units in sub-funds. The value of the units rises and falls according to the investment performance of the sub-fund. The value of the policy-holder's portfolio is measured by the number of units acquired and can be checked against the current price of the individual units. This method of allocating units to policies provides flexibility with the fund manager, or individual policy-holders, being able to choose which sub-funds should be used and, if necessary, switching between them when market trends change. With a unit linked pension, for example, it may be wise to switch into a safe fixed-interest sub-fund when retirement is imminent in order to preserve the value of units accumulated over the years against any sudden fall in the stock market. The insurance company takes its costs and charges by simply reducing the amount of money from the fund used to buy units. Bonus allocations of units can also be made by the company. The unit linked system is being increasingly used for endowment mortgage policies and personal pensions, as well as for life assurance policies and investment bonds.

Unit trust A fund formed to manage investments collectively on behalf of a number of investors, under terms and conditions laid down by a TRUST DEED. Aimed particularly at small investors, unit trusts are supposed to be a cheaper and safer way of buying stocks and shares. The trust is professionally managed by the company setting it up and normally has its own fund manager. By combining the resources of many investors together, the trust is able to buy a bigger range of stocks and shares in order to spread the risk of individual shares losing value. Larger purchases also enable the cost of dealing commissions to be reduced. The value of the securities bought is divided up into units of equal worth and allocated to the individual investors, according to the size of their investment. The investors' profit or loss is based on the change in the value of the units, which is calculated by taking into account the current market price of the underlying securities held by the fund, and deducting costs and charges.

The value of the units varies according to whether they are being bought (the offer price) or sold (the bid price). The spread, or gap, between the offer and bid prices covers the managers' initial charge for creating units and is also used to encourage or discourage purchases and sales. The maximum size of the bid/offer spread is regulated; but within that range the trust can go on to a bid basis, where the bid price is set close to the cancellation level – that is, the amount received if the trust's holdings were all to be sold. This discourages selling and encourages buying, since the offer price is also fixed at the lower end of the range. Alternatively, if the trust is doing well, the offer price is set at the top end of the range and the bid price is also raised for the benefit of existing unit-holders. All the securities bought by the trust are held by especially appointed independent trustees (normally a bank), who then issue or cancel units in line with the increase or decline in the amount of money invested in the trust. They are thus OPEN-ENDED FUNDS, whose size varies in accordance with demand for the units. The trustees are also responsible for ensuring that the fund managers act in accordance with the conditions laid down in the deed which created the trust and obey the relevant rules and regulations.

The deed sets out the objectives of the trust and specifies which markets it is allowed to operate in. A unit trust specifically formed to invest, say, in Japanese stocks, and sold as such, would not be allowed to buy German or British stocks instead. A global, or international, trust would, however, be permitted to invest in markets worldwide. Unit trusts can be used either to invest in specific countries or sectors, or in stocks and shares generally. They can also be used either to provide a regular source of income by investing in fixed-interest securities and high yielding stocks, or to concentrate on achieving growth in the value of capital invested by buying shares or stocks whose market prices rise and push up the value of the units.

The advantages of collective investment, with a professional manager, are to some extent offset by the charges made for providing the management and selling units in the trust, so the individual investor does not necessarily gain much extra financial benefit unless the fund manager achieves above-average investment performance. But unit trusts should be safer, less time-consuming, and have the additional advantage, not enjoyed by INVESTMENT BONDS, of not being liable to capital gains tax on the purchases and sales made within the fund. However, the trust, unless it is a special tax-exempt fund for charities or pensions, does pay tax at the standard rate on the dividends received. The investor may be liable to pay additional higher rate tax on income received from the fund, and may also be subject to capital gains tax on any profits made by selling units at a higher price than their purchase price.

Unlike their rival INVESTMENT TRUSTS, unit trusts are not shares quoted on the Stock Exchange. The price of units is based primarily on the value of the underlying assets; with investment trusts, the price also depends on supply and demand for the shares, whose value is often at a discount to the value of assets held. See UNITIZATION.

Unit Trust Association Organization formed by unit trust groups to look after their interests, collate statistics and promote the industry generally. See USEFUL ADDRESSES.

Unit trust ombudsman Independent official appointed to settle disputes between those unit trust groups which are members of the scheme, and their customers. Similar to the banking, building society and insurance industry ombudsmen. Unlike arbitration, the Ombudsman's rulings are not legally binding on the complainant, who can pursue the matter in the courts if dissatisfied with the decision. See INVESTMENT REFEREE, OMBUDSMAN and USEFUL ADDRESSES.

Universal (life) plans Assurance policies, kept in force until death or a specified age. They can be varied to provide different types of cover, such as against losses suffered from ill-health, all under the same policy. Also known as 'flexible policies'.

Unlimited company Company, for example a partnership, where the members do not have limited liability and are, therefore, liable to pay in full any debts and losses that the company might incur.

Unlisted investment Shares in companies which are not quoted on a recognized stock exchange and are therefore difficult to buy and sell freely – as well as possibly being artificially priced.

Unlisted securities market (USM) Special section of the London Stock Exchange, introduced in 1980 for companies which do not qualify for, or do not want, a listing on the full market. USM companies are often of too small a size, or are not established long enough, to meet the minimum qualifications for a full listing; alternatively, they may not want to meet the costs involved in a full listing, or are not prepared to offer a sufficient percentage of their total shareholdings to the public with the risk of losing control. By joining the USM, companies can raise money from a new source (the public) for expansion, possibly as a prelude to a full listing. At the same time a public quotation enables the owners and directors of the company to realize their gains at a share market value by selling their stock. Shares on the junior market, as the USM is often called, tend to be more risky and volatile in price, lacking an established track record on which to base the value, and sometimes a dearth of market-makers. But while the risks are higher, so too the rewards of investing in a young, rapidly expanding company can be that much greater. The THIRD (tier) MARKET introduced on to the Exchange in 1986 covers companies, previously traded over the counter, that do not qualify for listing on the full market or the USM.

Unquoted securities Shares which are dealt in on the London stock market, but which have no official status and are not subject to the rules and regulations of the Stock Exchange. They are normally small companies or new, highly speculative ventures, like exploration companies.

Unsecured creditor, debenture, debt or loan Where the borrower has provided no security, or collateral, to the lender in case of defaulting on repayment. See DEBENTURE, MORTGAGE; LOAN STOCK.

Unsecured loan stock Company stock that pays a fixed interest; but repayment of the loan is not backed by any of the company's assets in the event of the company failing.

Unvalued policy An insurance contract which sets a maximum sum to be paid in the event of a claim, but which leaves the value of different objects covered by the policy to be decided upon, if and when a claim is made.

Upper earnings limit The top (or ceiling) level of salary that fixes the maximum of NATIONAL INSURANCE contributions to be paid. See BAND EARNINGS and LOWER EARNINGS LIMIT.

Upset price The lowest price at an auction which the seller is prepared to accept. More commonly known as RESERVE PRICE.

Usance The normal period which foreign exchange bills take to be honoured between two countries.

USM See UNLISTED SECURITIES MARKET.

Usurer Derogatory term for a moneylender who charges higher-than-normal rates of interest.

Usury Lending money at excessive rates of interest.

UTA See UNIT TRUST ASSOCIATION and USEFUL ADDRESSES.

V

Vacant possession Promise by the seller of a property that it is ready for occupation by the buyer immediately, or at an agreed date in the future.

Valorization Artificially fixing a price or value for a commodity or currency, backed by suitable measures to sustain it in the market-place.

Valuation Estimating the value of a property or other assets and possessions. A house valuation for the purpose of obtaining a mortgage is not a survey to discover any structural faults or defects; it is simply to assess the current market value of the property and check it in relation to the size of the loan. If the loan sought exceeds the valuation, the mortgage offer is likely to be reduced; or the lender might insist on some form of indemnity insurance if the valuation is close to the size of the loan.

Value added The increase in the value of a product as a result of processing, packaging or marketing it.

Value added tax (VAT) An indirect form of government taxation, which is charged as a percentage of the selling price. Introduced into the UK in 1973, it replaced the old purchase tax, but is applied to a much wider range of products and services. It is levied at every stage of production and distribution as an output tax, but is effectively passed on down the line by the ability to reclaim it as an input tax until reaching the final stage. The revenue from VAT helps to finance the contributions from individual member countries towards the costs of the European Community.

Valuer Professional person who gives advice, for a fee, on the market value of assets or property.

Variable annuity A life assurance annuity policy under which the payments to the beneficiary change according to the income generated by the stocks and shares purchased by the proceeds of the policy.

Variable costs Accounting term for costs that vary according to the level of production.

VAT See VALUE ADDED TAX.

Vendor The actual seller of a property or other goods, as opposed to an agent.

Vendors' share Class of share issued (instead of making a cash payment) to the persons selling a business for formation into a company.

Venture capital Loans made by individuals or institutions to help new or developing businesses, often in exchange for a percentage of the shares. See RISK CAPITAL.

Vesting date The day on which an assurance policy matures and the company starts to make any payments due.

Visible reserves Reserves that are clearly shown on a company balance sheet.

Voluntary liquidation When a partnership is dissolved by agreement, or a company decides to cease trading with the agreement of the creditors but not necessarily under the supervision of the court.

Voteless share See NON-VOTING SHARES.

Voting share Class of share that gives the holder the right to vote at general meetings of the company.

Voucher Receipt for payment of money or proof of entitlement to a sum of money, goods or service.

W

Wagering contract A bet which is not legally binding in court under the Gaming Act.

Wager policy An insurance policy that is supposed to cover the insured against losses arising from a chance event. As it can be viewed as a wagering (or gaming) contract, however, the insurer may not be legally liable to pay up. Also known as an 'aleatory contract'.

Waiver Giving up a right or not pressing a legal claim by agreeing to end a contract. Life assurance, pension and permanent health insurance policies often include a waiver of premiums clause, allowing the holders to stop making payments if they are unable to work because of ill-health or become unemployed.

Wall Street Specifically refers to the New York Stock Exchange which is situated in Wall Street in New York. But often used as a more general term, like the City (of London), to describe all the stock exchanges and financial institutions in New York; often abbreviated to 'The Street'.

Warehousing Financial term to describe the action of a broker or investment group holding stocks or shares off the market to bolster the price.

War loan Fixed-interest government security (gilt), first issued after the Second World War; it is undated and thereby has no redemption date. See UNDATED STOCK.

Warrants Documents providing legal authority to do something (such as pay a dividend) or acting as a receipt for goods held in storage. Share warrants are certificates issued by some companies and investment trusts, giving the holder the right to buy shares at a specified price at some time in the future; but the name of the holder is not registered, so the warrants can be freely bought and sold and traded separately on the stock markets. They tend to be more volatile in price than the share of the underlying company or trust, since the 'gearing' element – buying the shares at a discount – tends to provide higher rewards and greater losses.

Warranty Condition attached to an insurance policy that must be fulfilled if any future claim is to be met. For example, a household contents policy might be dependent on special window-locks being installed; if this is not done, then the insurance company would reject any claim for burglary losses.

Wasting assets See ASSETS.

Watering stock The practice of issuing additional supplies of new shares without increasing the amount allocated for distribution as dividends; therefore the dividend per share is reduced.

Way-leave Special right to walk or drive over land belonging to someone else or to install something like drains or a road on someone else's property. Often a special way-leave payment has to be made and details included in property deeds.

Ways-and-means advances Short-term loans made to the Treasury by the Bank of England, or by other government departments, to supplement a temporary shortfall in revenue.

Wear and tear Accounting term for the decrease in value of assets, such as building and machinery, resulting from use and the passage of time.

Weather insurance Policy taken out to cover losses which may result from bad weather, such as the cancellation of a sale or sports match. See PLUVIUS INSURANCE.

Weighted average Mathematical calculation, used in compiling indices, that seeks to give the proper importance, or weight, to the individual items included in the index. This is aimed at avoiding distortion of the underlying trend by a few (possibly relatively unimportant) items.

Weighted ballot Method of allocating shares in a new issue to a particular type of investor sought. See NEW ISSUES.

Wheeler-dealer Slang name for trader or businessman who buys and sells frequently, and often uses unfair or even dishonest means to make a profit.

Whitsun See QUARTER DAY.

Whole life policy An assurance policy that pays out a sum insured only on death and gives no other benefits. Also known as straight life policy. Arrangements are often made for the payment of premiums to cease when the insured reaches

retirement age, in which case it becomes a whole life (with limited payments) policy.

Wholesale money Funds obtained from the MONEY MARKET – as opposed to retail money, obtained via retail outlets (like building societies), from individual investors and from depositors.

Wholesale price The amount charged for goods to a retailer or bulk purchaser.

Wide price When the gap or spread between the offer and sale price of a share on the stock market is much wider than usual.

Wider-range investments See TRUSTEE INVESTMENTS.

Wider share ownership council See USEFUL ADDRESSES.

Widow's allowances If before his death the husband made sufficient National Insurance contributions, his widow is entitled to various special payments from the government. These include mother's allowance, if the widow has dependent children, and a pension for those between 40 and 65 years of age.

Widow's bereavement allowance Special relief against paying tax, available for limited period after the death of a husband.

Widow's pension Payments made to a wife on the death of her husband, either by the state or under a private pension or insurance policy. Called a 'widow's mite' when the payment is extremely small.

Will Legal document in which a person states how his or her possessions should be distributed after death and by whom. The drawing up of a Will can be extremely important for the heirs and beneficiaries in avoiding future tax bills, and also in ensuring that the money goes to the right quarters. For example, if there is no Will, a wife may inherit only part of the estate and as a result find herself in financial difficulties.

Windfall Money or property received completely unexpectedly, either as the result of a gift or legacy, or as a surprise increase in the value of something.

Windfall profits Unexpected extra gains made. In company accounts, they are listed separately under 'exceptional items'.

Winding-up The legal process of bringing to an end the existence of a company or partnership and selling its assets to pay any debts or distribute the monies among the members. See VOLUNTARY LIQUIDATION.

Withholding tax Tax or levy imposed by many foreign countries on dividends paid by local companies to residents not liable to domestic taxation. This tax can often be reclaimed.

With-profits (endowment) policy An insurance policy which includes the right to receive a share of the extra profits made by the company, over and above the basic sum assured. The profits are added in the form of reversionary annual bonuses, which cannot be taken away once they have been declared, and a terminal bonus when the policy matures. These policies are commonly sold and promoted as a form of savings plan, even though the extra profits depend on the success or otherwise of the insurance company's investment strategy. Widely used with ENDOWMENT MORTGAGE policies, where the basic sum needed to repay the

mortgage loan on maturity is guaranteed, but where the policy-holder can normally expect to receive additional lump sums from profits made, when the policy matures. Most popular is the low-cost endowment. It has cheaper premiums because the guaranteed sum is below the amount required to pay off the mortgage, but the shortfall is calculated to be made up by investment profits, paid in the form of bonuses (annually and at the end of the policy term).

With rights See CUM DIVIDENDS.

Working capital The stock of money needed by a business to continue trading or production. It includes stocks, as well as liquid resources, which can quickly be turned into cash.

World Bank Popular name for International Bank for Reconstruction and Development, set up in 1944 under the Bretton Woods Agreement together with the INTERNATIONAL MONETARY FUND. It is a specialized agency of the United Nations and its basic purpose is to provide or guarantee long-term loans to finance expansion and aid projects in less-developed countries.

World money Anything that can be used for settlement of international debts, like gold or a currency which is acceptable everywhere.

Write off Reduce to nothing the value of an asset, investment or unpaid debt.

Written-down value Accounting term for the cost or valuation of an asset, taking into account depreciation. It does not, therefore, necessarily reflect the true value of the asset.

X

X.A. See EX ALL benefits.

X.B. See EX BONUS.

X.C. See EX CAP(ITALIZATION).

X.CP. See EX COUPON.

X.D. See EX DIVIDEND and EX BONUS (re ex distribution).

X.DIST. See EX BONUS (re ex distribution).

X.DIV. See EX DIVIDEND.

X.IN. See EX DIVIDEND (re ex interest).

X.R. See EX BONUS (re ex rights).

X.W. See EX BONUS (re ex warrant).

Y

Yankees Stock Exchange slang term for American stocks and shares.

Yard Slang term for a billion.

Yearlings Popular term for fixed-interest bonds, issued by local authorities in the UK, which are repayable after one year. See BOND.

Yearly plan Regular savings scheme offered by NATIONAL SAVINGS, with a minimum investment period of one year but with a higher rate of interest if retained for five years.

Year's purchase Value of a property or business estimated by dividing the proposed purchase price by the annual income, to assess the risk involved over a number of years.

Yield The rate of return on an investment or deposit. This can be calculated in a variety of ways, either as a gross figure without any deductions for charges and tax, or net to show the actual return on capital received by the investor. See DIVIDEND YIELD, EARNINGS YIELD, NET YIELD, NOMINAL YIELD, REDEMPTION YIELD.

Yield curve Measurement in graph form of the past and projected future movements in interest rates over selected periods of years; used to define an underlying trend.

Yield gap The difference between the average yield (rate of return) provided by investment in a 15-year government fixed-interest security (LONG GILT) and the average yield on investing in shares or property. Often used to assess whether shares on a stock market are over- or under-valued: if the yield gap becomes too wide it provides a clear signal that share prices are either too expensive or that interest rates are due to come down.

Yield method See DISCOUNTED CASH FLOW.

Z

Zero (coupon) bonds Bonds that pay no interest, but which are sold at a discount well below the fixed repayment price, so that investors make a guaranteed gain in capital rather than receiving income. Designed to appeal to investors who have sufficient income and are liable to pay high-rate income tax but who may require a capital gain some years hence when their tax liability is likely to decline, either as a result of retiring from work or moving overseas. See DEEP DISCOUNT BONDS.

Appendix 1: Local Currencies

Country	Currency
Afghanistan	Afghani
Albania	lek
Algeria	dinar
Andorra	French franc/Spanish peseta
Angola	kwanza
Antigua	East Caribbean dollar
Aruba	florin
Australia	Australian dollar
Austria	Schilling
Azores	Portuguese escudo
Bahamas	Bahamas dollar
Bahrain	dinar
Balearic Islands	Spanish peseta
Bangladesh	taka
Barbados	Barbados dollar
Belgium	Belgian franc
Belize	Belize dollar
Benin	Central African Federation franc
Bermuda	Bermudan dollar
Bhutan	ngultrum
Bolivia	boliviano
Botswana	pula
Brazil	cruzado
British Virgin Islands	US dollar
Brunei	Brunei dollar
Bulgaria	lev
Burkino Faso	Central African Federation franc
Burma	kyat
Burundi	Burundi franc
Cameroon	Central African Federation franc
Canada	Canadian dollar
Canary Islands	Spanish peseta
Cape Verde Islands	Cape Verde escudo
Central African Republic	Central African Federation franc
Chad	Central African Federation franc
Chile	Chilean peso
China	Renminbi yuan
Colombia	Colombian peso

Country	*Currency*
Comoro Islands	Central African Federation franc
Congo (Brazzaville)	Central African Federation franc
Costa Rica	colon
Cuba	Cuban peso
Cyprus	Cyprus pound
Czechoslovakia	koruna
Denmark	Danish kroner
Djibouti	Djibouti franc
Dominica	East Caribbean dollar
Dominican Republic	Dominican peso
Ecuador	sucre
Egypt	Egyptian pound
El Salvador	colon
Equatorial Guinea	Central African Federation franc
Ethiopia	birr
Falkland Islands	Falkland pound
Faroe Islands	Danish kroner
Fiji	Fiji dollar
Finland	markka
France	franc
Gabon	Central African Federation franc
Gambia	dalasi
Germany, East	Ostmark
Germany, West	Deutschmark
Ghana	cedi
Gibraltar	Gibraltarian pound
Greece	drachma
Greenland	Danish kroner
Grenada	East Caribbean dollar
Guadeloupe	Guadeloupe franc
Guam	US dollar
Guatemala	quetzal
Guinea	franc
Guinea-Bissau	peso
Guyana	Guyana dollar
Haiti	goude
Honduras	lempira
Hong Kong	Hong Kong dollar
Hungary	forint
Iceland	Icelandic kroner
India	rupee
Indonesia	rupiah
Iran	rial
Iraq	dinar
Irish Republic	punt
Israel	shekel

Country	Currency
Italy	lira
Ivory Coast	Central African Federation franc
Jamaica	Jamaican dollar
Japan	yen
Jordan	dinar
Kampuchea	riel
Kenya	shilling
Kiribati	Australian dollar
Korea, North	won
Korea, South	won
Kuwait	dinar
Laos	new kip
Lebanon	Lebanese pound
Lesotho	maluti
Liberia	Liberian dollar
Libya	dinar
Liechtenstein	Swiss franc
Luxembourg	Luxembourg franc
Macao	pataca
Madeira	Portuguese escudo
Malagasy Republic	Malagasy franc
Malawi	kwacha
Malaysia	ringgit
Maldive Islands	rufiya
Mali Republic	Central African Federation franc
Malta	Maltese pound
Martinique	Martinique franc
Mauritania	ougulya
Mauritius	rupee
Mexico	peso
Miquelon	Miquelon franc
Monaco	French franc
Mongolia	tugrik
Montserrat	East Caribbean dollar
Morocco	dirham
Mozambique	metical
Namibia	South African rand
Nauru Islands	Australian dollar
Nepal	rupee
Netherlands	guilder
Netherlands Antilles	Antilles guilder
New Zealand	New Zealand dollar
Nicaragua	cordoba
Niger Republic	Central African Federation franc
Nigeria	naira
Norway	Norwegian krone

Country	*Currency*
Oman	rial Omani
Pakistan	rupee
Panama	balboa
Papua New Guinea	kina
Paraguay	guarani
Peru	inti
Philippines	peso
Pitcairn Islands	pound sterling
Poland	zloty
Portugal	escudo
Puerto Rico	US dollar
Qatar	riyal
Réunion Islands	French franc
Romania	leu
Rwanda	franc
St Christopher	East Caribbean dollar
St Helena	pound sterling
St Lucia	East Caribbean dollar
St Pierre	French franc
St Vincent	East Caribbean dollar
San Marino	Italian lira
Sao Tome	dobra
Saudi Arabia	riyal
Senegal	Central African Federation franc
Seychelles	rupee
Sierra Leone	leone
Singapore	Singapore dollar
Solomon Islands	Solomon Islands dollar
Somali Republic	shilling
South Africa	rand
Soviet Union	rouble
Spain	peseta
Sri Lanka	rupee
Sudan Republic	pound
Surinam	guilder
Swaziland	lilangeni
Sweden	krona
Switzerland	Swiss franc
Syria	pound
Taiwan	Taiwan dollar
Tanzania	shilling
Thailand	baht
Togo Republic	Central African Federation franc
Trinidad and Tobago	East Caribbean dollar
Tunisia	dinar
Turkey	lira

Country	Currency
Turks and Caicos Islands	US dollar
Tuvalu	Australian dollar
Uganda	new shilling
United Arab Emirates	dirham
United Kingdom	pound sterling
United States of America	US dollar
Uruguay	peso
Vanuatu	vatu
Vatican	Italian lira
Venezuela	bolivar
Vietnam	dong
Virgin Islands	US dollar
Western Samoa	taia
Yemen	rial
Yemen, PDR	dinar
Yugoslavia	dinar
Zaire	zaire
Zambia	kwacha
Zimbabwe	Zimbabwe dollar

Appendix 2: Useful Addresses

Association of British Insurers (ABI)
Aldermary House, Queen Street,
London EC4N 1TT
(01-248 4477)
Association of Futures Brokers and
Dealers (AFBD)
B Section, 5th Floor, Plantation House,
4–16 Mincing Lane, London EC3M
3DX
(01-626 9763)
Association of Investment Trust
Companies (AITC)
Park House, 16 Finsbury Circus,
London EC2M 7JJ
(01-588 5347)

Baltic Exchange
24 St Mary Axe, London EC3A 8BU
(01-283 9300)
Banking Information Service
10 Lombard Street, EC3V 9AP
(01-626 8486)
Banking Ombudsman
Citadel House, 5–11 Fetter Lane,
London EC4A 1BR
(01-583 1395)
British Franchise Association
Franchise Chambers, 75a Bell Street,
Henley-on-Thames, Oxon RG9 2BD
(0491 578049)
British Insurance and Investment
Association (BIBA)
BIBA House, 14 Bevis Marks, London
EC3A 7NT
(01-623 9043)
Building Societies Association
3 Savile Row, London W1X 1AF
(01-437 0655)

Building Societies Ombudsman
35–37 Grosvenor Gardens, London
SW1X 7AW
(01-931 0044)

Campaign for Independent Financial
Advice (CAMIFA)
33 St John's Street, London EC1M
4AA
(01-253 5757)
Chartered Association of Certified
Accountants
29 Lincoln's Inn Fields, London WC2A
3EE
(01-242 6855)
Chartered Institute of Arbitrators
75 Cannon Street, London EC4N 5BH
(01-236 8761)
Company Pensions Information Centre
7 Old Park Lane, London W1Y 3LJ
(01-493 4757)
Consumer's Association
2 Marylebone Road, London NW1
4DX1
(01-486 5544)
Council for Licensed Conveyancers
Golden Cross House, Duncannon
Street, London WC2N 4JF
(01-210 4602)

Ethical Investment Research Information
Service (EIRIS)
Bondway Business Centre, 71
Bondway, London SW8 1SQ
(01-753 1351)

Finance Houses Association
18 Upper Grosvenor Street, London
W1X 9PB
(01-491 2783)

Financial Intermediaries, Managers and
Brokers Regulatory Association
(FIMBRA)
  Hertsmere House, Marsh Walk,
  London E14 9RW
  (01-538 8860)
Futures and Options Exchange (FOX)
  1 St Katharine's Dock, London EC1
  9AX
  (01-481 2080)

Investment Managers Regulatory
Organisation (IMRO)
  Centre Point, 103 New Oxford Street,
  London WC1A 1PT
  (01-379 0601)
Incorporated Society of Valuers and
Auctioneers
  3 Cadogan Gate, London SW1X 0AS
  (01-235 2282)
Inland Revenue
  Somerset House, Strand, London
  WC1R 1LB
  (01-438 6622)
Institute of Actuaries
  Staples Inn Hall, High Holborn, London
  WC1V 7QJ
  (01-242 0106)
Institute of Arbitrators
  75 Cannon Street, London EC4N 5BH
  (01-236 8761)
Institute of Bankers
  10 Lombard Street, London EC3V 9A5
  (01-623 3531)
Institute of Chartered Accountants
(England and Wales)
  Chartered Accountants Hall, Moorgate
  Place, London EC2P 2BJ
  (01-628 7060)
Institute of Chartered Accountants of
Scotland
  27 Queen Street, Edinburgh EH2 1LA
  (031-225 5673)
Institute of Taxation
  12 Upper Belgrave Street, London
  SW1X 8BB
  (01-235 9381)

Insurance Ombudsman
  31 Southampton Row, London WC1B
  5HJ
  (01-242 8613)

Land Registry
  32 Lincoln's Inn Fields, London WC2A
  3PH
  (01-405 3488)
Law Society
  113 Chancery Lane, London WC2A
  1DL
  (01-242 1222)
Law Society of Northern Ireland
  Law Society House, 90–106 Victoria
  Street, Belfast BT1 3JZ
  (0232 231614)
Law Society of Scotland
  26 Drumsheugh Gardens, Edinburgh
  EH3 7YR
  (031-226 7411)
Life Assurance and Unit Trust Regulatory
Association (LAUTRO)
  Centre Point, 103 New Oxford Street,
  London WC1A 1QH
  (01-379 0444)
Life Insurance Association (LIA)
  Citadel House, Station Approach,
  Chorleywood, Herts WD3 5PS
  (09278 5333)
Lloyd's of London (Insurance)
  1 Lime Street, London EC3M 7HA
  (01-623 7100)
London International Financial Futures
Exchange (LIFFE)
  The Royal Exchange, Cornhill, London
  EC3V 3PJ
  (01-623 0444)
London Metal Exchange (LME)
  Plantation House, Fenchurch Street,
  London EC3M 3AP
  (01-626 3311)
London Traded Options Market
(LTOM)
  International Stock Exchange, Old
  Bond Street, London EC2N 1HD
  (01-588 2355)

National Association of Conveyancers
    44 London Road, Kingston-on-Thames,
    Surrey KT2 6QF
    (01-549 3636)
National Consumer Council
    18 Queen Anne's Gate, London SW1H
    9AA
    (01-222 9501)
National Federation of Housing
Associations
    175 Grays Inn Road, London WC1X
    8UP
    (01-278 6571)

Occupational Pensions Advisory Service
(OPAS)
    8a Bloomsbury Square, London WC1
    2UA
    (01-831 5511)
Office of Fair Trading (OFT)
    Field House, Breams Building, London
    EC4A 1PR
    (01-242 2858)

Personal Insurance Arbitration Service
    Chartered Institute of Arbitrators,
    75 Cannon Street, London EC4N 5BH
    (01-236 8761)

Rating and Valuation Association
    115 Ebury Street, London SW1W 9QT
    (01-730 7258)
Registrar of Companies
    Companies House, Crown Way,
    Maindy, Cardiff, CF4 3UZ
    (0222 388588)
Registry of Friendly Societies
    15 Great Marlborough Street, London
    W1V 2AX
    (01-437 9992)
Royal Institution of Chartered Surveyors
    12 Great George Street, Parliament
    Square, London SW1P 3AD
    (01-222 7000)

Securities and Investment Board (SIB)
    3 Royal Exchange Buildings, London
    EC3V 3NL
    (01-283 2474)
(The) Securities Association (TSA)
    The Stock Exchange, Old Broad
    Street, London EC2N 1EQ
    (01-256 9000)
Society of Pension Consultants
    Ludgate House, Ludgate Circus,
    London EC4A 2AB
    (01-353 1688)
Special Commissioners of Income Tax
    Turnstile House, 94 High Holborn,
    London WC1 6LQ
    (01-831 5253)
Stock Exchange
    Old Broad Street, London EC2N 1HP
    (01-588 2355)

Timeshare Developers Association
    23 Buckingham Gate, London SW1E
    6LB
    (01-821 8845)

Unit Trust Association
    Park House, 16 Finsbury Circus,
    London EC2M 7JP
    (01-638 3071)
Unit Trust Ombudsman
    31 Southampton Row, London WC1B
    5HJ
    (01-242 8613)

Wider Share Ownership Council
    Juxon House, 94 St Paul's Churchyard,
    London EC4M 8EH
    (01-248 9155)